ACCA

PRACTICE & REVISION KIT

PAPER F6

TAXATION (UK)

FA 2010 and F(No.2)A 2010

BPP Learning Media is the **sole ACCA Platinum Approved Learning Partner – content** for the ACCA qualification. In this, **the only Paper F6 Practice and Revision Kit to be reviewed by the examiner**:

- We discuss the **best strategies** for revising and taking your ACCA exams

- We show you how to be **well prepared** for your exam

- We give you **lots of great guidance** on tackling questions

- We show you how you can **build your own exams**

- We provide you with **three** mock exams including the **December 2010 exam**

Our **i-Pass** product also supports this paper.

FOR EXAMS IN 2011

BPP
LEARNING MEDIA

First edition 2007
Fifth edition January 2011

ISBN 9780 7517 9402 1
(previous ISBN 9780 7517 8044 4)
ebook ISBN 9780 7517 8724 5

British Library Cataloguing-in-Publication Data
A catalogue record for this book
is available from the British Library

Published by

BPP Learning Media Ltd
BPP House, Aldine Place
London W12 8AA

www.bpp.com/learningmedia

Printed in the United Kingdom

We are grateful to the Association of Chartered Certified
Accountants for permission to reproduce past
examination questions. The suggested solutions in the
exam answer bank have been prepared by BPP Learning
Media Ltd, except where otherwise stated.

Contents

Question index

The headings in this checklist/index indicate the main topics of questions, but questions often cover several different topics.

Questions set under the old syllabus exam are included in this Kit (labelled BTX) because their style and content are similar to those that appear in the new syllabus exam. The questions have been amended as appropriate to reflect the current syllabus exam format.

Planning your question practice

Our guidance from page xxi shows you how to organise your question practice, either by attempting questions from each syllabus area or **by building your own exams** – tackling questions as a series of practice exams.

Using your BPP Learning Media products

This Kit gives you the question practice and guidance you need in the exam. Our other products can also help you pass:

- **Learning to Learn Accountancy** gives further valuable advice on revision

- **Passcards** provide you with clear topic summaries and exam tips

- **Success CDs** help you revise on the move

- **i-Pass CDs** offer tests of knowledge against the clock

You can purchase these products by visiting www.bpp.com.

Topic index

Listed below are the key Paper F6 syllabus topics and the numbers of the questions in this Kit covering those topics.

If you need to concentrate your practice and revision on certain topics or if you want to attempt all available questions that refer to a particular subject, you will find this index useful.

Syllabus topic	Question numbers
Administration of tax – individuals	2, 3, 9, 19, 20, ME1 Qu 1, ME3 Qu 1, ME Qu 5
Administration of tax – companies	35, 36
Capital allowances	18, 31, 33, 36, 41, 43
Chargeable gains – reliefs	21, 22, 23, 24, 25, 26, 38, ME1 Qu 3, ME 3 Qu 3
Chargeable gains – companies	37, 38, ME2 Qu 2, ME 3 Qu 3
Chargeable gains – individuals	10, 21, 22, 23, 24, 25, 26, ME1 Qu 3, ME 3 Qu 3
Companies – calculation of taxable total profits	31, 32, 33, 36, 39, 41, 43, 47, 48, 49, ME1 Qu 2, ME2 Qu 2, ME3 Qu 2
Companies – calculation of tax	32, 34, 35, 43, ME1 Qu 2, ME2 Qu 2, ME 3 Qu 2, ME 3 Qu 4
Companies – groups	44, 45, 46, 47, 48, 49,
Companies – losses	36, 39, 40, 41, 45
Companies – overseas aspects	42, 43, ME2 Qu 2, ME3 Qu 2
Income tax computation	1, 5, 7, 9, 33, ME1 Qu 1, ME1 Qu 5, ME3 Qu 1
Individuals – employment income	2, 3, 4, 5, 7, 13, ME1 Qu 1, ME2 Qu 1, ME3 Qu 1, ME3 Qu 4
Individuals – property income	4, 6, 7, ME1 Qu 1,
Individuals – trading income	2, 5, 9, 10, 12, 13, 18, ME1 Qu 4
Individuals – losses	11, 13, 14
Inheritance tax	27, 28, 29, 30, ME2 Qu 5, ME 3 Qu 5
National insurance contributions	10, 33, ME1 Qu 5, ME2 Qu 1, ME 3 Qu 4
Partnerships	15, 16, 17, 18
Pensions	2, 8, ME2 Qu 4
Value added tax	13, 31, 50, 51, 52, 53, 54, ME1 Qu 2, ME2 Qu 1, ME3 Qu 2

ME1 is Mock Exam 1, ME2 is Mock Exam 2 and ME3 is Mock Exam 3

Helping you with your revision – the ONLY F6 Practice and Revision Kit to be reviewed by the examiner!

BPP Learning Media – the sole Platinum Approved Learning Partner - content

As ACCA's **sole Platinum Approved Learning Partner – content**, BPP Learning Media gives you the **unique opportunity** to use **examiner-reviewed** revision materials for the 2011 exams. By incorporating the examiner's comments and suggestions regarding syllabus coverage, the BPP Learning Media Practice and Revision Kit provides excellent, **ACCA-approved** support for your revision.

Tackling revision and the exam

You can significantly improve your chances of passing by tackling revision and the exam in the right ways. Our advice is based on feedback from ACCA examiners.

- We look at the dos and don'ts of revising for, and taking, ACCA exams
- We focus on Paper F6; we discuss revising the syllabus, what to do (and what not to do) in the exam, how to approach different types of question and ways of obtaining easy marks

Selecting questions

We provide signposts to help you plan your revision.

- A full **question index**
- A **topic index** listing all the questions that cover key topics, so that you can locate the questions that provide practice on these topics, and see the different ways in which they might be examined
- **BPP's question plan** highlighting the most important questions and explaining why you should attempt them
- **Build your own exams**, showing how you can practise questions in a series of exams

Making the most of question practice

At BPP Learning Media we realise that you need more than just questions and model answers to get the most from your question practice.

- Our **Top tips** included for certain questions provide essential advice on tackling questions, presenting answers and the key points that answers need to include
- We show you how you can pick up **Easy marks** on some questions, as we know that picking up all readily available marks often can make the difference between passing and failing
- We include **marking guides** to show you what the examiner rewards
- We include **examiners' comments** to show you where students struggled or performed well in the actual exam
- We refer to the **FA 2010 and F(No.2)A 2010 BPP Study Text** (for exams in June and December 2011) for detailed coverage of the topics covered in questions

Attempting mock exams

There are three mock exams that provide practice at coping with the pressures of the exam day. We strongly recommend that you attempt them under exam conditions. **Mock exams 1** and **2** reflect the question styles and syllabus coverage of the exam and **Mock exam 3** is the December 2010 paper.

Revising F6

Topics to revise

Any part of the syllabus could be tested in the examination, therefore it is essential that you learn the **entire syllabus** to maximise your chances of passing. There are no short cuts – trying to spot topics is dangerous and will significantly reduce the likelihood of success.

Question practice

You should use the Passcards and any brief notes you have to revise the syllabus, but you mustn't spend all your revision time passively reading. **Question practice is vital;** doing as many questions as you can in full will help develop your ability to analyse scenarios and produce relevant discussion and recommendations. The question plan on page xxi tells you what questions cover so that you can choose questions covering a variety of syllabus areas.

Also ensure that you attempt all three mock exams under exam conditions.

Passing F6

BPP Learning Media is committed to giving you the best possible support in your quest for exam success. With this in mind, we have produced **guidance** on how to revise and techniques you can apply to **improve your chances of passing** the exam. This guidance can be found on the BPP Learning Media web site at the following link:

www.bpp.com/acca/examtips/revising-for-ACCA-exams.doc

A paper copy of this guidance is available by writing to learningmedia@bpp.com.

As well as written guidance, an excellent presentation entitled '**Exam technique – advice from the experts at BPP Learning Media**' is available at the following link:

http://www.bppprofessionaldevelopment.com/elearning/Assets/audiovisual/ACCAExamSkills/NewSyllabus/player.html?cmp=get_ataste

Topics to revise

That said, you must have sound knowledge in the following fundamental areas if you are to stand a chance of passing the exam. You should therefore revise the following areas particularly well.

- Income tax computation including the personal allowance and the tax bands and rates.

- The calculation of benefits from employment, such as company car and/or fuel, use of an employer's asset and low cost loans. Make sure you can spot tax free benefits too.

- Capital allowances proforma paying particular attention to the availability of annual investment allowance. Note particularly the difference in the calculation rules between individuals (sole traders and partners) and companies.

- Calculation of taxable total profits, in relation to companies. Be aware that you may need to calculate the various elements that make up the taxable total profits such as property business income, interest income, gains and so on.

- Computation of chargeable gains paying attention to whether the disposal is made by an individual or a company, particularly for aspects such as indexation allowance and annual exempt amount.

- Inheritance tax computations including lifetime transfers and the death estate.

- How to calculate VAT payable or repayable depending on the type of supply (ie standard rated, zero rated or exempt).

- The different classes of NIC payable by employees and their employers compared to those due from self employed individuals or partners.

Question practice

You should use the Passcards and any brief notes you have to revise the syllabus, but you mustn't spend all your revision time passively reading. **Question practice is vital**; doing as many questions as you can in full will help develop your ability to analyse scenarios and produce relevant discussion and recommendations. The question plan on page xxi tells you what questions cover so that you can choose questions covering a variety of syllabus areas.

Passing the F6 exam

Displaying the right qualities

The examiner expects students to display the following qualities.

Qualities required	
Knowledge development	Questions will test your knowledge of underlying principles and major technical areas of taxation, as they affect the activities of individuals and businesses, across the breadth of the F6 syllabus. You will also be expected to apply this knowledge to the facts of each particular question and also to identify the compliance issues for your client.
Computation skills	Although you will be expected to be able to calculate the tax liability, note that you will also be marked on the methods you use. So, if your numbers are not perfect you will not necessarily lose too many marks so long as your method is correct and you have stated any assumptions you have made.
Ability to explain	Whilst the main focus of the exam is on the computation of tax liabilities, you may also be required to explain rules and conditions, so take care to practise the written elements of the answers also.
Identification capability	You must know who you are calculating tax liabilities for – is the client a company or an individual? Be sure who you are advising as this will seriously impact your answers.

You will not always produce the exact same answer as we have in our answer section. This does not necessarily mean that you have failed the question, but if you do use the suggested proformas and methods you will maximise the number of marks you can achieve.

Avoiding weaknesses

We give details of the examiner's comments and criticisms throughout this Kit. These hardly varied over the last few years. His reports always emphasise the need for thorough preparation for the exam, but there are various things you can do on the day of the exam to enhance your chances. Although these all sound basic, the examiner has commented that many scripts don't:

- Make the most of the information given in the question
- Follow the question requirements
- Set out workings clearly

Using the reading time

You will have 15 minutes' reading time for Paper F6. Here are some helpful tips on how to best utilise this time.

- Speed read through the question paper, jotting down any ideas that come to you about any of the questions.

- Decide the order which you're likely to tackle questions (probably easiest questions first, most difficult questions last).

- Spend the remainder of reading time reading the question(s) you'll do first in detail jotting down proformas and plans (any plans or proformas written on the question paper should be reproduced in the answer booklet).

- When you can start writing, get straight on with the question(s) you've planned in detail.

If you have looked at all of the questions during the reading time, this should hopefully mean that you will find it easier to answer the more difficult questions when you come to them, as you will have been generating ideas and remembering facts while answering the easier questions.

Choosing which questions to answer first

There are five compulsory questions, with a larger number of marks awarded for the first two questions.

- Many students prefer to answer the questions with the largest number of allocated marks first. Others prefer to answer a question on their most comfortable topic.

- Whatever the order, make sure you leave yourself **sufficient time** to tackle all the questions. Don't get so bogged down in the calculations in the first question you do, especially if it's your favourite topic, that you have to rush the rest of the paper.

- Allocate your time carefully between different question parts. If a question is split into a number of requirements, use the number of marks available for each to allocate your time effectively.

Tackling questions

You'll improve your chances by following a step-by-step approach along the following lines.

Step 1   **Read the requirement**

Identify the knowledge areas being tested and see precisely what the examiner wants you to do. This will help you focus on what's important in the question.

Step 2   **Check the mark allocation**

This helps you allocate time.

Step 3   **Read the question actively**

You will already know which knowledge area(s) are being tested from having read the requirement so whilst you read through the question underline or highlight key words and figures as you read. This will mean you are thinking about the question rather than just looking at the words blankly, and will allow you to identify relevant information for use in your calculations.

Step 4   **Plan your answer**

You may only spend five minutes planning your answer but it will be five minutes well spent. Identify the calculations you will need to do and whether you have appropriate proformas to assist in these. If there is a written element to the question, determine whether you can you use bullet points or if you need a more formal format.

Step 5   **Write your answer**

Stick carefully to the time allocation for each question, and for each part of each question.

Gaining the easy marks

There are two main ways to obtain easy marks in the F6 exam.

Proformas

There will always be basic marks available for straightforward tasks such as putting easy figures into proformas, for example putting the cost figure for an addition into a capital allowances proforma. Do not miss out on these easy marks by not learning your proformas properly. Make it easy for yourself to pick up the easy marks.

Deadlines and dates

An important component of your knowledge of the different taxes is the administrative, or compliance, details such as filing deadlines and tax payment dates. This element of the requirement can often be answered even before you make any calculations, for example stating the submission deadline for an individual's self assessment tax return.

Exam information
The exam paper

The syllabus is assessed by a three-hour paper-based examination.

The paper will be predominantly computational and will have five questions, all of which will be compulsory.

- Question one will focus on income tax and question two will focus on corporation tax. The two questions will be for a total of 55 marks, with one of the questions being for 30 marks and the other being for 25 marks.

- Question three will focus on chargeable gains (either personal or corporate) and will be for 15 marks.

- Questions four and five will be on any area of the syllabus, can cover more than one topic and will be for 15 marks each.

There will always be at a minimum of 10 marks on value added tax. These marks will normally be included within question one or question two, although there might be a separate question on value added tax.

National insurance contributions will not be examined as a separate question, but may be examined in any question involving income tax or corporation tax.

Inheritance tax could be examined in either of questions 4 or 5 for a maximum of 15 marks.

Groups and overseas aspects of corporation tax may be examined in either question two or question five.

Questions one or two might include a small element of chargeable gains.

Any of the five questions might include the consideration of issues relating to the minimisation or deferral of tax liabilities.

December 2010

		Question in this Kit
1	Employment benefits. Taxable income. PAYE	Mock Exam 3 Question 1
2	Taxable total profits. Calculation of corporation tax. Overseas aspects of corporation tax VAT	Mock Exam 3 Question 2
3	Chargeable gains for individual. Valuation of deemed proceeds. Shares. Entrepreneurs' relief. Part disposal. Chargeable gains for company.	Mock Exam 3 Question 3
4	Salary or company car. Income tax and NIC aspects for employee and employer	Mock Exam 3 Question 4
5	Losses for individual	n/a

June 2010

Examiner's comments

This style of this paper was slightly different from recent papers, with more smaller sub-parts enabling more of the syllabus to be covered: Some of the other changes were that the VAT information needed for question 1 part (d) was not shown separately (instead being included within the main text), and in question 2 the group relief and capital allowance aspects were in separate sections (requiring explanations instead of straightforward computations) rather than being examined computationally as part of the main corporation tax question. Candidates cannot expect to have an easy income tax or benefits computation in every paper. The pass rate achieved was quite satisfactory.

December 2009

Examiner's comments

This was another good performance, and well prepared candidates had no difficulty in achieving a pass mark. Questions 3 (capital gains tax (CGT)) and 5 (corporate loss relief) caused the most problems, and the value added tax (VAT) aspects of question 2 were also not particularly well answered.

June 2009

Examiner's comments

This was another exceptionally good performance with many candidates achieving high marks. The simplification of capital gain tax for individuals, having a separate VAT question, and a fairly straightforward question five all contributed to the good pass rate. In addition, candidates seemed very well prepared for this examination. Areas, such as NIC, which a few diets ago were causing problems, are now handled with ease.

December 2008

Examiner's comments

This was an exceptionally good performance with many candidates achieving high marks. None of the questions caused any problems, and even candidates who did not do particularly well with questions 1, 2 and 3, often managed to achieve a pass mark by scoring good marks on questions 4 and 5.

June 2008

Examiner's comments

This was a reasonable performance. The main problem was caused by question four, which many candidates found surprisingly difficult. This question was usually left until last, and it was often obvious that insufficient time had been left to attempt it properly.

December 2007

Examiner's comments

This was a very good performance for the first sitting of this paper. Those candidates who marginally failed to achieve a pass mark generally did so because of poor time management. Also, many candidates that were obviously running out of time surprisingly opted to attempt question five, which was quite the most technically demanding on the paper, rather than question four where it was relatively easy to score 9 or 10 marks. Practicing questions under timed, exam-style conditions prior to sitting the examination would have helped as regards time management.

Pilot paper

Analysis of past papers

The table below provides details of when each element of the syllabus has been examined and the question number and section in which each element appeared. Further details can be found in the Exam Focus Points in the relevant chapters. Note that the exam structure for 2011 is slightly different from that in previous years and that inheritance tax has been added to the syllabus.

Covered in Text chapter		December 2010	June 2010	Dec 2009	June 2009	Dec 2008	June 2008
	UK TAX SYSTEM						
1	Introduction to the UK tax system						
	INCOME TAX AND NATIONAL INSURANCE CONTRIBUTIONS						
2	The computation of taxable income and the income tax liability	1a	1a, 2d	1c, 4b	1a	1a	1b, 1c
3	Employment income	1a			1a, 5	1a	1a
4	Taxable and exempt benefits. The PAYE system	1a, 4			1a	1a	1a
5	Pensions	1a			1a	5	
6	Property income					1a	
7	Computing trading income		1b	1b 4a, 4b	1a		1a
8	Capital allowances		2c				
9	Assessable trading income			1a	5		
10	Trading losses	5					
11	Partnerships and limited liability partnerships		1b			4	
12	National insurance contributions	4	1c, 2d	4b	5	1b	
	CHARGEABLE GAINS FOR INDIVIDUALS						
13	Computing chargeable gains	3		3a, 3b, 3c, 4b	3		3
14	Chattels and the principal private residence exemption			3c	3		
15	Business reliefs	3		3a, 3b	3		3
16	Shares and securities	3		3b	3		
	TAX ADMINISTRATION FOR INDIVIDUALS						
17	Self assessment and payment of tax for individuals	1a	4	1c, 1d	1b		4
	INHERITANCE TAX						
18	Inheritance tax	n/a	n/a	n/a	n/a	n/a	n/a
	CORPORATION TAX						
19	Computing taxable total profits	2a, 4	2a	2a	2a	2a	2a, 5
20	Computing the corporation tax liability	2a, 4	5	2a	2b	3a	5
21	Chargeable gains for companies	3	3a, 3b			3a, 3b	
22	Losses		2a	5		2a	
23	Groups		2b		2d		
24	Overseas matters for companies	2a		2a			2a
25	Self assessment and payment of tax by companies				2c	2a	
	VALUE ADDED TAX						
26	An introduction to VAT	2b	1d	2b	4	2b	2b
27	Further aspects of VAT	2b	1d	2b	4	2b	

Useful websites

The websites below provide additional sources of information of relevance to your studies for *Taxation*.

- www.accaglobal.com

  ACCA's website. The students' section of the website is invaluable for detailed information about the qualification, past issues of *Student Accountant* (including technical articles) and even interviews with the examiners.

- www.bpp.com

  Our website provides information about BPP products and services, with a link to the ACCA website.

Planning your question practice

We have already stressed that question practice should be right at the centre of your revision. Whilst you will spend some time looking at your notes and Paper F6 Passcards, you should spend the majority of your revision time practising questions.

We recommend two ways in which you can practise questions.

- Use **BPP Learning Media's question plan** to work systematically through the syllabus and attempt key and other questions on a section-by-section basis

- **Build your own exams** – attempt questions as a series of practice exams

These ways are suggestions and simply following them is no guarantee of success. You or your college may prefer an alternative but equally valid approach.

BPP Learning Media's question plan

The BPP Learning Media plan below requires you to devote a **minimum of 36 hours** to revision of Paper F6. Any time you can spend over and above this should only increase your chances of success.

Step 1   For each section of the syllabus, **review your notes** and the relevant chapter summaries in the Paper F6 **Passcards**.

Step 2   **Answer the questions** for that section as shown in **white boxes** in the table below. Try to complete your answers without referring to our solutions. In some cases we suggest that you make notes for the written part of a question or make answer plans, if you are short of time. You must make sure that you attempt a variety of questions from the whole syllabus and not just concentrate on a few aspects.

Step 3   Once you have worked through all of the syllabus sections attempt **Mock exam 1** under strict exam conditions. Then have a go at **Mock exam 2**, again under strict exam conditions. Just before the exam, if you have time, attempt **Mock exam 3**, again under strict exam conditions This is the December 2010 paper.

Syllabus section	Passcards chapters	Questions in this Kit	Comments	Done ☑
Revision period 1 Income tax computations	1, 2, 3	1	Work through this question carefully. It covers the basic income tax computation you will have to do in the exam.	☐
Revision period 2 Pensions and property income	5	8	Pensions are topical so work through this question very carefully.	☐
	6	6, 7	Property income can appear as part of a longer question or as a question on its own like this one.	☐
Revision periods 3/4 Employees	3, 4, 5, 6, 12, 17	2, 3, 5	These questions are typical of Question 1 in the exam. If you are short of time, prioritise Q2 and Q5 which are recent exam questions.	☐
Revision periods 5/6 Trading profits and losses for individuals Adjustment of profits	2, 7, 8, 9, 12, 13, 15, 17	9, 13	Important questions that also include basis period rules for an individual. Q9 and Q13 also covers employment income: a good comparison with trading income. You should ignore the disposal in Q10 if you are short of time.	☐
Change of accounting date	2, 9	12	You should make sure that you are happy with the calculations in this question.	☐
Losses	10	11, 14	Losses are a key area so answer these questions carefully.	☐
Revision period 7 Partnerships	5, 7, 8, 11, 12	15 to 18	Useful questions covering this important topic.	☐
Revision period 8 Self assessment	17	19, 20	Self assessment is a key topic. If you are short of time, make bullet points for the written elements of these questions.	☐
Revision period 9 NIC	2, 12, 13 – 16	4	A question covering a number of taxes. Work through carefully.	☐
Revision period 10 Capital gains			Gains will be tested in Question 3 in the exam and may also be tested in any of the other questions. The gains rules are therefore key for your exam.	☐
Basics	13 – 16	21	You can attempt part (a) of this question now. Leave part (b) until you have revised reliefs in Revision period 12.	☐

Syllabus section	Passcards chapters	Questions in this Kit	Comments	Done ☑
Revision period 11 Additional aspects of capital gains	13 – 16	22, 23	The gains rules for shares, chattels and immoveable property, including PPR relief. These are important questions. Make sure you understand the calculations.	☐
Revision period 12 Capital gains reliefs	13 – 16	24, 25, 26	It is likely that you will not be able to avoid reliefs for gains in the exam.	☐
Revision period 13/14 Inheritance tax	18	27, 28, 29 30	This is a new topic so is highly likely to be examined. Make sure that you can deal with both lifetime transfers and the death estate	☐
Revision periods 14/15 Computing corporation tax Computation of taxable total profits and CT	8, 13 – 16, 19, 20, 25, 26	31, 32, 33 34, 35, 36 37, 38	Vitally important questions that you must work through in full. These are similar to the type of question that you could see as Question 2 in the exam. Questions 37 and 38 deal with gains for companies. This could be tested in Question 3 in the exam.	☐
Revision period 15 Corporation tax losses Single company losses	13 – 16, 19, 20, 21, 22	39, 40, 41	Important questions covering a single company's losses.	☐
Revision period 16 Corporation tax groups Group losses	8, 13, 15, 19, 20, 21, 23, 25	44, 45, 46, 47 48	Important questions. Group losses are a popular exam question.	☐
Revision period 17 Overseas aspects of corporation tax	8, 20, 22, 24	42, 43	Make sure you can deal with DTR. This topic may be tested in Question 2 in the exam.	☐
Revision period 18 VAT	26, 27	50 to 54	Essential questions. There will be at least 10 marks for VAT in your paper so be prepared. You might see a whole question on VAT or it could be tested as part of a longer question.	☐

Build your own exams

Having revised your notes and the BPP Passcards, you can attempt the questions in the Kit as a series of practice exams. You can organise the questions in the following ways.

- Either you can attempt complete past exam papers; recent papers are listed below:

	June 10 Questions in Kit	December 09 Question in Kit	June 09 Question in Kit
1	18	9	2
2	33	32	49
3	38	26	25
4	20	10	54
5	35	40	ME1 Qu 5

- Or you can make up practice exams, either yourself or using the suggestions we have listed below.

	Practice Exam					
	1	2	3	4	5	6
1	3	18	9	13	5	2
2	32	33	39	48	41	45
3	37	21	38	22	25	26
4	6	27	20	28	10	29
5	40	19	14	11	35	52

Questions

TAXATION OF INDIVIDUALS

Questions 1 to 18 cover the taxation of individuals and their income from employment and self-employment, the subject of Part B of the BPP Study Text for Paper F6. Questions 19 and 20 cover tax administration for individuals, the subject of Part D of the BPP Study Text for Paper F6.

1 Brad, Lauren, Tom and Sarah

36 mins

(a) Brad, an advertising executive, and his wife Lauren, an IT consultant, have one son. Having made a large gain on the sale of a property when they got married, they have acquired a considerable number of investments. They now require assistance in preparing their taxation returns for tax year 2010/11 and have listed out their income and expenditure:

Brad

	£
Salary (before deduction of PAYE)	104,500
Premium Bond winnings	5,000
Interest received on National Savings & Investments Certificates	300
Building society interest (Joint account – total net interest credited)	4,400 (net)

Lauren

	£
Salary (before deduction of PAYE)	46,000
ISA account – dividends	350
– interest	125
Dividend received on Virgin plc shares	2,250
Building society interest (Joint account – total net interest credited)	4,400 (net)
Interest received on 2013 5% Treasury Stock (received gross)	2,000
Gift Aid payment to Dogs Trust (actual amount paid)	1,000

Required

Calculate Brad and Lauren's income tax liability for tax year 2010/11. **(10 marks)**

(b) Lauren's father, Tom, a widower, who is 69, has the following income for tax year 2010/11.

	£
State retirement pension	4,226
Pension from former employer (before deduction of PAYE)	6,390
Building society interest (net interest credited)	13,520

Tom gave £3,200 to Oxfam (a registered charity) on 21 September 2010 under Gift Aid. This was the actual amount paid.

Required

Calculate Tom's income tax liability for tax year 2010/11. **(5 marks)**

(c) Sarah, Brad's sister, is self-employed and has the following income for tax year 2010/11:

	£
Trading profits	164,000
Bank interest received from Santander (net interest credited)	8,000
Dividends from BP plc (actual amount received)	4,950

Sarah paid £16,000 (net) into her personal pension scheme during 2010/11.

Required

Calculate Sarah's income tax liability for tax year 2010/11. **(5 marks)**

(Total = 20 marks)

2 Domingo, Erigo and Fargo (TX 06/09)

45 mins

Domingo, Erigo and Fargo Gomez are three brothers. The following information is available for the tax year 2010/11:

Domingo Gomez

(1)   Domingo is aged 67.

(2)   During the tax year 2010/11 he received the state pension of £4,500 and a private pension of £2,300.

(3)   In addition to his pension income Domingo received building society interest of £14,400 and interest of £600 on the maturity of a savings certificate from National Savings and Investments during the tax year 2010/11. These were the actual cash amounts received.

(4)   During the tax year 2010/11 Domingo made donations of £300 (gross) to local charities. These were not made under the gift aid scheme.

Erigo Gomez

(1)   Erigo is aged 56.

(2)   He is employed as a business journalist by Economical plc, a magazine publishing company. During the tax year 2010/11 Erigo was paid a gross annual salary of £36,000.

(3)   During the tax year 2010/11 Erigo used his private motor car for business purposes. He drove 18,000 miles in the performance of his duties for Economical plc, for which the company paid an allowance of 20 pence per mile.

(4)   During June 2010 Economical plc paid £11,400 towards the cost of Erigo's relocation when he was required to move his place of employment. Erigo's previous main residence was 140 miles from his new place of employment with the company. The £11,400 covered the cost of disposing of Erigo's old property and of acquiring a new property.

(5)   Erigo contributed 6% of his gross salary of £36,000 into Economical plc's HM Revenue and Customs' registered occupational pension scheme.

(6)   During the tax year 2010/11 Erigo donated £100 (gross) per month to charity under the payroll deduction scheme.

Fargo Gomez

(1)   Fargo is aged 53.

(2)   He commenced self-employment as a business consultant on 6 July 2010. Fargo's tax adjusted trading profit based on his draft accounts for the nine-month period ended 5 April 2011 is £64,800. This figure is before making any adjustments required for:

   (i)   Advertising expenditure of £2,600 incurred during May 2010. This expenditure has not been deducted in calculating the profit of £64,800.

   (ii)   Capital allowances.

(3)   The only item of plant and machinery owned by Fargo is his motor car. This cost £11,000 on 6 July 2010 and had CO_2 emissions of 150g/km. During the nine-month period ended 5 April 2011 Fargo drove a total of 24,000 miles, of which 8,000 were for private journeys.

(4)   During the tax year 2010/11 Fargo contributed £5,200 (gross) into a personal pension scheme, and made gift aid donations totalling £2,400 (net) to national charities.

Tax returns

For the tax year 2010/11 Domingo wants to file a paper self-assessment tax return and have HM Revenue and Customs prepare a self-assessment on his behalf. Erigo also wants to file a paper tax return but will prepare his own self-assessment. Fargo wants to file his tax return online.

Required

(a) Calculate the respective income tax liabilities for the tax year 2010/11 of:

(i)	Domingo Gomez;	**(6 marks)**
(ii)	Erigo Gomez;	**(6 marks)**
(iii)	Fargo Gomez.	**(7 marks)**

(b) Advise Domingo, Erigo and Fargo Gomez of the latest dates by which their respective self-assessment tax returns for the tax year 2010/11 will have to be submitted given their stated filing preferences.   **(3 marks)**

(c) Advise Domingo, Erigo and Fargo Gomez as to how long they must retain the records used in preparing their respective tax returns for the tax year 2010/11, and the potential consequences of not retaining the records for the required period.   **(3 marks)**

(Total = 25 marks)

3 Vigorous plc (BTX)   45 mins

Vigorous plc runs a health club. The company has three employees who received taxable benefits during tax year 2010/11, and it therefore needs to prepare forms P11D for them. Each of the three employees is paid an annual salary of £35,000. The following information is relevant:

Andrea Lean

(1) Andrea was employed by Vigorous plc throughout tax year 2010/11.

(2) Throughout tax year 2010/11 Vigorous plc provided Andrea with a petrol powered company motor car with a list price of £19,400. The official CO_2 emission rate for the motor car is 255 grams per kilometre. Vigorous plc paid for all of the motor car's running costs of £6,200 during tax year 2010/11, including petrol used for private journeys. Andrea pays £150 per month to Vigorous plc for the use of the motor car.

(3) Vigorous plc has provided Andrea with living accommodation since 1 November 2008. The property was purchased on 1 January 2006 for £130,000. The company spent £14,000 improving the property during March 2006, and a further £8,000 was spent on improvements during May 2010. The value of the property on 1 November 2008 was £170,000, and it has an annual value of £7,000. The furniture in the property cost £6,000 during November 2008. Andrea personally pays for the annual running costs of the property amounting to £4,000.

(4) Throughout tax year 2010/11 Vigorous plc provided Andrea with a mobile telephone costing £500. The company paid for all business and private telephone calls.

Ben Slim

(1) Ben commenced employment with Vigorous plc on 1 July 2010.

(2) On 1 July 2010 Vigorous plc provided Ben with an interest free loan of £120,000 so that he could purchase a new main residence. He repaid £20,000 of the loan on 1 October 2010.

(3) During tax year 2010/11 Vigorous plc paid £9,300 towards the cost of Ben's relocation. His previous main residence was 125 miles from his place of employment with the company. The £9,300 covered the cost of disposing of Ben's old property and of acquiring his new property.

(4) During the period from 1 October 2010 until 5 April 2011 Vigorous plc provided Ben with a new diesel powered company motor car which has a list price of £11,200. The official CO_2 emission rate for the motor car is 126 grams per kilometre. Ben reimburses Vigorous plc for all the diesel used for private journeys.

Chai Trim

(1) Chai was employed by Vigorous plc throughout tax year 2010/11.

(2) During tax year 2010/11 Vigorous plc provided Chai with a two-year old company van, although the van was unavailable during the period 1 August to 30 September 2010. No fuel was provided for private journeys.

(3) Vigorous plc has provided Chai with a television for her personal use since 6 April 2008. The television cost Vigorous plc £800 in April 2008. On 6 April 2010 the company sold the television to Chai for £150, although its market value on that date was £250.

(4)   Throughout tax year 2010/11 Vigorous plc provided Chai with free membership of its health club. The normal annual cost of membership is £800. This figure is made up of direct costs of £150, fixed overhead costs of £400 and profit of £250. The budgeted membership for the year has been exceeded, but the health club has surplus capacity.

(5)   On 6 April 2010 Vigorous plc provided Chai with a new computer costing £1,900. She uses the computer at home for personal study purposes.

Required

(a)   Explain what is meant by the term 'P11D employee'.   **(3 marks)**

(b)   Calculate the taxable benefit figures that Vigorous plc will have to include on the forms P11D for Andrea, Ben, and Chai for tax year 2010/11.   **(19 marks)**

(c)   Explain how the income tax liability in respect of taxable benefits is collected by HMRC.   **(3 marks)**

(Total = 25 marks)

4 Bryan Thompson   49 mins

Bryan Thompson (age 48) is a full-time director of Watnot Ltd.

During tax year 2010/11 he was paid a salary of £75,000 and had the private use of a car provided by his employer. The car had a list price of £25,000 and an emissions rating (petrol) of 150g/km.

In September 2010, the company offered to replace his car with a more expensive model. Bryan declined the offer and instead on 5 October 2010 the company purchased a car with a list price of £7,500 and an emissions rating (petrol) of 130g/km for use by his wife. Bryan pays for all petrol used in his car with the company credit card. His wife pays for the petrol for use in the car provided for her use personally.

Bryan pays 10% of his salary (excluding his benefits) into his employer's occupational pension scheme. His employer matches his contribution.

Since March 2010, the company has paid £100 a month medical insurance to cover Bryan and his family. In January 2011, his son had a minor operation on his leg costing £1,800 which was paid for by the insurance company.

During August 2010, Bryan attended an international business conference in Florida. His wife went with him for a holiday. They stayed for the five nights that the conference lasted and the cost of the double room was £100 per night upgraded from £75 per night for the single room originally booked for Bryan. The return air fares were £1,000 each. All costs were paid by the company.

In December 2010, Bryan was transferred to the new head office 200 miles from his original office which necessitated moving house. The company paid the following expenses in connection with his move:

	£
Agents' fees	4,500
Removal costs	750
Stamp Duty Land Tax	10,500
Legal fees	1,800

Bryan and his wife also receive income from a furnished house they jointly own. During tax year 2010/11 the income and expenses were:

	£
Rental income	20,000
Caretaker's wages	2,600
Heat and light	1,400
Interest on loan to purchase property	6,000

In February 2011 Bryan received net interest of £3,200 from a two year high interest savings account which had matured. He received a dividend of £1,800 from Adams plc, a UK company in June 2010.

(a)   Calculate Bryan's taxable income and tax liability for tax year 2010/11.   **(25 marks)**

(b)   Calculate the NICs payable by Bryan for tax year 2010/11.   **(2 marks)**

(Total = 27 marks)

5 Sam and Kim White (TX 06/08)   45 mins

Sam and Kim White are a married couple. Sam is aged 36 and Kim is aged 38. The following information is available for the tax year 2010/11:

Sam White

(1)   Sam is self-employed running a retail clothing shop. His income statement for the year ended 5 April 2011 is as follows:

	Note	£	£
Gross profit			140,300
Depreciation		7,600	
Motor expenses	2	8,800	
Patent royalties	3	700	
Professional fees	4	1,860	
Other expenses	5	71,340	
			(90,300)
Net profit			50,000

(2)   During the year ended 5 April 2011 Sam drove a total of 25,000 miles, of which 5,000 miles were driven when he visited his suppliers in Europe. The balance of the mileage is 25% for private journeys and 75% for business journeys in the United Kingdom.

(3)   During the year ended 5 April 2011 Sam paid patent royalties of £700 (gross) in respect of specialized technology that he uses when altering clothes for customers.

(4)   The figure for professional fees consists of £1,050 for legal fees in connection with an action brought against a supplier for breach of contract and £810 for accountancy. Included in the figure for accountancy is £320 in respect of personal capital gains tax advice for the tax year 2009/10.

(5)   The figure for other expenses of £71,340 includes £560 for gifts to customers of food hampers costing £35 each and £420 for gifts to customers of pens carrying an advertisement for the clothing shop costing £60 each.

(6)   Sam uses one of the eight rooms in the couple's private house as an office for when he works at home. The total running costs of the house for the year ended 5 April 2011 were £5,120. This cost is not included in the income statement expenses of £90,300.

(7)   Sam uses his private telephone to make business telephone calls. The total cost of the private telephone for the year ended 5 April 2011 was £1,600, and 25% of this related to business telephone calls. The cost of the private telephone is not included in the income statement expenses of £90,300.

(8)   During the year ended 5 April 2011 Sam took goods out of the clothing shop for his personal use without paying for them and no entry has been made in the accounts to record this. The goods cost £820, and had a selling price of £1,480.

(9)   The tax written down values for capital allowance purposes at 6 April 2010 were as follows:

	£
Main pool	18,500
Expensive motor car (acquired June 2008)	20,200

The expensive motor car is used by Sam.

Kim White

(1)   Kim is employed as a sales person by Sharp-Suit plc, a clothing manufacturing company. During the tax year 2010/11 she was paid a gross annual salary of £21,600.

(2)   On 1 June 2010 Sharp-Suit plc provided Kim with an interest free loan of £12,000 so that she could purchase a new motor car.

(3)   During the period from 1 June 2010 to 5 April 2011 Kim used her private motor car for business and private purposes. She received no reimbursement from Sharp-Suit plc for any of the expenditure incurred. Kim's mileage during this period included the following:

	Miles
Normal daily travel between home and permanent workplace	3,400
Travel between permanent workplace and Sharp-Suit plc's customers	11,200
Travel between home and a temporary workplace for a period of one month	1,300

(4)   During the tax year 2010/11 Kim paid interest of £140 (gross) on a personal loan taken out on 1 January 2010 to purchase a laptop computer for use in her employment with Sharp-Suit plc.

Joint income – Building society deposit account

The couple have savings of £25,000 in a building society deposit account which is in their joint names.

During the tax year 2010/11 Sam and Kim received building society interest of £1,200 in total from this joint account.

This was the actual cash amount received.

Required

(a)   Calculate Sam's tax adjusted trading profit for the year ended 5 April 2011.

Note: Your computation should start with net profit for the period of £50,000 and should list all of the items in the income statement indicating by the use of a zero (0) any items that do not require adjustment.

(11 marks)

(b)   Calculate Sam and Kim's respective income tax liabilities for the tax year 2010/11.

Note: you should ignore any capital allowances that Kim might be entitled to. **(10 marks)**

(c)   Explain to Sam and Kim how their overall income tax liability could be reduced if they were to either:
   (i)   transfer their joint building society deposit account into individual savings accounts (ISAs); or
(2 marks)
   (ii)   transfer their joint building society deposit account into Kim's sole name. **(2 marks)**

(Total = 25 marks)

6 Edmond Brick (TX 12/07)   27 mins

Edmond Brick owns four properties which are let out. The following information relates to the tax year 2010/11:

Property one

This is a freehold house that qualifies as a trade under the furnished holiday letting rules. The property was purchased on 6 April 2010. During the tax year 2010/11 the property was let for eighteen weeks at £370 per week. Edmond spent £5,700 on furniture and kitchen equipment during April 2010. Due to a serious flood £7,400 was spent on repairs during November 2010. The damage was not covered by insurance. The other expenditure on this property for the tax year 2010/11 amounted to £2,710, and this is all allowable.

Property two

This is a freehold house that is let out furnished. The property was let throughout the tax year 2010/11 at a monthly rent of £575, payable in advance. During the tax year 2010/11 Edmond paid council tax of £1,200 and insurance of £340 in respect of this property. He claims the wear and tear allowance for this property.

Property three

This is a freehold house that is let out unfurnished. The property was purchased on 6 April 2010, and it was empty until 30 June 2010. It was then let from 1 July 2010 to 31 January 2011 at a monthly rent of £710, payable in advance. On 31 January 2011 the tenant left owing three months rent which Edmond was unable to recover. The property was not re-let before 5 April 2011. During the tax year 2010/11 Edmond paid insurance of £290 for this property and spent £670 on advertising for tenants. He also paid loan interest of £6,700 in respect of a loan that was taken out to purchase this property.

Property four

This is a leasehold office building that is let out unfurnished. Edmond pays an annual rent of £6,800 for this property, but did not pay a premium when he acquired it. On 6 April 2010 the property was sub-let to a tenant, with Edmond receiving a premium of £15,000 for the grant of a five-year lease. He also received the annual rent of £4,600 which was payable in advance. During the tax year 2010/11 Edmond paid insurance of £360 in respect of this property.

Furnished room

During the tax year 2010/11 Edmond rented out one furnished room of his main residence. During the year he received rent of £5,040, and incurred allowable expenditure of £1,140 in respect of the room. Edmond always computes the taxable income for the furnished room on the most favourable basis.

Required

(a)   State the income tax advantages of property one being treated as a trade under the furnished holiday letting rules.   **(3 marks)**

(b)   Calculate Edmond's furnished holiday letting loss in respect of property one for the tax year 2010/11.
                                                                                                           (3 marks)

(c)   Calculate Edmond's property business profit in respect of the other three properties and the furnished room for the tax year 2010/11.   **(9 marks)**

                                                                                            (Total = 15 marks)

7 Peter Chic (TX 12/08)   45 mins

Peter Chic is employed by Haute-Couture Ltd as a fashion designer. The following information is available for the tax year 2010/11:

Employment

(1)   During the tax year 2010/11 Peter was paid a gross annual salary of £45,600 by Haute-Couture Ltd. Income tax of £14,670 was deducted from this figure under PAYE.

(2)   In addition to his salary, Peter received two bonus payments from Haute-Couture Ltd during the tax year 2010/11. The first bonus of £4,300 was paid on 30 April 2010 and was in respect of the year ended 31 December 2009. Peter became entitled to this first bonus on 10 April 2010. The second bonus of £3,600 was paid on 31 March 2011 and was in respect of the year ended 31 December 2010. Peter became entitled to this second bonus on 25 March 2011.

(3)   Throughout the tax year 2010/11 Haute-Couture Ltd provided Peter with a diesel powered motor car which has a list price of £22,500. The motor car cost Haute-Couture Ltd £21,200, and it has an official CO_2 emission rate of 222 grams per kilometre. Peter made a capital contribution of £2,000 towards the cost of the motor car when it was first provided to him. Haute-Couture Ltd also provided Peter with fuel for private journeys.

(4)   Haute-Couture Ltd has provided Peter with living accommodation since 1 January 2008. The company had purchased the property in 2006 for £160,000, and it was valued at £185,000 on 1 January 2008. Improvements costing £13,000 were made to the property during June 2009 The annual value of the property is £8,225.

(5)   Throughout the tax year 2010/11 Haute-Couture Ltd provided Peter with two mobile telephones. The telephones had each cost £250 when purchased by the company in January 2010.

(6)   On 5 January 2011 Haute-Couture Ltd paid a health club membership fee of £510 for the benefit of Peter.

(7)   During February 2011 Peter spent five nights overseas on company business. Haute-Couture Ltd paid Peter a daily allowance of £10 to cover the cost of personal expenses such as telephone calls to his family.

Property income

(1)   Peter owns two properties, which are let out. Both properties are freehold houses, with the first property being let out furnished and the second property being let out unfurnished.

(2)   The first property was let from 6 April 2010 to 31 August 2010 at a monthly rent of £500, payable in advance. On 31 August 2010 the tenant left owing two months' rent which Peter was unable to recover. The property was not re-let before 5 April 2011. During March 2011 Peter spent £600 repairing the roof of this property.

(3)   The second property was purchased on 1 July 2010, and was then let from 1 August 2010 to 5 April 2011 at a monthly rent of £820, payable in advance. During July 2010 Peter spent £875 on advertising for tenants. For the period 1 July 2010 to 5 April 2011 he paid loan interest of £1,800 in respect of a loan that was taken out to purchase this property.

(4)   Peter insured both of his rental properties at a total cost of £660 for the year ended 30 June 2010, and £1,080 for the year ended 30 June 2011. The insurance is payable annually in advance.

(5)   Where possible, Peter claims the wear and tear allowance.

Other information

(1)   During the tax year 2010/11 Peter received building society interest of £1,760 and dividends of £720. These were the actual cash amounts received.

(2)   On 4 August 2010 Peter received a premium bond prize of £100.

(3)   During the tax year 2010/11 Peter made Gift Aid donations totaling £2,400 (net) to national charities.

Required

(a)   Calculate the income tax payable by Peter Chic for the tax year 2010/11.   **(21 marks)**

(b)   Calculate the total amount of national insurance contributions that will have been paid by Peter Chic and Haute-Couture Ltd in respect of Peter's earnings and benefits for the tax year 2010/11.   **(4 marks)**

(Total = 25 marks)

8 Peach, Plum and Pear (TX 12/08)   13 mins

You are a trainee accountant and your manager has asked for your help regarding three taxpayers who have all made personal pension contributions during the tax year 2010/11.

Ann Peach

Ann, aged 30, is self-employed as an estate agent. Her trading profit for the year ended 5 April 2011 was £49,100. Ann made contributions of £52,000 (gross) into a personal pension scheme during the tax year 2010/11.

Basil Plum

Basil, aged 42, is employed by the Banana Bank plc as a fund manager. During the tax year 2010/11 Basil was paid a gross salary of £330,000. Basil made contributions of £270,000 (gross) into a personal pension scheme during the tax year 2010/11. He is not a member of Banana Bank plc's occupational pension scheme.

Chloe Pear

Chloe, aged 54, lets out unfurnished property. For the tax year 2010/11 her property business profit was £25,000. Chloe made contributions of £8,200 (gross) into a personal pension scheme during the tax year 2010/11.

Neither Ann nor Basil nor Chloe has any other income.

Required

For each of the three taxpayers Ann Peach, Basil Plum and Chloe Pear, state, giving reasons the amount of personal pension contributions that will have qualified for tax relief for the tax year 2010/11. Calculate the income tax liabilities for that year for Ann and Chloe and explain how Basil's income tax liability will be affected by his personal pension contribution.

Note: marks are allocated: Ann Peach 3 marks; Basil Plum 2 marks; and Chloe Pear 2 marks.   **(Total = 7 marks)**

9 Na Style (TX 12/09)

Na Style commenced self-employment as a hairdresser on 1 January 2008. She had tax adjusted trading profits of £25,200 for the six-month period ended 30 June 2008 and £21,600 for the year ended 30 June 2009.

The following information is available for the tax year 2010/11:

Trading profit for the year ended 30 June 2010

(1)   Na's income statement for the year ended 30 June 2010 is as follows:

	Note	£	£
Income			61,300
Expenses			
Depreciation		1,300	
Motor expenses	2	2,200	
Professional fees	3	1,650	
Property expenses	4	12,900	
Purchases	5	4,700	
Other expenses	6	16,550	
			(39,300)
Net profit			22,000

(2)   Na charges all the running expenses for her motor car to the business. During the year ended 30 June 2010 Na drove a total of 8,000 miles, of which 7,000 were for private journeys.

(3)   The figure for professional fees consists of £390 for accountancy and £1,260 for legal fees in connection with the grant of a new five-year lease of parking spaces for customers' motor cars.

(4)   Na lives in a flat that is situated above her hairdressing studio, and one-third of the total property expenses of £12,900 relate to this flat.

(5)   During the year ended 30 June 2010 Na took goods out of the hairdressing business for her personal use without paying for them, and no entry has been made in the accounts to record this. The goods cost £250 and had a selling price of £450.

(6)   The figure for other expenses of £16,550 includes £400 for a fine in respect of health and safety regulations, £80 for a donation to a political party and £160 for a trade subscription to the Guild of Small Hairdressers.

(7)   Na uses her private telephone to make business telephone calls. The total cost of the private telephone for the year ended 30 June 2010 was £1,200, and 20% of this related to business telephone calls. The cost of the private telephone is not included in the income statement expenses of £39,300.

(8)   Capital allowances for the year ended 30 June 2010 are £810.

Other information

(1)   During the tax year 2010/11 Na received dividends of £1,080, building society interest of £560, interest of £310 from an individual savings account (ISA), interest of £1,100 on the maturity of a savings certificate from the National Savings & Investments Bank and interest of £810 from government stocks (gilts). These were the actual cash amounts received in each case.

(2)   Na's payments on account of income tax in respect of the tax year 2010/11 totalled £3,200.

Required

(a)   Calculate the amount of trading profits that will have been assessed on Na Style for the tax years 2007/08, 2008/09 and 2009/10 respectively, clearly identifying the amount of any overlap profits.   **(5 marks)**

(b)   Calculate Na Style's tax adjusted trading profit for the year ended 30 June 2010.

Note: your computation should commence with the net profit figure of £22,000, and should list all of the items referred to in notes (1) to (8) indicating by the use of zero (0) any items that do not require adjustment.   **(8 marks)**

(c)   (i)   Calculate the income tax payable by Na Style for the tax year 2010/11.   **(6 marks)**

(ii)   Calculate Na Style's balancing payment for the tax year 2010/11 and her payments on account for the tax year 2011/12, stating the relevant due dates.

Note: you should ignore national insurance contributions.   **(3 marks)**

(d)   Advise Na Style of the consequences of not making the balancing payment for the tax year 2010/11 until 31 May 2012.

Note: your answer should include calculations as appropriate.   **(3 marks)**

(Total = 25 marks)

10 Simon House (TX 12/09)   **27 mins**

On 30 April 2010 Simon House purchased a derelict freehold house for £127,000. Legal fees of £1,800 were paid in respect of the purchase.

Simon then renovated the house at a cost of £50,600, with the renovation being completed on 10 August 2010. He immediately put the house up for sale, and it was sold on 30 August 2010 for £260,000. Legal fees of £2,600 were paid in respect of the sale.

Simon financed the transaction by a bank loan of £150,000 that was taken out on 30 April 2010 at an annual interest rate of 6%. The bank loan was repaid on 30 August 2010.

Simon had no other income or capital gains for the tax year 2010/11 except as indicated above.

Simon has been advised that whether or not he is treated as carrying on a trade will be determined according to the six following 'badges of trade':

(1)   Subject matter of the transaction.
(2)   Length of ownership.
(3)   Frequency of similar transactions.
(4)   Work done on the property.
(5)   Circumstances responsible for the realisation.
(6)   Motive.

Required

(a)   Briefly explain the meaning of each of the six 'badges of trade' listed in the question.

Note: you are not expected to quote from decided cases.   **(3 marks)**

(b)   Calculate Simon House's income tax liability and his Class 2 and Class 4 national insurance contributions for the tax year 2010/11, if he is treated as carrying on a trade in respect of the disposal of the freehold house.

(8 marks)

(c)   Calculate Simon House's capital gains tax liability for the tax year 2010/11, if he is not treated as carrying on a trade in respect of the disposal of the freehold house.   **(4 marks)**

(Total = 15 marks)

11 Malcolm
27 mins

(a)   Malcolm started in business as a self-employed builder on 1 August 2009. His adjusted trading results, after capital allowances, were:

	£
Period ended 30 November 2009	(10,000) Loss
Year ended 30 November 2010	(20,000) Loss
Year ended 30 November 2011	17,000 Profit

Prior to being self-employed Malcolm was employed as a builder when his earnings were:

	£
2009/10 (to 31 July 2009)	7,600
2008/09	8,000
2007/08	Nil

He received annual building society interest income of £3,040 (net) from 2008/09 onwards. In 2009/10 he realised a capital gain on the disposal of a non-business asset of £9,900 before the annual exempt amount.

Required

Show how Malcolm's trading losses can be utilised most effectively, giving your reasoning.

You may assume the 2010/11 rates and allowances apply to all years relevant to this question.   **(12 marks)**

(b)   You are required to state by what date(s) the claims you are proposing in part (a) should be submitted.

(3 marks)

(Total = 15 marks)

12 Robert Sax
27 mins

Robert Sax commenced trading on 1 June 2003 drawing up accounts to 30 September. His adjusted profits were as follows:

	£
1.6.03 – 30.9.04	30,000
y/e 30.9.05	40,000
y/e 30.9.06	50,000
y/e 30.9.07	60,000
y/e 30.9.08	55,000

He decided to change his accounting date to 31 December. Profits were as follows:

	£
1.10.08 – 31.12.09	75,000
y/e 31.12.10	40,000

He decided to retire on 31 March 2011. His profits of his final 3 months of trade were £12,000.

Required

Calculate the assessments for all years. **(15 marks)**

13 Vanessa Serve and Serene Volley (TX 12/07)   54 mins

(a)   Vanessa Serve and Serene Volley, aged 32 and 35 years respectively, are sisters. The following information is available for the tax year 2010/11:

Vanessa Serve

(1)   Vanessa is self-employed as a tennis coach. Her tax adjusted trading profit for the year ended 30 June 2010 is £52,400. However, this figure is before taking account of capital allowances.

(2)   The only item of plant and machinery owned by Vanessa is her motor car. This originally cost £19,000 in July 2007 and at 1 July 2009 had a tax written down value of £13,000. During the year ended 30 June 2010 Vanessa drove a total of 20,000 miles, of which 6,000 were for private journeys.

(3)   Vanessa contributed £6,400 (gross) into a personal pension scheme during the tax year 2010/11.

(4)   In addition to her self-employed income, Vanessa received interest of £1,100 from an investment account at National Savings & Investments during the tax year 2010/11. This was the actual cash amount received.

(5)   Vanessa's payments on account in respect of the tax year 2010/11 totalled £8,460.

Serene Volley

(1)   Serene is employed as a sports journalist by Backhand plc, a newspaper publishing company. During the tax year 2010/11 she was paid a gross annual salary of £26,400. Income tax of £4,490 was deducted from this figure under PAYE.

(2)   Throughout the tax year 2010/11 Backhand plc provided Serene with a petrol powered motor car which has a list price of £16,400. The official CO_2 emission rate for the motor car is 182 grams per kilometre. The company did not provide Serene with any fuel for private journeys.

(3)   Serene contributed 5% of her gross salary of £26,400 into Backhand plc's HM Revenue and Customs' registered occupational pension scheme.

(4)   In addition to her employment income, Serene received interest of £1,200 on the maturity of a savings certificate from National Savings & Investments during the tax year 2010/11. This was the actual cash amount received.

(5)   Serene did not make any payments on account in respect of the tax year 2010/11.

Required

(i)   Calculate the income tax payable by Vanessa and Serene respectively for the tax year 2010/11.

                                                                                                (11 marks)

(ii)   Calculate the national insurance contributions payable by Vanessa and Serene respectively for the tax year 2010/11.   **(4 marks)**

(iii) Calculate Vanessa and Serene's respective balancing payments for the tax year 2010/11 and their payments on account, if any, for the tax year 2011/12. You should state the relevant due dates.
                                                                                                (5 marks)

(b)   Note that in answering this part of the question you are not expected to take account of any of the information provided in part (a) above.

Unless stated otherwise all of the figures below are exclusive of VAT.

Vanessa Serve is registered for value added tax (VAT), and is in the process of completing her VAT return for the quarter ended 31 March 2011. The following information is available:

(1)   There were no transactions before 4 January 2011.

(2)   Sales invoices totalling £18,000 were issued in respect of standard rated sales. All of Vanessa's customers are members of the general public.

(3)   During the quarter ended 31 March 2011 Vanessa spent £600 on mobile telephone calls, of which 40% related to private calls.

(4)   On 3 February 2011 Vanessa purchased a motor car for £12,000. On 18 March 2011 £987 was spent on repairs to the motor car. The motor car is used by Vanessa in her business, although approximately 10% of the mileage is for private journeys. Both figures are inclusive of VAT at the standard rate.

(5)   On 29 March 2011 tennis coaching equipment was purchased for £1,760. Vanessa paid for the equipment on this date, but did not take delivery of the equipment or receive an invoice until 3 April 2011. This purchase was standard rated.

(6)   In addition to the above, Vanessa also had other standard rated expenses amounting to £2,200 in the quarter ended 31 March 2011 This figure includes £400 for entertaining customers.

Required

(i)   Calculate the amount of VAT payable by Vanessa for the quarter ended 31 March 2011.   **(5 marks)**

(ii)   Advise Vanessa of the condition that she must satisfy before being permitted to use the VAT flat rate scheme, and the advantages of joining the scheme. The relevant flat rate scheme percentage for Vanessa's trade as notified by HM Revenue and Customs is 8.5%.

Note: your answer should be supported by appropriate calculations of the amount of tax saving if Vanessa had used the flat rate scheme to calculate the amount of VAT payable for the quarter ended 31 March 2011.   **(5 marks)**

(Total = 30 marks)

14 Samantha Fabrique (TX 12/07)   18 mins

Samantha Fabrique has been a self-employed manufacturer of clothing since 1998. She has the following gross income and chargeable gains for the tax years 2008/09 to 2011/12:

	2008/09	2009/10	2010/11	2011/12
	£	£	£	£
Trading profit/(loss)	6,290	51,600	(84,000)	12,390
Building society interest	–	2,100	3,800	1,500
Chargeable gains/(loss)	20,100	23,300	(3,400)	13,500

The chargeable gains are stated before taking account of loss relief and the annual exempt amount.

Required

(a)   State the factors that will influence an individual's choice of loss relief claims.   **(3 marks)**

(b)   Calculate Samantha's taxable income and taxable gains for each of the tax years 2008/09, 2009/10, 2010/11 and 2011/12 on the assumption that she relieves the trading loss of £84,000 for the tax year 2010/11 on the most favourable basis.

You should assume that the tax rates and allowances for the tax year 2010/11 apply throughout.   **(7 marks)**

(Total = 10 marks)

15 Wright and Wong   18 mins

Geoff Wright and Sam Wong are in partnership running a design studio, with profits being shared in the ratio 4:1. They both wish to start saving for their retirement and would like to make maximum contributions to a pension. The partnership's trading profit for tax year 2010/11 is £175,000. Neither Geoff or Sam has any other income.

Required

(a)   Advise Geoff and Sam of the maximum amount they can each contribute in tax year 2010/11 to obtain tax relief.

(4 marks)

(b)   Explain the method by which Geoff and Sam will be given tax relief for their pension contributions and show their income tax liability.   **(5 marks)**

(c)   Explain how they will be able to continue to contribute to their pensions if the partnership ceases trading on 5 April 2011 and they no longer have earnings. **(1 mark)**

(Total = 10 marks)

16 Amy Bwalya (BTX)   27 mins

(a)   Amy Bwalya commenced in self-employment on 1 August 2008, preparing accounts to 31 May. Her trading profits for the first two periods of trading were as follows:

	£
Ten-month period ended 31 May 2009	38,500
Year ended 31 May 2010	52,800

Required

Calculate the amount of trading profits that will have been assessed on Amy for the tax years 2008/09, 2009/10 and 2010/11. Your answer should show the amount of overlap profits.   **(5 marks)**

(b)   Cedric Ding and Eli Fong commenced in partnership on 6 April 2006, preparing accounts to 5 April. Cedric resigned as a partner on 31 December 2010, and Gordon Hassan joined as a partner on 1 January 2011. The partnership's trading profit for the year ended 5 April 2011 is £90,000. Profits were shared as follows:

   (1)   Eli was paid an annual salary of £6,000.
   (2)   Interest was paid at the rate of 10% on the partners' capital accounts, the balances on which were:

	£
Cedric	40,000
Eli	70,000
Gordon (from 1 January 2011)	20,000

Cedric's capital account was repaid to him on 31 December 2010.

   (3)   The balance of profits were shared:

	Cedric	Eli	Gordon
	%	%	%
6 April 2010 to 31 December 2010	60	40	
1 January 2011 to 5 April 2011		70	30

Required

Calculate the trading income assessments of Cedric, Eli and Gordon for the tax year 2010/11.   **(5 marks)**

(c)   Ivan Jha ceased trading on 31 December 2010. He had commenced in self-employment on 1 October 2003, initially preparing accounts to 30 September. His overlap profits for the period 1 October 2003 to 5 April 2004 were £4,500. Ivan subsequently changed his accounting date to 30 June by preparing accounts for the nine month period to 30 June 2009. His trading profits for the final four periods of trading were as follows:

	£
Year ended 30 September 2008	36,000
Nine-month period ended 30 June 2009	23,400
Year ended 30 June 2010	28,800
Six-month period ended 31 December 2010	10,800

Required

Calculate the amount of trading profits that will have been assessed on Ivan for the tax years 2008/09, 2009/10 and 2010/11.   **(5 marks)**

(Total = 15 marks)

17 Ae, Bee, Cae, Dee and Eu (TX 12/08)   27 mins

(a)   Ae and Bee commenced in partnership on 1 July 2008 preparing accounts to 30 June. Cae joined as a
       partner on 1 July 2010. Profits have always been shared equally. The partnership's trading profits since the
       commencement of trading have been as follows:

	£
Year ended 30 June 2009	54,000
Year ended 30 June 2010	66,000
Year ended 30 June 2011	87,000

Required

Calculate the trading income assessments of Ae, Bee and Cae for each of the tax years 2008/09, 2009/10
and 2010/11.   **(5 marks)**

(b)   Dee commenced in self-employment on 6 April 2007. She initially prepared accounts to 5 April, but changed
       her accounting date to 31 July by preparing accounts for the four-month period to 31 July 2009. Dee's
       trading profits since she commenced trading have been as follows:

	£
Year ended 5 April 2008	35,160
Year ended 5 April 2009	32,880
Four-month period ended 31 July 2009 05.04.09 – 31.07.09	16,240
Year ended 31 July 2010	54,120

Required

(i)   Calculate the amount of trading profits that will have been assessed on Dee for each of the tax years
       2008/09, 2009/10 and 2010/11.   **(4 marks)**

(ii)   State the amount of Dee's unrelieved overlap profits as at 5 April 2011.   **(1 mark)**

(c)   Eu ceased trading on 30 September 2010, having been self-employed since 1 July 2002.

(1)   Eu's trading profits for the final three periods of trading were as follows:

	£
Year ended 30 June 2009	62,775
Year ended 30 June 2010	57,600
Three-month period ended 30 September 2010	14,400

These figures are before taking account of capital allowances.

(2)   The tax written-down value of the capital allowances main pool at 1 July 2008 was £7,875. On
       15 September 2010 Eu purchased office furniture for £2,400. All of the items included in the main
       pool were sold for £4,300 on 30 September 2010.

(3)   Until the final period of trading Eu had always prepared accounts to 30 June. Her overlap profits for
       the period 1 July 2002 to 5 April 2003 were £19,800.

Required

Calculate the amount of trading profits that will have been assessed on Eu for each of the tax years 2009/10
and 2010/11.   **(5 marks)**

                                                                                (Total = 15 marks)

18 Auy Man and Bim Men (TX 06/10)   54 mins

Auy Man and Bim Men have been in partnership since 6 April 2001 as management consultants. The following
information is available for the tax year 2010/11:

Personal information

Auy is aged 32. During the tax year 2010/11 she spent 190 days in the United Kingdom. Bim is aged 56. During the
tax year 2010/11 she spent 100 days in the United Kingdom. Bim has spent the same amount of time in the United
Kingdom for each of the previous five tax years.

Income statement for the year ended 5 April 2011

The partnership's summarised income statement for the year ended 5 April 2011 is as follows:

	Note	£	£
Sales revenue	1		142,200
Expenses	2		
Depreciation		3,400	
Motor expenses	3	4,100	
Other expenses	4	1,800	
Wages and salaries	5	50,900	
			(60,200)
Profit before taxation			82,000

(1)   The sales figure of £142,200 is exclusive of output value added tax (VAT) of £21,600.

(2)   The expenses figures are exclusive of recoverable input VAT of:

Motor expenses £180

Other expenses £140

(3)   The figure of £4,100 for motor expenses includes £2,600 in respect of the partners' motor cars, with 30% of this amount being in respect of private journeys.

(4)   The figure of £1,800 for other expenses includes £720 for entertaining employees. The remaining expenses are all allowable.

(5)   The figure of £50,900 for wages and salaries includes the annual salary of £4,000 paid to Bim (see the profit sharing note below), and the annual salary of £15,000 paid to Auy's husband, who works part-time for the partnership. Another part-time employee doing the same job is paid a salary of £10,000 per annum.

Plant and machinery

On 6 April 2010 the tax written down values of the partnership's plant and machinery were as follows:

	£
Main pool	3,100
Motor car [1]	18,000
Motor car [2]	14,000

The following transactions took place during the year ended 5 April 2011:

		Cost/(proceeds) £
8 May 2010	Sold motor car [2]	(13,100)
8 May 2010	Purchased motor car [3]	11,600
21 November 2010	Purchased motor car [4]	14,200
14 January 2011	Purchased motor car [5]	8,700

Motor car [1] has a CO_2 emission rate of 185 grams per kilometre. It is used by Auy and 70% of the mileage is for business journeys. It was acquired before 6 April 2009.

Motor car [2] had a CO_2 emission rate of 145 grams per kilometre. It was used by Bim and 70% of the mileage was for business journeys. It was acquired before 6 April 2009.

Motor car [3] purchased on 8 May 2010 has a CO_2 emission rate of 105 grams per kilometre. It is used by Bim and 70% of the mileage is for business journeys.

Motor car [4] purchased on 21 November 2010 has a CO_2 emission rate of 135 grams per kilometre. Motor car [5] purchased on 14 January 2011 has a CO_2 emission rate of 200 grams per kilometre. These two motor cars are used by employees of the business.

Profit sharing

Profits are shared 80% to Auy and 20% to Bim. This is after paying an annual salary of £4,000 to Bim, and interest at the rate of 5% on the partners' capital account balances. The capital account balances are:

	£
Auy Man	56,000
Bim Men	34,000

VAT

The partnership has been registered for VAT since 6 April 2001. However, the partnership has recently started invoicing for its services on new payment terms, and the partners are concerned about output VAT being accounted for at the appropriate time.

Required

(a) Explain why both Auy Man and Bim Men will each be treated for tax purposes as resident in the United Kingdom for the tax year 2010/11. **(2 marks)**

(b) Calculate the partnership's tax adjusted trading profit for the year ended 5 April 2011 and the trading income assessments of Auy Man and Bim Men for the tax year 2010/11.

Note: Your computation should commence with the profit before taxation figure of £82,000, and should also list all of the items referred to in notes (2) to (5) indicating by the use of zero (0) any items that do not require adjustment. **(15 marks)**

(c) Calculate the Class 4 national insurance contributions payable by Auy Man and Bim Men for the tax year 2010/11. **(3 marks)**

(d) (i) Advise the partnership of the VAT rules that determine the tax point in respect of a supply of services; **(3 marks)**

(ii) Calculate the amount of VAT paid by the partnership to HM Revenue & Customs throughout the year ended 5 April 2011;

Note: you should ignore the output VAT scale charges due in respect of fuel for private journeys. **(2 marks)**

(iii) Advise the partnership of the conditions that it must satisfy in order to join and continue to use the VAT flat rate scheme, and calculate the tax saving if the partnership had used the flat rate scheme to calculate the amount of VAT payable throughout the year ended 5 April 2011.

Note: you should assume that the relevant flat rate scheme percentage for the partnership's trade was11% throughout the whole of the year ended 5 April 2011. **(5 marks)**

(Total = 30 marks)

19 Pi Casso (TX 06/08) 27 mins

Pi Casso has been a self-employed artist since 1992, making up her accounts to 30 June. Pi's tax liabilities for the tax years 2008/09, 2009/10 and 2010/11 are as follows:

	2008/09 £	2009/10 £	2010/11 £
Income tax liability	3,240	4,100	2,730
Class 2 national insurance contributions	120	125	125
Class 4 national insurance contributions	1,240	990	990
Capital gains tax liability	–	4,880	–

No income tax has been deducted at source.

Required

(a) Prepare a schedule showing the payments on account and balancing payments that Pi will have made or will have to make during the period from 1 July 2010 to 31 March 2012 if Pi makes any appropriate claims to reduce her payments on account, clearly identifying the relevant due date of each payment **(8 marks)**

(b) State the implications if Pi had made a claim to reduce her payments on account for 2010/11 to nil.

(2 marks)

(c) Advise Pi of the latest submission date for her 2010/11 self-assessment tax return. **(2 marks)**

(d)   State the date by which HMRC will have to notify Pi if they intend to enquire into her self-assessment tax return for 2010/11 and the possible reasons why such an enquiry would be made.   **(3 marks)**

(Total = 15 marks)

20 Ernest Vader (TX 06/10)   27 mins

You should assume that today's date is 30 June 2012.

You are a trainee Chartered Certified Accountant and are dealing with the tax affairs of Ernest Vader.

Ernest's self-assessment tax return for the tax year 2010/11 was submitted to HM Revenue & Customs (HMRC) on 15 May 2011 and Ernest paid the resulting income tax liability by the due date of 31 January 2012. However, you have just discovered that during the tax year 2010/11 Ernest disposed of a freehold property, the details of which were omitted from his self-assessment tax return. The capital gains tax liability in respect of this disposal is £18,000 and this amount has not been paid.

Ernest has suggested that since HMRC's right to raise an enquiry into his self-assessment tax return for the tax year 2010/11 expired on 15 May 2012, no disclosure should be made to HMRC of the capital gain.

Required

(a)   Briefly explain the difference between tax evasion and tax avoidance, and how HMRC would view the situation if Ernest Vader does not disclose his capital gain.   **(3 marks)**

(b)   Briefly explain from an ethical viewpoint how you, as a trainee Chartered Certified Accountant, should deal with the suggestion from Ernest Vader that no disclosure is made to HMRC of his capital gain.   **(3 marks)**

(c)   State the action HMRC will take should they wish to obtain information from Ernest Vader regarding his capital gain.   **(1 mark)**

(d)   Explain why, even though the right to raise an enquiry has expired, HMRC will still be entitled to raise an assessment should they discover that Ernest Vader has not disclosed his capital gain.   **(2 marks)**

(e)   Assuming that HMRC discover the capital gain and raise an assessment in respect of Ernest Vader's capital gains tax liability of £18,000 for the tax year 2010/11, and that this amount is then paid on 31 July 2012:

   (i)   Calculate the amount of interest that will be payable;

         Note: you should assume that the rates for the tax year 2010/11 continue to apply.   **(2 marks)**

   (ii)   Advise Ernest Vader as to the amount of penalty that is likely to be charged as a result of the failure to notify HMRC and how this could have been reduced if the capital gain had been disclosed.

                                                                                              (4 marks)

(Total = 15 marks)

CHARGEABLE GAINS FOR INDIVIDUALS

Questions 21 to 26 cover the taxation of chargeable gains for individuals, the subject of Part C of the BPP Study Text for Paper F6.

21 Jack Chan   27 mins

Jack Chan has been in business as a sole trader since 1 May 2003. On 28 February 2011 he transferred the business to his daughter Jill, at which time the following assets were sold to her:

(1)   Goodwill with a market value of £60,000. The goodwill has been built up since 1 May 2003, and has a nil cost. Jill paid Jack £50,000 for the goodwill.

(2)   A freehold office building with a market value of £130,000. The office building was purchased for £110,000 and has always been used by Jack for business purposes. Jill paid Jack £105,000 for the office building.

(3)   A freehold warehouse with a market value of £140,000. The warehouse was purchased for £95,000 and has never been used by Jack for business purposes. Jill paid Jack £135,000 for the warehouse.

Where possible, Jack and Jill have elected to hold over any gains arising.

Jack also made the following disposals during the year.

(4)   He sold his entire holding of 12,000 ordinary shares (a 1% holding) in Coleman plc for £16,000 on 1 September 2010. He had purchased 10,000 shares in January 2004 for £8,000. In December 2005 there was a 1:5 bonus issue.

(5)   He sold three acres of a twelve acre plot of land for £45,600 on 1 November 2010. He had acquired the original plot of land for £125,000. He refused an offer of £250,000 for the remaining nine acres.

Jack has unused capital losses of £6,100 brought forward from 2009/10. He had taxable income of £24,000 in tax year 2010/11 and made a gift aid payment of £1,200 in December 2010.

Required

(a)   Calculate Jack's capital gains tax liability for tax year 2010/11, and advise him by when this should be paid. Assume that gift relief is claimed where possible and entrepreneurs' relief is not claimed.   **(11 marks)**

(b)   Recalculate Jack's capital gains tax liability assuming he claims entrepreneurs' relief but does not claim gift relief. Assume that Jack has not made any previous claims for entrepreneurs' relief.   **(4 marks)**

                                                                             (Total = 15 marks)

22 Peter Shaw   27 mins

Peter Shaw made the following disposals in tax year 2010/11:

(1)   On 10 August 2010 he sold a building for £600,000. He had purchased the building for £200,000 which he let commercially as offices to an unquoted company.

(2)   He held 20,000 shares in Forum Follies plc which he purchased in May 1999 for £50,000. In March 2011, Exciting Enterprises plc acquired all the share capital of Forum Follies plc. Under the terms of the take-over for every two shares previously held in Forum Follies plc shareholders received three ordinary shares in Exciting Enterprises plc plus £1 cash. Immediately after the take-over the ordinary shares in Exciting Enterprises plc were quoted at £3 each. Peter's shareholding represented less than a 1% holding in each company.

(3)   Peter purchased shares in Dassau plc, a quoted company, as follows.

	No. of shares	Cost
		£
December 1985	1,000	2,000
April 2001 1 for 2 rights issue		£2 per share

In November 2010 he sold 1,200 shares for £9,500. Peter has never worked for Dassau plc.

Peter had capital losses brought forward from 2009/10 of £6,400. His taxable income in tax year 2010/11 is £15,000.

Peter's wife Janet has a 12% shareholding in Dot Ltd, an unquoted trading company where she has worked for the past ten years. She sold her shares in March 2011 and realised a gain of £900,000. She is concerned that she will have to pay 28% capital gains tax on the gain. Her taxable income in the tax year 2010/11 is £45,000. The only other disposal that she has made for CGT is the disposal of a painting in November 2010 realising a gain of £10,100.

Required

(a) Calculate the CGT payable by Peter for tax year 2010/11 and state when it is due. **(11 marks)**

(b) Advise Janet whether she will have a 28% capital gains tax liability on the disposal of the shares in Dot Ltd.

(4 marks)

(Total = 15 marks)

23 David and Angela Brook (TX 12/07)   36 mins

David and Angela Brook are a married couple. They each had taxable income in excess of £37,400 in tax year 2010/11. Until tax year 2010/11 they had made no disposals of assets for capital gains tax. They disposed of the following assets during the tax year 2010/11:

Jointly owned property

(1) On 29 July 2010 David and Angela sold a classic Ferrari motor car for £34,400. The motor car had been purchased for £27,200.

(2) On 30 September 2010 David and Angela sold a house for £393,900. The house had been purchased on 1 October 1989 for £86,000. David and Angela occupied the house as their main residence from the date of purchase until 31 March 1993.

The house was then unoccupied between 1 April 1993 and 31 December 1996 due to Angela being required by her employer to work elsewhere in the United Kingdom.

From 1 January 1997 until 31 December 2004 David and Angela again occupied the house as their main residence. The house was then unoccupied until it was sold on 30 September 2010.

Throughout the period 1 October 1989 to 30 September 2010 David and Angela did not have any other main residence.

David Brook

(1) On 18 July 2010 David sold an antique table for £5,600. The antique table had been purchased for £3,200.

(2) On 5 August 2010 David transferred his entire shareholding of 20,000 £1 ordinary shares in Bend Ltd, an unquoted investment company, to Angela. On that date the shares were valued at £64,000. David's shareholding had been purchased on 21 June 2006 for £48,000.

(3) On 14 February 2011 David made a gift of 15,000 £1 ordinary shares in Galatico plc to his son. On that date the shares were quoted on the Stock Exchange at £2.90 – £3.10. David had originally purchased 8,000 shares in Galatico plc on 15 June 2007 for £17,600, and he purchased a further 12,000 shares on 24 August 2007 for £21,600. On 10 July 2008 Galatico plc made a rights issue of 1 for 4 at £2 per share. David purchased his full entitlement of rights issue shares. David's total shareholding was less than 1% of Galatico plc's issued share capital.

Angela Brook

(1) On 5 July 2010 Angela sold an antique clock for £7,200. The antique clock had been purchased for £3,700.

(2) On 7 July 2010 Angela sold 15,000 of the 20,000 £1 ordinary shares in Bend Ltd that had been transferred to her from David. The sale proceeds were £62,400.

(3) On 1 November 2010 Angela sold her sole trader business which she had run since February 2001. Her shop was sold for £180,000 and goodwill for £40,000. The shop had been purchased for £102,000. The goodwill had no cost.

Compute David and Angela's respective capital gains tax liabilities for the tax year 2010/11.   **(20 marks)**

24 Wilson Biazma (TX 06/08)   **36 mins**

Wilson Biazma is resident and ordinarily resident in the United Kingdom for tax purposes. In tax year 2010/11, his taxable income was £10,000. He disposed of the following assets during the tax year 2010/11:

(1)   On 21 July 2010 Wilson sold a freehold office building for £246,000. The office building had been purchased for £144,000. Wilson has made a claim to rollover the gain on the office building against the replacement cost of a new freehold office building that was purchased on 14 January 2010 for £136,000. Both office buildings have always been used entirely for business purposes in a wholesale business run by Wilson as a sole trader.

(2)   On 26 August 2010 Wilson incorporated a retail business that he had run as a sole trader since 1 June 2006. The market value of the business on 26 August 2010 was £100,000. All of the business assets were transferred to a new limited company, with the consideration consisting of 70,000 £1 ordinary shares valued at £70,000 and £30,000 in cash. The only chargeable asset of the business was goodwill and this was valued at £40,000 on 26 August 2010. The goodwill has a nil cost. Wilson took full advantage of the available incorporation relief.

(3)   On 17 August 2010 Wilson made a gift of his entire holding of 10,000 £1 ordinary shares (a 100% holding) in Gandua Ltd, an unquoted trading company, to his daughter. The market value of the shares on that date was £160,000. The shares had been purchased on 8 January 2010 for £112,000. On 17 August 2010 the market value of Gandua Ltd's chargeable assets was £180,000, of which £150,000 was in respect of chargeable business assets. Wilson and his daughter have elected to hold over the gain on this gift of a business asset.

(4)   On 3 October 2010 an antique vase owned by Wilson was destroyed in a fire. The antique vase had been purchased for £49,000. Wilson received insurance proceeds of £68,000 on 20 December 2010 and on 22 December 2010 he paid £69,500 for a replacement antique vase. Wilson has made a claim to defer the gain arising from the receipt of the insurance proceeds.

(5)   On 9 March 2011 Wilson sold ten acres of land for £85,000. He had originally purchased twenty acres of land as an investment for £120,000. The market value of the unsold ten acres of land as at 9 March 2011 was £65,000.

(6)   On 17 November 2010 Wilson sold 6,000 ordinary shares (a 10% holding) in WJD Ltd which is a trading company. Wilson had paid £1 for each share in June 2000 and received sale proceeds of £13 per share. He had worked for WJD Ltd since June 2001.

Wilson has made claims for entrepreneurs' relief where relevant. He has not made any claims for this relief prior to tax year 2010/11.

Required

(a)   Briefly explain when a person will be treated as resident or ordinarily resident in the United Kingdom for a particular tax year and state how a person's residence status establishes whether or not they are liable to capital gains tax.

   Note: you are not expected to explain the rules concerning people leaving or coming to the United Kingdom.

   (4 marks)

(b)   Calculate Wilson's liability to capital gains tax for the tax year 2010/11, clearly identifying the effects of the reliefs claimed in respect of disposals (1) to (6).   **(16 marks)**

   (Total = 20 marks)

25 Nim and Mae (TX 06/09)

36 mins

Nim and Mae Lom are a married couple. They disposed of the following assets during the tax year 2010/11:

Nim Lom

(1) On 20 July 2010 Nim made a gift of 10,000 £1 ordinary shares in Kapook plc to his daughter. On that date the shares were quoted on the Stock Exchange at £3.70 – £3.90, with recorded bargains of £3.60, £3.75 and £3.80. Nim has made the following purchases of shares in Kapook plc:

19 February 2001	8,000 shares for £16,200
6 June 2006	6,000 shares for £14,600
24 July 2010	2,000 shares for £5,800

Nim's total shareholding was less than 5% of Kapook plc, and so holdover relief is not available.

(2) On 13 August 2010 Nim transferred his entire shareholding of 5,000 £1 ordinary shares in Jooba Ltd, an unquoted company, to his wife, Mae. On that date the shares were valued at £28,200. Nim's shareholding had been purchased on 11 January 2007 for £16,000.

(3) On 26 November 2010 Nim sold an antique table for £8,700. The antique table had been purchased for £5,200.

(4) On 2 April 2011 Nim sold UK Government securities (Gilts) for £12,400. The securities had been purchased for £10,100.

Mae Lom

(1) On 28 August 2010 Mae sold 2,000 of the 5,000 £1 ordinary shares in Jooba Ltd that had been transferred to her from Nim (see (2) above). The sale proceeds were £30,400. Entrepreneurs' relief is not available in respect of this disposal.

(2) On 30 September 2010 Mae sold a house for £186,000. The house had been purchased on 1 October 2000 for £122,000. Throughout the period of ownership the house was occupied by Nim and Mae as their main residence, but one of the house's eight rooms was always used exclusively for business purposes by Mae. Entrepreneurs' relief is not available in respect of this disposal.

(3) On 30 November 2010 Mae sold a business that she had run as a sole trader since 1 December 2002. The sale resulted in the following capital gains:

	£
Goodwill	80,000
Freehold office building	136,000
Investment property	34,000

The assets were all owned for more than one year prior to the date of disposal. The investment property has always been rented out.

Mae claimed entrepreneurs' relief in respect of this disposal. This is her first claim for entrepreneurs' relief.

(4) On 31 March 2011 Mae sold a copyright for £9,600. The copyright had been purchased on 1 April 2006 for £10,000 when it had an unexpired life of 20 years.

Other information

Nim has unused capital losses of £16,700 brought forward from the tax year 2009/10.

Mae has unused capital losses of £8,500 brought forward from the tax year 2009/10.

Nim has taxable income of £10,000 in tax year 2010/11.

Mae has taxable income of £25,000 in tax year 2010/11.

Required

Compute Nim and Mae Lom's respective capital gains tax liabilities, if any, for the tax year 2010/11. In each case, the amount of unused capital losses carried forward to future tax years, if any, should be clearly identified.

(20 marks)

You are a trainee accountant and your manager has asked for your help regarding three taxpayers who have all disposed of assets during the tax year 2010/11.

(a) **Amanda Moon**

On 30 June 2010 Amanda incorporated a business. She had run the business as a sole trader since 1 July 2004.

The market value of the business assets on 30 June 2010 was £300,000. This figure, along with the respective cost of each asset, is made up as follows:

	Market value	Cost
	£	£
Goodwill	90,000	Nil
Freehold shop	165,000	120,000
Net current assets	45,000	45,000
	300,000	

The freehold shop has always been used by Amanda for business purposes. All of the business assets were transferred to a new limited company, Ammoon Ltd, with the consideration consisting of 300,000 £1 ordinary shares valued at £300,000. Amanda took full advantage of the available incorporation relief.

Required

(i) Calculate Amanda Moon's chargeable gains, if any, for the tax year 2010/11, and the base cost of her 300,000 £1 ordinary shares in Ammoon Ltd. **(4 marks)**

(ii) Explain how your answer to (i) above would have differed if the consideration for the transfer of Amanda Moon's business had instead consisted of 200,000 £1 ordinary shares and £100,000 in cash. **(3 marks)**

Note: You should ignore entrepreneurs' relief.

(b) **Bo Neptune**

On 31 July 2010 Bo made a gift of his entire holding of 50,000 £1 ordinary shares (a 100% holding) in Botune Ltd, an unquoted trading company, to his son. The market value of the shares on that date was £210,000. The shares had been purchased by Bo on 22 January 2004 for £94,000. Bo and his son have elected to hold over the gain as a gift of a business asset.

Required

(i) Calculate Bo Neptune's chargeable gain, if any, for the tax year 2010/11, and the base cost of his son's 50,000 £1 ordinary shares in Botune Ltd. **(3 marks)**

(ii) Explain how your answer to (i) above would have differed if the shares in Botune Ltd had instead been sold to Bo Neptune's son for £160,000. **(2 marks)**

Note: You should ignore entrepreneurs' relief.

(c) **Charles Orion**

On 30 September 2010 Charles sold a house for £282,000. The house had been purchased on 1 October 1998 for £110,000.

He occupied the house as his main residence from the date of purchase until 31 March 2000. The house was then unoccupied between 1 April 2000 and 31 December 2008 when Charles went to live with his parents due to his father's illness. From 1 January 2009 until 30 September 2010 Charles again occupied the house as his main residence.

Throughout the period 1 October 1998 to 30 September 2010 Charles did not have any other main residence.

Required

(i)   Calculate Charles Orion's chargeable gain, if any, for the tax year 2010/11.   **(5 marks)**

(ii)   Explain how your answer to (i) above would have differed if Charles Orion had rented out his house during the period 1 April 2000 to 31 December 2008.   **(3 marks)**

(Total = 20 marks)

INHERITANCE TAX

Questions 27 to 30 cover inheritance tax, the subject of Part E of the BPP Study Text for Paper F6.

27 Naomi

27 mins

On 6 May each year, Naomi gave quoted shares worth £3,000 to her son Marcus.

She also made the following gifts in her lifetime:

Date	Gift	Donee
15 August 2002	Cash of £300,000	Trust (Trustees paid the IHT due)
12 September 2007	3,000 shares in BCD Ltd (see below)	Marcus
14 February 2009	House valued at £90,000	Trust (Naomi paid the IHT due)

BCD Ltd was an investment company owned by Naomi and her brother and sister. Naomi had owned 5,000 shares in the company since its incorporation. These shares had a market value of £50,000 immediately before the gift to Marcus. At 12 September 2007, the 3,000 shares gifted had a market value of £18,000 and the remaining 2,000 shares retained by Naomi had a market value of £4,000. In April 2010, Naomi sold the remainder of her shares to an outside investor.

Naomi died on 12 October 2010. At her death, the value of the house gifted in 2009 was £110,000.

Naomi left a net estate of £550,000 at her death. In her Will, she left a legacy of £250,000 to her husband, Robert, and the residue of her estate to Marcus.

Required

(a) Describe the inheritance tax implications of the gifts made during Naomi's lifetime whilst Naomi was still alive and calculate any inheritance due during Naomi's lifetime. **(7 marks)**

Nil rate bands for previous years
2002/03	£250,000
2007/08	£300,000
2008/09	£312,000

(b) Describe the inheritance tax implications of Naomi's death on the gifts made during her lifetime. Calculate any inheritance tax due on these gifts as the result of her death. **(6 marks)**

(c) Describe the inheritance tax implications of the terms of Naomi's Will. Compute any inheritance tax due on the death estate. **(2 marks)**

(Total = 15 marks)

28 Malakai and Moira

27 mins

(a) Malakai married Jasmine in 2000. They had one child, Tamara, who was born in 2003. Malakai died on 26 September 2010 leaving the following assets:

	£
Quoted share portfolio	210,000
House	325,000
Chattels	10,000
Cash in ISA	11,500
Car	15,000

Malakai also had the following debts at his death:

	£
Mortgage secured on house (N)	100,000
Credit card	7,000
Bank overdraft	4,500
Council tax	800
Gambling debt owed to friend Joe	1,000

Note: The mortgage was an endowment mortgage and was paid off in full by the proceeds of an insurance policy which matured on Malakai's death.

In his Will, Malakai left £100,000 to Jasmine and the remainder of his estate on trust for the benefit of Tamara. He appointed Jasmine and Joe to be the trustees of the trust for Tamara and his brother, Ezra, to be the sole executor of his Will.

Ezra paid Malakai's funeral expenses of £5,600 on 10 January 2011.

Ezra filed an IHT account for Malakai's death estate on 20 February 2011.

In his lifetime, the only transfer of value that Malakai had made was a cash gift of £256,000 to his brother in August 2008.

Required

Compute Malakai's death estate and the inheritance tax payable on it. State who is liable to pay this tax and the due date for payment.

(10 marks)

(b) Moira and Stuart were married for many years. 90% of Stuart's nil rate band was used when he died on 5 May 2005.

Moira gave quoted shares worth £340,000 to one of her nephews in September 2009. This was the only lifetime gift that she made. Moira died in January 2011 leaving a net death estate of £600,000 to a trust for her nephews and nieces.

Required

Explain the inheritance tax implications of Moria's death, assuming any beneficial claims are made. State the due date for payment of the inheritance tax on her death estate.

(5 marks)

(Total = 15 marks)

29 Artem   27 mins

Artem died on 15 December 2010. During his lifetime he made the following cash gifts:

Date	Donee	£
10 December 2002	Daughter	65,000
17 January 2007	Trust	296,000
	(Artem paid the IHT)	
15 February 2007	Nephew	200
18 August 2007	Sister	46,000
17 June 2008	Trust	103,000
	(Trustees paid the IHT)	
1 August 2009	Grandson on the occasion of his marriage	66,000
5 September 2009	Wife	40,000

Required

(a) Explain the inheritance tax implications of these gifts during Artem's lifetime and compute any lifetime inheritance tax payable. **(9 marks)**

> **Nil rate bands**
> | | |
> |---|---|
> | 2002/03 | £250,000 |
> | 2006/07 | £285,000 |
> | 2007/08 | £300,000 |
> | 2008/09 | £312,000 |
> | 2009/10 | £325,000 |

(b) Explain the inheritance tax implications of these gifts as a result of Artem's death on 15 December 2010 and compute the resulting inheritance tax payable. **(6 marks)**

(Total = 15 marks)

30 IHT transfers   27 mins

Describe the inheritance tax effects of the following events:

(a) Bilal gives his daughter £20,000 on her marriage in June 2010. This is the first gift made by Bilal in his lifetime. **(3 marks)**

(b) Sammy gives her grandson and granddaughter £200 spending money each when they go on holiday in August 2010. **(1 mark)**

(c) Terry sells a vase to his friend Alan for £1,000 which both Terry and Alan believe to be the market value of the vase. Alan takes the vase to the Antiques Roadshow and an expert tells him that the vase is, in fact, worth £20,000. **(3 marks)**

(d) Lucas gives 2,000 shares (a 20% holding) in A Ltd, an investment company, to a trust for his children in December 2010.

Before the transfer, Lucas owned 8,000 shares in A Ltd (an 80% holding).

The following values per share applied at the date of the transfer:

%shareholding	Value per share
	£
80%	37.50
60%	18.75
20%	7.50

The only other lifetime gift that Lucas has made is a gift of quoted shares worth £3,000 each year to his son on 30 April each year. **(3 marks)**

(e) Donald decides to give his grandson £1,000 each month to pay university living expenses for at least four years. Donald will use income surplus to his living requirements to make these payments. **(2 marks)**

(f)   Jas wants to make a gift to his son in November 2010. He can either give the son £100,000 in cash or shares in a newly incorporated investment company worth £100,000. These are the only shares Jas owns in the company. Jas thinks that the shares in the company will be worth five times their current value in three years' time. Jas gives £3,000 to his sister in June each year. He made a lifetime chargeable transfer of £500,000 in July 2010.

(3 marks)

(Total = 15 marks)

TAXATION OF COMPANIES

Questions 31 to 49 cover corporate businesses, the subject of Part F of the BPP Study Text for Paper F6.

31 Wireless Ltd (TX 06/08)   50 mins

(a)   Wireless Ltd, a United Kingdom resident company, commenced trading on 1 October 2010 as a manufacturer of computer routers. The company prepared its first accounts for the six-month period ended 31 March 2011.

The following Information is available:

Trading profit

The tax adjusted trading profit based on the draft accounts for the six-month period ended 31 March 2011 is £75,788. This figure is before making any adjustments required for:

(1)   Capital allowances.

(2)   Director's remuneration of £23,000 paid to the managing director of Wireless Ltd, together with the related employer's Class 1 national insurance contributions. The remuneration is in respect of the period ended 31 March 2011 but was not paid until 5 April 2011. No accrual has been made for this remuneration in the draft accounts. The managing director received no other remuneration from Wireless Ltd during the tax year 2010/11.

Plant and machinery

Wireless Ltd purchased the following assets in respect of the six-month period ended 31 March 2011:

		£
20 September 2010	Office equipment	3,400
5 October 2010	Machinery	10,200
11 October 2010	Building alterations necessary for the installation of the machinery	4,700
18 February 2011	Motor car CO$_2$ emissions 148g/km	10,600

The motor car purchased on 18 February 2011 is used by the sales manager, and 15% of the mileage is for private journeys.

Construction of factory

Wireless Ltd had a new factory constructed at a cost of £200,000 that the company brought into use on 1 November 2010. The cost was made up as follows:

	£
Land	60,000
Site preparation	8,000
Canteen for employees	22,000
General offices	42,000
Factory	68,000
	200,000

The factory is used for industrial purposes.

Loan interest received

Loan interest of £1,110 was received on 31 March 2011. The loan was made for non-trading purposes.

Donation

A donation to charity of £1,800 was paid on 20 March 2011. The donation was made under the gift aid scheme.

Required

(i)   Explain when an accounting period starts for corporation tax purposes.   **(2 marks)**

(ii)   Calculate Wireless Ltd's taxable total profits for the six-month period ended 31 March 2011. Ignore VAT.   **(12 marks)**

(b)   Note that in answering this part of the question you are not expected to take account of any of the information provided in part (a) above.

Wireless Ltd's sales since the commencement of trading on 1 October 2010 have been as follows:

		£
2010	October	9,700
	November	18,200
	December	21,100
2011	January	14,800
	February	23,300
	March	24,600

The above figures are stated exclusive of value added tax (VAT).

The company's sales are all standard rated and are made to VAT registered businesses.

Wireless Ltd only sells goods and since registering for VAT has been issuing sales invoices to customers that show (1) the invoice date and the tax point, (2) Wireless Ltd's name and address, (3) the VAT-exclusive amount for each supply, (4) the total VAT-exclusive amount and (5) the amount of VAT payable. The company does not offer any discount for prompt payment.

Required

(i)   Explain from what date Wireless Ltd was required to compulsorily register for VAT and state what action the company then had to take as regards notifying HM Revenue and Customs (HMRC) of the registration.   **(4 marks)**

(ii)   Explain the circumstances in which Wireless Ltd would have been allowed to recover input VAT incurred on goods purchased and services incurred prior to the date of VAT registration.

                                                                                                         (4 marks)

(iii)   Explain why it would have been beneficial for Wireless Ltd to have voluntarily registered for VAT from 1 October 2010.   **(3 marks)**

(iv)   State the additional information that Wireless Ltd must show on its sales invoices in order for them to be valid for VAT purposes.   **(3 marks)**

                                                                                              (Total = 28 marks)

32 Crash-Bash Ltd (TX 12/09)   54 mins

(a)   Crash-Bash Ltd commenced trading on 1 July 2010 as a manufacturer of motor cycle crash helmets in the United Kingdom. The company is incorporated overseas, although its directors are based in the United Kingdom and hold their board meetings in the United Kingdom.

Crash-Bash Ltd prepared its first accounts for the nine-month period ended 31 March 2011. The following information is available:

UK trading profit

The tax adjusted UK trading profit based on the draft accounts for the nine-month period ended 31 March 2011 is £445,900. This figure is **before** making any adjustments required for:

(1)   Capital allowances.

(2)   Advertising expenditure of £12,840 incurred during June 2010. This expenditure has not been deducted in arriving at the tax adjusted trading profit for the period ended 31 March 2011 of £445,900.

Plant and machinery

The accounts for the nine-month period ended 31 March 2011 showed the following additions and disposals of plant and machinery:

		Cost/(Proceeds) £
2 October 2010	Purchased machinery	100,000
28 November 2010	Purchased a motor car	13,200
12 February 2011	Sold machinery	(3,600)

The motor car purchased on 28 November 2010 for £13,200 has a CO_2 emission rate of 108 grams per kilometre. The machinery sold on 12 February 2011 for £3,600 originally cost £5,300 and is part of the machinery purchased on 2 October 2010 for £100,000.

Industrial building

Crash-Bash Ltd purchased a new factory from a builder on 1 January 2011 for £320,000 (including £100,000 for the land). The factory was immediately brought into use for industrial purposes.

Overseas branch profits

Crash-Bash Ltd also had overseas trading profits of £20,000 (gross) for the nine-month period ended 31 March 2011 from its sales through an overseas branch. Overseas tax was payable on these profits at the rate of 28.75%.

Overseas dividend received

On 31 March 2011 Crash-Bash Ltd received a dividend of £14,250 from a 100% owned subsidiary company, Safety Inc, that is resident overseas.

UK dividends received

During the period ended 31 March 2011 Crash-Bash Ltd received dividends of £36,000 from Flat-Out plc, an unconnected United Kingdom company. This figure was the actual cash amount received.

Export of crash helmets to Safety Inc

Safety Inc, Crash-Bash Ltd's 100% owned overseas subsidiary company, sells crash helmets that have been manufactured by Crash-Bash Ltd. Crash-Bash Ltd is a large company for the purposes of transfer pricing legislation.

Other information

With the exception of Safety Inc, Crash-Bash Ltd does not have any associated companies.

Required

(i) Explain why Crash-Bash Ltd is treated as being resident in the United Kingdom. **(2 marks)**

(ii) Calculate Crash-Bash Ltd's corporation tax liability for the nine-month period ended 31 March 2011 after taking account of double taxation relief. **(14 marks)**

(iii) Explain the corporation tax implications if Crash-Bash Ltd were to invoice Safety Inc for the exported crash helmets at a price that was less than the market price. **(4 marks)**

(b)   Note that in answering this part of the question you are not expected to take account of any of the
        information provided in part (a) above.

        Crash-Bash Ltd's outputs and inputs for the first two months of trading from 1 July 2010 to 31 August 2010
        were as follows:

	July £	August £
Outputs		
Sales	13,200	18,800
Inputs		
Goods purchased	94,600	193,100
Services incurred	22,300	32,700

        The above figures are stated exclusive of value added tax (VAT). On 1 September 2010 Crash-Bash Ltd
        realised that its sales for September 2010 were going to exceed £100,000, and therefore immediately
        registered for VAT. On that date the company had a stock of goods that had cost £108,600 (exclusive of
        VAT).

        During February 2011 Crash-Bash Ltd discovered that a number of errors had been made when completing
        its VAT return for the quarter ended 30 November 2010. As a result of these errors the company will have to
        make an additional payment of VAT to HM Revenue and Customs (HMRC).

        Required

        (i)   Explain why Crash-Bash Ltd was required to compulsorily register for VAT from 1 September 2010,
                and state what action the company then had to take as regards notifying HM Revenue and Customs of
                the registration.   **(3 marks)**

        (ii)   Calculate the amount of input VAT that Crash-Bash Ltd was able to recover in respect of inputs
                incurred prior to registering for VAT on 1 September 2010. Your answer should include an
                explanation as to why the input VAT is recoverable.   **(4 marks)**

        (iii)   Explain how Crash-Bash Ltd could have voluntarily disclosed the errors relating to the VAT return for
                the quarter ended 30 November 2010, and state the circumstances in which default interest would
                have been due.   **(3 marks)**

                                                                                              (Total = 30 marks)

33 Mice Ltd (TX 06/10)   45 mins

(a)   **You should assume that today's date is 28 March 2011.**

        Mice Ltd commenced trading on 1 July 2007 as a manufacturer of computer peripherals. The company
        prepares accounts to 31 March, and its results for the first three periods of trading were as follows:

	Period ended 31 March 2008 £	Year ended 31 March 2009 £	Year ended 31 March 2010 £
Trading profit	83,200	24,700	51,200
Property business profit	2,800	7,100	12,200
Gift aid donations	(1,000)	(1,500)	-

The following information is available in respect of the year ended 31 March 2011:

Trading loss

Mice Ltd expects to make a trading loss of £180,000.

Property business income

Mice Ltd lets out three office buildings that are surplus to requirements.

The first office building is owned freehold. The property was let throughout the year ended 31 March 2011 at a quarterly rent of £3,200, payable in advance. Mice Ltd paid business rates of £2,200 and insurance of £460 in respect of this property for the year ended 31 March 2011. During June 2010 Mice Ltd repaired the existing car park for this property at a cost of £1,060 and then subsequently enlarged the car park at a cost of £2,640.

The second office building is owned leasehold. Mice Ltd pays an annual rent of £7,800 for this property, but did not pay a premium when the lease was acquired. On 1 April 2010 the property was sub-let to a tenant, with Mice Ltd receiving a premium of £18,000 for the grant of an eight-year lease. The company also received the annual rent of £6,000 which was payable in advance. Mice Ltd paid insurance of £310 in respect of this property for the year ended 31 March 2011.

The third office building is also owned freehold. Mice Ltd purchased the freehold of this building on 1 January 2011 and it will be empty until 31 March 2011. The building is to be let from 1 April 2011 at a monthly rent of £640, and on 15 March 2011 Mice Ltd received three months rent in advance. On 1 January 2011 Mice Ltd paid insurance of £480 in respect of this property for the year ended 31 December 2011, and during February 2011 spent £680 on advertising for tenants. Mice Ltd paid loan interest of £1,800 in respect of the period 1 January 2011 to 31 March 2011 on a loan that was taken out to purchase this property.

Loan interest received

On 1 July 2010 Mice Ltd made a loan for non-trading purposes. Loan interest of £6,400 was received on 31 December 2010 and £3,200 will be accrued at 31 March 2011.

Overseas dividend

On 15 October 2010 Mice Ltd received a dividend of £7,400 (net) from a 3% shareholding in USB Inc, a company that is resident overseas. Withholding tax was withheld from this dividend at the rate of 7.5%.

Chargeable gain

On 20 December 2010 Mice Ltd sold its 3% shareholding in USB Inc. The disposal resulted in a chargeable gain of £10,550, after taking account of indexation.

Required

(i)   Calculate Mice Ltd's property business profit for the year ended 31 March 2011;   **(8 marks)**

(ii)   Assuming that Mice Ltd claims relief for its trading loss as early as possible, calculate the company's taxable total profits for the nine-month period ended 31 March 2008, and each of the years ended 31 March 2009, 2010 and 2011.   **(7 marks)**

(b)   Mice Ltd has owned 100% of the ordinary share capital of Web-Cam Ltd since it began trading on 1 April 2010. For the three-month period ended 30 June 2010 Web-Cam Ltd made a trading profit of £28,000 and is expected to make a trading profit of £224,000 for the year ended 30 June 2011. Web-Cam Ltd has no other taxable profits or allowable losses.

Required

Assuming that Mice Ltd does not make any loss relief claim against its own profits, advise Web-Cam Ltd as to the maximum amount of group relief that can be claimed from Mice Ltd in respect of the trading loss of £180,000 for the year ended 31 March 2011.   **(3 marks)**

(c)   Mice Ltd has surplus funds of £125,000 which it is planning to spend before 31 March 2011. The company will either purchase new equipment for £125,000, or alternatively it will purchase a new ventilation system for £125,000, which will be installed as part of its factory.

Required

Explain the maximum amount of capital allowances that Mice Ltd will be able to claim for the year ended 31 March 2011 in respect of each of the two alternative purchases of assets.

Note: you are not expected to recalculate Mice Ltd's trading loss for the year ended 31 March 2011, or redo any of the calculations made in parts (a) and (b) above. **(4 marks)**

(d)   Mice Ltd is planning to pay its managing director a bonus of £40,000 on 31 March 2011. The managing director has already been paid gross director's remuneration of £50,000 during the tax year 2010/11 and the bonus of £40,000 will be paid as additional director's remuneration. The managing director has no other income in 2010/11.

Required

Advise the managing director as to the additional amount of income tax and national insurance contributions (both employee's and employer's) that will be payable as a result of the payment of the additional director's remuneration of £40,000.

Note: you are not expected to recalculate Mice Ltd's trading loss for the year ended 31 March 2011, or redo any of the calculations made in parts (a) and (b) above. **(3 marks)**

(Total = 25 marks)

34 Do-Not-Panic Ltd (TX 06/08)   18 mins

Do-Not-Panic Ltd is a United Kingdom resident company that installs burglar alarms. The company commenced trading on 1 January 2010 and its results for the fifteen-month period ended 31 March 2011 are summarised as follows:

(1)   The trading profit as adjusted for tax purposes is £285,000. This figure is before taking account of capital allowances.

(2)   Do-Not-Panic Ltd purchased equipment for £8,000 on 20 February 2011.

(3)   Do-Not-Panic Ltd bought some loan stock on 1 January 2011 as an investment. Interest of £7,500 was received on 31 March 2011 which was also the amount accrued to that date.

(4)   On 21 December 2010 Do-Not-Panic Ltd disposed of some investments and this resulted in a capital loss of £4,250. On 28 March 2011 the company made a further disposal and this resulted in a chargeable gain of £42,000.

(5)   Franked investment income of £25,000 was received on 22 February 2011.

Do-Not-Panic Ltd has no associated companies.

Required

Calculate Do-Not-Panic Ltd's corporation tax liabilities in respect of the fifteen-month period ended 31 March 2011 and advise the company by when these should be paid. **(10 marks)**

35 Quagmire plc (TX 06/10)   18 mins

For the year ended 31 January 2011 Quagmire plc had taxable total profits of £1,200,000 and franked investment income of £200,000. For the year ended 31 January 2010 the company had taxable total profits of £1,600,000 and franked investment income of £120,000.

Quagmire plc's profits accrue evenly throughout the year.

Quagmire plc has one associated company.

Required

(a)   Explain why Quagmire plc will have been required to make quarterly instalment payments in respect of its corporation tax liability for the year ended 31 January 2011. **(3 marks)**

(b)   Calculate Quagmire plc's corporation tax liability for the year ended 31 January 2011 and explain how and when this will have been paid. **(3 marks)**

(c) Explain how your answer to part (b) above would differ if Quagmire plc did not have an associated company. Your answer should include a calculation of the revised corporation tax liability for the year ended 31 January 2011.

(4 marks)

(Total = 10 marks)

36 Thai Curry Ltd (BTX)   50 mins

Thai Curry Ltd is a manufacturer of ready to cook food. The following information is available in respect of the year ended 31 March 2011:

Trading loss

The trading loss is £35,700. This figure is before taking account of capital allowances.

Plant and machinery

On 1 April 2010 the tax written down values of plant and machinery were as follows:

	£
Main pool	10,600
Expensive motor car (acquired December 2007)	16,400
Short-life asset	2,900

The following transactions took place during the year ended 31 March 2011:

		Cost/ (Proceeds) £
1 May 2010	Sold equipment	(12,800)
15 June 2010	Sold the short-life asset	(800)
8 July 2010	Purchased equipment	7,360
14 July 2010	Sold the expensive motor car	(9,700)
26 August 2010	Purchased motor car (1) CO_2 emissions 149g/km	15,800
19 November 2010	Purchased motor car (2) CO_2 emissions 103g/km	9,700
20 March 2011	Purchased a new freehold office building	220,000

The equipment sold on 1 May 2010 for £12,800 originally cost £27,400.

The cost of the new freehold office building purchased on 20 March 2011 included £8,500 for the central heating system, £7,200 for sprinkler equipment and the fire alarm system and £7,050 for the ventilation system.

Industrial building

On 1 May 2010 Thai Curry Ltd purchased a new factory for £360,000 (including £70,000 for the cost of land).

Income from property

Thai Curry Ltd lets out two warehouses that are surplus to requirements.

The first warehouse was let from 1 April 2010 until 30 November 2010 at a monthly rent of £2,200. On that date the tenant left owing two months rent which Thai Curry Ltd was not able to recover. During February 2011 £8,800 was spent on painting the warehouse. The warehouse was not re-let until 1 April 2011.

The second warehouse was empty from 1 April 2010 until 31 July 2010, but was let from 1 August 2010. On that date Thai Curry Ltd received a premium of £60,000 for the grant of a four-year lease, and the annual rent of £18,000 which is payable in advance.

Loan interest received

Loan interest of £8,000 was received on 30 September 2010 relating to the period from 1 April 2010 and £3,500 was accrued at 31 March 2011. The loan was made for non-trading purposes.

Dividends received

During the year ended 31 March 2011 Thai Curry Ltd received dividends of £36,000 from African Spice plc, an unconnected UK company. This figure was the actual cash amount received.

Profit on disposal of shares

On 28 July 2010 Thai Curry Ltd sold 10,000 £1 ordinary shares in African Spice plc, making a capital gain of £152,300 on the disposal.

Other information

Thai Curry Ltd has three associated companies.

Required

(a) Calculate Thai Curry Ltd's tax adjusted trading loss for the year ended 31 March 2011. You should assume that the company claims the maximum available capital allowances. **(11 marks)**

(b) Assuming that Thai Curry Ltd claims relief for its trading loss against total profits, calculate the company's corporation tax liability for the year ended 31 March 2011. **(11 marks)**

(c) (i) State the date by which Thai Curry Ltd's self-assessment corporation tax return for the year ended 31 March 2011 should be submitted, and advise the company of the penalties that will be due if the return is not submitted until 30 November 2012. **(3 marks)**

(ii) State the date by which Thai Curry Ltd's corporation tax liability for the year ended 31 March 2011 should be paid, and advise the company of the interest that will be due if the liability is not paid until 30 November 2012. **(3 marks)**

(Total = 28 marks)

37 Hawk Ltd (TX 12/08) 36 mins

Hawk Ltd sold the following assets during the year ended 31 March 2011:

(1) On 30 April 2010 a freehold office building was sold for £260,000. The office building had been purchased on 2 July 1993 for £81,000, and had been extended at a cost of £43,000 during May 2005. Hawk Ltd incurred legal fees of £3,200 in connection with the purchase of the office building, and legal fees of £5,726 in connection with the disposal. The office building has always been used by Hawk Ltd for business purposes. The relevant retail prices indexes (RPIs) are as follows:

July 1993 140.6
May 2005 192.0
April 2010 222.8

(2) On 29 August 2010 5,000 £1 ordinary shares in Albatross plc were sold for £42,500. Hawk Ltd had purchased 6,000 shares in Albatross plc on 1 August 2010 for £18,600, and purchased a further 2,000 shares on 17 August 2010 for £9,400.

(3) On 27 October 2010 10,000 £1 preference shares in Cuckoo plc were sold for £32,000. Hawk Ltd had originally purchased 5,000 £1 ordinary shares in Cuckoo plc on 2 October 2010 for £60,000. On 18 October 2010 Cuckoo plc had a reorganisation whereby each £1 ordinary share was exchanged for three new £1 ordinary shares and two £1 preference shares. Immediately after the reorganisation each new £1 ordinary share was quoted at £4.50 and each £1 preference share was quoted at £2.25.

(4) On 28 March 2011 two acres of land were sold for £120,000. Hawk Ltd had originally purchased three acres of land on 1 March 2011 for £203,500. The market value of the unsold acre of land as at 28 March 2011 was £65,000. The land has never been used by Hawk Ltd for business purposes.

Hawk Ltd's only other income for the year ended 31 March 2011 was a trading profit of £125,000.

Hawk Ltd does not have any associated companies.

Required

(a)   Calculate Hawk Ltd's corporation tax liability for the year ended 31 March 2011.   **(16 marks)**

(b)   Advise Hawk Ltd of:

(i)   The minimum amount that will have to be reinvested in qualifying replacement business assets in order for the company to claim the maximum possible amount of rollover relief in respect of its chargeable gains for the year ended 31 March 2011.   **(2 marks)**

(ii)   The period during which the reinvestment must take place.   **(1 mark)**

(iii)   The amount of corporation tax that will be deferred if the maximum possible amount of rollover relief is claimed for the year ended 31 March 2011.   **(1 mark)**

(Total = 20 marks)

38 Problematic Ltd (TX 06/10)   36 mins

Problematic Ltd sold the following assets during the year ended 31 March 2011:

(1)   On 14 June 2010 16,000 £1 ordinary shares in Easy plc were sold for £54,400. Problematic Ltd had originally purchased 15,000 shares in Easy plc on 26 June 1995 for £12,600. On 28 September 2007 Easy plc made a 1 for 3 rights issue. Problematic Ltd took up its allocation under the rights issue in full, paying £2.20 for each new share issued. The relevant retail prices indexes (RPIs) are as follows:

June 1995	149.8
September 2007	208.0
June 2010	225.0

(2)   On 1 October 2010 an office building owned by Problematic Ltd was damaged by a fire. The indexed cost of the office building on that date was £169,000. The company received insurance proceeds of £36,000 on 10 October 2010 and spent a total of £41,000 during October 2010 on restoring the office building. Problematic Ltd has made a claim to defer the gain arising from the receipt of the insurance proceeds. The office building has never been used for business purposes.

(3)   On 28 January 2011 a freehold factory was sold for £171,000. The indexed cost of the factory on that date was £127,000. Problematic Ltd has made a claim to holdover the gain on the factory against the cost of a replacement leasehold factory under the rollover relief (replacement of business assets) rules. The leasehold factory has a lease period of 20 years, and was purchased on 10 December 2010 for £154,800. The two factory buildings have always been used entirely for business purposes.

(4)   On 20 February 2011 an acre of land was sold for £130,000. Problematic Ltd had originally purchased four acres of land, and the indexed cost of the four acres on 20 February 2011 was £300,000. The market value of the unsold three acres of land as at 20 February 2011 was £350,000. Problematic Ltd incurred legal fees of £3,200 in connection with the disposal. The land has never been used for business purposes.

Problematic Ltd's only other income for the year ended 31 March 2011 is a tax adjusted trading profit of £108,509.

Required

(a)   Calculate Problematic Ltd's taxable total profits for the year ended 31 March 2011.   **(16 marks)**

(b)   Advise Problematic Ltd of the carried forward indexed base costs for capital gains purposes of any assets included in (1) to (4) above that are still retained at 31 March 2011.   **(4 marks)**

(Total = 20 marks)

39 Spacious Ltd (BTX)

54 mins

Spacious Ltd is a UK resident company that commenced trading on 1 July 2009 as a manufacturer of engineering equipment. The company's summarised income statement for the year ended 31 March 2011 is as follows:

	£	£
Gross profit		138,505
Operating expenses		
Depreciation	54,690	
Patent royalties (note 1)	9,400	
Professional fees (note 2)	22,500	
Repairs and renewals (note 3)	27,700	
Other expenses (note 4)	149,490	
		(263,780)
Operating loss		(125,275)
Profit from sale of fixed assets		
Disposal of office building (note 5)		54,400
Income from investments		
Bank interest (note 6)		7,000
		(63,875)
Interest payable (note 7)		(23,000)
Loss before taxation		(86,875)

Notes

(1) *Patent royalties*

Patent royalties of £3,900 were paid on 30 September 2010, with a further £5,500 being paid on 31 March 2011. These relate to the year ended 31 March 2011.

(2) *Professional fees*

Professional fees are as follows:

	£
Accountancy and audit fee	3,600
Legal fees in connection with the issue of share capital	8,800
Legal fees in connection with the issue of debentures (see note 7)	6,900
Legal fees in connection with the defence of the company's Internet domain name	2,300
Legal fees in connection with a court action and fine for not complying with health and safety legislation	900
	22,500

(3) *Repairs and renewals*

The figure of £27,700 for repairs includes £9,700 for constructing a new wall around the company's premises and £5,400 for replacing the roof of a warehouse because it was in a bad state of repair.

(4) *Other expenses*

Other expenses include £4,215 for entertaining customers, £600 for entertaining employees and a donation of £1,000 made to a national charity under the Gift Aid scheme.

(5) *Disposal of office building*

The profit of £54,400 is in respect of a freehold office building that was sold on 30 June 2010 for £380,000. The indexed cost of the building on 30 June 2010 was £345,400. The building has always been used by Spacious Ltd for trading purposes. The company has claimed to rollover the gain arising on the office building against the cost of a new factory that was purchased on 1 July 2010 for £360,000 (see note 8). The new factory is used 100% for trading purposes by Spacious Ltd.

(6) *Bank interest received*

The bank interest was received on 31 March 2011. The bank deposits are held for non-trading purposes.

(7) *Interest payable*

Spacious Ltd raised a debenture loan on 1 October 2010, and this was used for trading purposes. Interest of £23,000 in respect of the first six months of the loan was paid on 31 March 2011.

(8) *Industrial building*

Spacious Ltd purchased a new factory from a builder on 1 July 2010 for £360,000 and this was immediately brought into use. The figure of £360,000 includes £135,000 for land, £61,500 for general offices and £54,000 for a drawing office.

(9) *Long-life asset*

On 1 September 2010 Spacious Ltd installed a new overhead crane costing £110,000 in the new factory. The crane is a long-life asset.

(10) *Plant and machinery*

On 1 April 2010 the tax written down values of plant and machinery were as follows:

	£
Main pool	28,400
Expensive motor car (acquired June 2008)	14,800

The following transactions took place during the year ended 31 March 2011:

		Cost/(Proceeds) £
10 April 2010	Purchased equipment	30,200
5 February 2011	Sold the expensive motor car	(9,800)
5 February 2011	Purchased a motor car CO_2 emissions 175g/km	27,200
20 March 2011	Sold a lorry	(17,600)
31 March 2011	Purchased a motor car CO_2 emissions 133g/km	9,400

The lorry sold on 20 March 2011 for £17,600 originally cost £18,200. The motor car purchased on 31 March 2011 for £9,400 is used by the sales manager, and 20% of the mileage is for private journeys.

(11) *Other information*

Spacious Ltd has no associated companies.

The company's results for the nine-month period ended 31 March 2010 were as follows:

	£
Trading income profit	218,200
Interest income profit	5,200
Capital loss	(4,900)
Gift aid donation	(800)

Spacious Ltd's taxable total profits for the year ended 31 March 2012 are expected to be £495,000, of which £450,000 represents trading income profit.

Required

(a) Calculate Spacious Ltd's trading loss for the year ended 31 March 2011. Your answer should commence with the loss before taxation figure of £86,875 and should list all of the items in the income statement indicating by the use of a zero (0) any items that do not require adjustment. You should assume that the company claims the maximum available capital allowances. **(19 marks)**

(b) Assuming that Spacious Ltd claims relief for its trading loss against total profits, calculate the company's taxable total profits for the nine-month period ended 31 March 2010 and the year ended 31 March 2011. **(8 marks)**

(c) Explain why it would probably have been beneficial for Spacious Ltd to have carried its trading loss forward, rather than making the claim against total profits. Assume that the rates of corporation tax in FY 11 are the same as in FY 10. **(3 marks)**

(Total = 30 marks)

40 Volatile Ltd (TX 12/09)

18 mins

Volatile Ltd commenced trading on 1 July 2006. The company's results for its first five periods of trading are as follows:

	Period ended 31 December 2006	Year ended 31 December 2007	Year ended 31 December 2008	Period ended 30 September 2009	Year ended 30 September 2010
	£	£	£	£	£
Trading profit/(loss)	44,000	(73,800)	95,200	78,700	(186,800)
Property business profit	9,400	6,600	6,500	–	–
Chargeable gains	5,100	–	–	9,700	–
Gift Aid donations	(800)	(1,000)	(1,200)	–	–

Required

(a) State the factors that will influence a company's choice of loss relief claims.

Note: You are not expected to consider group relief. **(3 marks)**

(b) Assuming that Volatile Ltd claims relief for its trading losses as early as possible, calculate the company's taxable total profits for the six-month period ended 31 December 2006, each of the years ended 31 December 2007 and 2008 and the nine-month period ended 30 September 2009. Your answer should also clearly identify the amount of any unrelieved trading losses as at 30 September 2010.

(7 marks)

(Total = 10 marks)

41 Jogger Limited (TX 12/08)

54 mins

(a) Jogger Ltd is a manufacturer of running shoes. The company's summarised income statement for the year ended 31 March 2011 is as follows:

	Note	£	£
Operating loss	1		(9,140)
Income from investments			
Bank interest	4	8,460	
Loan interest	5	24,600	
Income from property	6	144,000	
Dividends	7	45,000	
			222,060
Profit from sale of fixed assets			
Disposal of shares	8		102,340
Profit before taxation			315,260

Note 1 – Operating loss

Depreciation of £58,840 has been deducted in arriving at the operating loss of £9,140.

Note 2 – Plant and machinery

On 1 April 2010 the tax written down values of plant and machinery were as follows:

	£
Main Pool	21,600
Expensive motor car (acquired January 2004)	8,800

The following transactions took place during the year ended 31 March 2011:

		Cost/(proceeds) £
20 July 2010	Sold the expensive motor car	(11,700)
31 July 2010	Purchased motor car	11,800
	CO_2 emissions 135g/km	
30 September 2010	Purchased machinery	105,000
14 March 2011	Sold a lorry	(8,600)

The expensive motor car sold on 20 July 2010 for £11,700 originally cost £18,400. The lorry sold on 14 March 2011 for £8,600 originally cost £16,600.

Note 3 – Industrial building

On 1 April 2010 Jogger Ltd purchased a new factory for £250,000 (excluding the cost of land). It brought the factory into industrial use immediately.

Note 4 – Bank interest received

The bank interest was received on 31 March 2011. The bank deposits are held for non-trading purposes.

Note 5 – Loan interest receivable

The loan was made for non-trading purposes on 1 July 2010. Loan interest of £16,400 was received on 31 December 2010, and interest of £8,200 was accrued at 31 March 2011.

Note 6 – Income from property

Jogger Ltd lets out an unfurnished freehold office building that is surplus to requirements. The office building was let throughout the year ended 31 March 2011. On 1 April 2010 Jogger Ltd received a premium of £100,000 for the grant of a ten-year lease, and the annual rent of £44,000 which is payable in advance.

Note 7 – Dividends received

During the year ended 31 March 2011 Jogger Ltd received dividends of £45,000 from Sprinter plc, an unconnected UK company. This figure was the actual cash amount received.

Note 8 – Profit on disposal of shares

The profit on disposal of shares is in respect of a shareholding that was sold on 5 December 2010. The disposal resulted in a chargeable gain of £98,300. This figure is after taking account of indexation.

Note 9 – Other information

Jogger Ltd has two associated companies.

Required

Ignore VAT throughout part (a).

(i)   Calculate Jogger Ltd's tax adjusted trading loss for the year ended 31 March 2011.

Notes: (1)   Your computation should start with the operating loss of £(9,140).

(2)   You should assume that the company claims the maximum available capital allowances.

(7 marks)

(ii)   Assuming that Jogger Ltd claims relief for its trading loss against total profits, calculate the company's corporation tax liability for the year ended 31 March 2011.   **(8 marks)**

(iii)   State the date by which Jogger Ltd's self-assessment corporation tax return for the year ended 31 March 2011 should be submitted, and advise the company of the penalties that will be due if the return is submitted eight months late.

Note: you should assume that the company pays its corporation tax liability at the same time that the self-assessment tax return is submitted.   **(4 marks)**

(b) *Note:* In answering this part of the question you are not expected to take account of any of the information provided in part (a) above.

Jogger Ltd has been registered for value added tax (VAT) since 1 April 2004. From that date until 30 June 2009 the company's VAT returns were all submitted on time. Since 1 July 2009 the company's VAT returns have been submitted as follows:

Quarter ended	VAT paid £	Submitted
30 September 2009	42,700	One month late
31 December 2009	41,200	On time
31 March 2010	38,900	One month late
30 June 2010	28,300	On time
30 September 2010	49,100	On time
31 December 2010	63,800	On time
31 March 2011	89,100	Two months late

Jogger Ltd always pays any VAT that is due at the same time as the related return is submitted.

Required

(i)   State, giving appropriate reasons, the default surcharge consequences arising from Jogger Ltd's submission of its VAT returns for the quarter ended 30 September 2009 to the quarter ended 31 March 2011 inclusive, at the times stated. **(6 marks)**

(ii) Advise Jogger Ltd why it might be beneficial to use the VAT annual accounting scheme, and state the conditions that it will have to satisfy before being permitted to do so. **(5 marks)**

(Total = 30 marks)

42 B Ltd   18 mins

B Ltd acquired 80% of the voting rights of W Ltd in December 2010. Both companies are resident in the United Kingdom. B Ltd also has an overseas permanent establishment (branch), which is subject to overseas tax at 20%.

The following information relates to B Ltd for its twelve-month accounting period ended 31 March 2011.

	£
Income	
Adjusted trading profits	296,000
Capital gains	30,000
Branch profits, net of tax	1,600
Loan stock interest received 30 November 2010 (non-trading investment)	8,000
FII (inclusive of tax credit) received in May 2010	32,000
Payments	
Gift Aid to charity	18,000

There were no accruals of loan stock interest at the beginning or end of the year. The loan stock interest was received gross from another UK company.

Required

Compute the corporation tax payable by B Ltd for the above accounting period, assuming all appropriate claims are made.

Show clearly your treatment of double tax relief. **(10 marks)**

43 Sirius Ltd (BTX)

Sirius Ltd is a manufacturing company with no associated companies. The income statement for the year ended 31 March 2011 show a trading loss of £125,000. This figure includes the following items:

	£
Director's fees	47,000
Depreciation	42,750
Loss on disposal of computer equipment	5,260
Loss on sale of factory	39,500
Bank overdraft interest charged	10,000
Gift Aid donation to Oxfam paid on 15 November 2010	25,000
Dividend paid on 27 January 2011	21,000
Dividend received on 15 March 2011	180,000 18,000

Notes

(1) The written down values of plant and equipment at 1 April 2010 were as follows.

	£
Plant and machinery	42,000
Expensive car (acquired March 2005)	13,000
Short life asset (computer system)	3,600

On 1 June 2010 a new computer system was purchased for £12,000. The existing system, which had cost £9,600 three years earlier, was sold for £250.

On 5 November 2010 a new van was purchased at a cost of £21,680 for the sole use of the transport manager, whose mileage was 75% business and 25% private.

(2) In July 2010 a freehold factory was sold for £1,750,000. It had been acquired in September 2000 for £85,000. As at 1 April 2010 the company had capital losses brought forward of £37,155.

(3) The taxable total profits for the year ended 31 March 2010 were £3 million and the budgeted figure for the year ended 31 March 2012 is £105,000.

Future plans

Sirius is planning to set up an overseas operation next year, but is unsure whether to operate overseas through a branch or a 100% subsidiary. A subsidiary would be resident overseas. Regardless of the type of business structure chosen, the overseas operation is expected to make a tax adjusted trading profit of £200,000 for the year ended 31 March 2012. The overseas corporation tax on these profits will be £40,000.

If the overseas operation is set up as a branch then profits of £80,000 will be remitted to the UK during the year ended 31 March 2012. This remittance would not be subject to any withholding tax.

All of the above figures are in pounds Sterling.

Required

(a) (i) Calculate the corporation tax due for the year ended 31 March 2011 assuming that the trading loss is set off so as to obtain relief as early as possible. The RPI for September 2000 is 171.7 and in July 2010 is 226.4. **(10 marks)**

(ii) State when the corporation tax payment is due and when the company's tax return must be submitted. **(2 marks)**

(iii) State any alternative ways in which the company may set off its trading loss for the year ended 31 March 2011, ignoring any profit from overseas sources in the future. **(3 marks)**

(b) Explain the taxation factors that should be considered when deciding whether to operate overseas through a branch or a 100% subsidiary. You are not expected to discuss double taxation relief.

(5 marks)

(c) Calculate Sirius Ltd's UK corporation tax liability for the year ended 31 March 2012 if the overseas operation is set up as a branch.

(4 marks)

You should assume that Sirius Ltd has no other income or expenditure in the year and that the FY 2010 corporation tax rates continue to apply in the future.

(Total = 24 marks)

44 A Ltd   18 mins

On 1 July 2010 A Ltd, a manufacturing company resident in the United Kingdom, acquired 100% of the share capital of B Ltd, also a manufacturing company.

B Ltd makes up accounts each year to 30 June. For its year ended 30 June 2011, it sustained a trading loss of £68,000 and had no other profits.

A Ltd produced the following information in relation to its nine-month period of accounts to 31 December 2010.

Income

	£
Trading income	342,000
Property income	10,000
Loan interest receivable (received gross) (including £2,000 accrued at 31 December 2010)	16,000
Franked investment income (FII) (including tax credit; received August 2010)	1,000

Payments

Gift Aid donation (paid September 2010)	17,000

A Ltd wishes to claim maximum group relief in respect of B Ltd's trading loss.

Required

(a) Compute the corporation tax payable by A Ltd for the nine-month period to 31 December 2010. **(8 marks)**

(b) State the due date for payment of the corporation tax payable by A Ltd for the nine-month period to 31 December 2010. **(1 mark)**

(c) State the date by which A Ltd must file the corporation tax return for the nine-month period to 31 December 2010. **(1 mark)**

(Total = 10 marks)

45 Gold Ltd (BTX)   54 mins

Gold Ltd owns 100% of the ordinary share capital of Silver Ltd. Gold Ltd has an accounting date of 31 December, whilst Silver Ltd has an accounting date of 30 June. The results of Gold Ltd are as follows:

	Year ended 31 December	
	2009	2010
	£	£
Trading income	177,000	90,000
Property business income	5,000	–
Capital gain	–	12,000
Gift Aid donation	(2,000)	(2,000)

For the year ended 30 June 2009 Silver Ltd had taxable total profits of £260,000. Information for the year ended 30 June 2010 is as follows.

	£
Operating loss (note 1)	(167,464)
Income from investments	
Dividends (note 2)	116,514
Loss before taxation	(50,950)

Notes

(1)   *Operating loss*

Depreciation of £35,160 has been deducted in arriving at the operating loss of £167,464.

(2)   *Dividends received*

The dividends were all received from unconnected UK companies. The figure shown is the actual cash amount received.

(3)   *Plant and machinery*

On 1 July 2009 the tax written down values of plant and machinery were as follows:

	£
Main pool	46,650
Expensive motor car (1) (acquired January 2005)	11,750
Short-life asset	2,700

The following transactions took place during the year ended 30 June 2010:

		Cost/ (proceeds) £
5 July 2009	Sold the expensive motor car (1)	(18,700)
31 August 2009	Purchased motor car (2) CO_2 emissions 180g/km	23,250
7 October 2009	Sold a van	(12,220)
12 November 2009	Purchased motor car (3) CO_2 emissions 135g/km	9,500
16 April 2010	Sold the short-life asset	(555)

The expensive motor car sold on 5 July 2009 originally cost £31,240. The van sold on 7 October 2009 originally cost £11,750.

(4)   *Industrial building*

On 1 June 2010 Silver Ltd purchased a factory for £295,000 (including £85,000 for the land and £62,750 for general offices). The factory was brought into industrial use immediately.

No information is available regarding the year ended 30 June 2011.

Gold Ltd has no other associated companies.

Required

(a)   Calculate Silver Ltd's trade loss for the year ended 30 June 2010.   **(15 marks)**

(b)   Assuming that the maximum possible claim for group relief is made in respect of Silver Ltd's trading loss, calculate Gold Ltd's corporation tax liabilities for the year ended 31 December 2009 and the year ended 31 December 2010.   **(8 marks)**

(c)   Explain how loss relief should be allocated within a group of companies in order to maximise the potential benefit of the relief for the group as a whole.   **(4 marks)**

(d)   Based on the information available, advise Silver Ltd of the most beneficial way of relieving its trading loss.   **(3 marks)**

       (Total = 30 marks)

46 Apple Ltd

27 mins

You should assume that today's date is 30 November 2011.

Apple Ltd has owned 80% of the ordinary share capital of Bramley Ltd and 85% of the ordinary share capital of Cox Ltd since these two companies were incorporated on 1 April 2008. Cox Ltd acquired 80% of the ordinary share capital of Delicious Ltd on 1 April 2010, the date of its incorporation.

The tax adjusted trading profits/(losses) of each company for the years 31 March 2010, 2011 and 2012 are as follows.

	Year ended 31 March		
	2010	*2011*	*2012 (forecast)*
	£	£	£
Apple Ltd	620,000	250,000	585,000
Bramley Ltd	(64,000)	52,000	70,000
Cox Ltd	83,000	(58,000)	40,000
Delicious Ltd	n/a	90,000	(15,000)

The following information is also available.

(1)   Apple Ltd sold a freehold office building on 10 March 2011 for £380,000, and this resulted in a capital gain of £120,000.

(2)   Apple Ltd sold a freehold warehouse on 5 October 2011 for £365,000, and this resulted in a capital gain of £80,000.

(3)   Cox Ltd purchased a freehold factory on 20 September 2011 for £360,000.

(4)   Delicious Ltd is planning to sell a leasehold factory building on 15 February 2012 for £180,000, and this will result in a capital loss of £44,000.

Because each of the subsidiary companies has minority shareholders, the managing director of Apple Ltd has proposed that:

(1)   Trading losses should initially be carried back and relieved against profits of the loss making company, with any unrelieved amount then being carried forward.

(2)   Chargeable gains and allowable losses should not be transferred between group companies, and rollover relief should only be claimed where reinvestment is made by the company that incurred the chargeable gain.

Required

(a)   Assuming that the managing director's proposals are followed, calculate the taxable total profits for each of the companies in the Apple Ltd group for the years ended 31 March 2010, 2011 and 2012 respectively.

(5 marks)

(b)   Advise the Apple Ltd group of the amount of corporation tax that could be saved for the years ended 31 March 2010, 2011 and 2012 if reliefs were instead claimed in the most beneficial manner.

(10 marks)

Assume that Financial Year 2010 rates apply throughout.

(Total = 15 marks)

47 Tock-Tick Ltd (BTX)

54 mins

Tock-Tick Ltd is a clock manufacturer. The company's summarised income statement for the year ended 31 March 2011 is as follows:

	£	£
Gross profit		825,020
Operating expenses		
Impairment losses (note 1)	9,390	
Depreciation	99,890	
Gifts and donations (note 2)	3,090	
Professional fees (note 3)	12,400	
Repairs and renewals (note 4)	128,200	
Other expenses (note 5)	426,920	
		(679,890)
Operating profit		145,130
Profit from sale of fixed assets		
Disposal of office building (note 6)		78,100
Income from investments		
Loan interest (note 7)		12,330
		235,560
Interest payable (note 8)		(48,600)
Profit before taxation		186,960

Notes

(1) *Impairment losses*

Impairment losses are as follows:

	£
Trade debts recovered from previous years	(1,680)
Trade debts written off	4,870
Non-trade debts written off	6,200
	9,390

(2) *Gifts and donations*

Gifts and donations are as follows:

	£
Gifts to customers (pens costing £45 each displaying Tock-Tick Ltd's name)	1,080
Gifts to customers (food hampers costing £30 each)	720
Long service award to an employee	360
Donation to a national charity (made under the gift aid scheme)	600
Donation to a national charity (not made under the gift aid scheme)	250
Donation to a local charity (Tock-Tick Ltd received free advertising in the charity's magazine)	80
	3,090

(3) *Professional fees*

Professional fees are as follows:

	£
Accountancy and audit fee	5,400
Legal fees in connection with the issue of share capital	2,900
The cost of registering the company's trademark	800
Legal fees in connection with the renewal of a 35-year property lease	1,300
Debt collection	1,100
Legal fees in connection with a court action for not complying with health and safety legislation	900
	12,400

(4) *Repairs and renewals*

The figure of £128,200 for repairs and renewals includes £41,800 for replacing the roof of an office building, which was in a bad state of repair, and £53,300 for extending the office building.

(5) *Other expenses*

Other expenses include £2,160 for entertaining suppliers; £880 for counseling services provided to two employees who were made redundant; and the cost of seconding an employee to a charity of £6,400. The remaining expenses are all fully allowable.

(6) *Disposal of office building*

The profit of £78,100 is in respect of a freehold office building that was sold on 20 February 2011 for £300,925. The office building was purchased on 18 November 2000 for £197,900. The indexation allowance from November 2000 to February 2011 is £72,223.

The building has always been used by Tock-Tick Ltd for trading purposes.

(7) *Loan interest received*

The loan interest is in respect of a loan that was made on 1 July 2010. Interest of £8,280 was received on 31 December 2010, and interest of £4,050 was accrued at 31 March 2011. The loan was made for non-trading purposes.

(8) *Interest payable*

The interest payable is in respect of a debenture loan that is used for trading purposes. Interest of £24,300 was paid on 30 September 2010 and again on 31 March 2011.

(9) *Plant and machinery*

On 1 April 2010 the tax written down values of plant and machinery were as follows:

	£
Main pool	12,200
Expensive motor car (acquired May 2008)	20,800
Short-life asset	3,100

The following transactions took place during the year ended 31 March 2011:

		Cost/(Proceeds) £
28 May 2010	Sold the expensive motor car	(34,800)
7 June 2010	Purchased a motor car	14,400
1 August 2010	Sold the short-life asset	(460)
15 August 2010	Purchased equipment	6,700

The expensive motor car sold on 28 May 2010 for £34,800 originally cost £33,600. The motor car purchased on 7 June 2010 has CO_2 emission rate of 105 grams per kilometre .

Required

(a) Calculate Tock-Tick Ltd's tax adjusted trading income for the year ended 31 March 2011. Your computation should commence with the profit before taxation figure of £186,960 and should list all of the items in the income statement indicating by the use of a zero (0) any items that do not require adjustment.

(19 marks)

(b) Calculate Tock-Tick Ltd's taxable total profits for the year ended 31 March 2011. **(5 marks)**

(c) State the effect on Tock-Tick Ltd's taxable total profits for the year ended 31 March 2011 if Tock-Tick Ltd had:

(i) Claimed the maximum possible group relief from a 100% owned subsidiary company that had made a trading loss of £62,400 for the year ended 31 December 2010; **(3 marks)**

(ii) Made a claim to rollover the gain arising on the sale of the office building (see note 6) against the cost of a new freehold office building that was purchased on 15 April 2011 for £284,925. The new office building is to be used 100% for trading purposes by Tock-Tick Ltd. **(3 marks)**

(Total = 30 marks)

48 Sofa Ltd (TX 12/07)

(a) Sofa Ltd is a manufacturer of furniture. The company's summarised income statement for the year ended 31 March 2011 is as follows:

	£	£
Gross profit		294,500
Operating expenses		
Depreciation	87,100	
Professional fees (note 1)	19,900	
Repairs and renewals (note 2)	22,800	
Other expenses (note 3)	363,000	(492,800)
Operating loss		(198,300)
Profit from sale of fixed assets		
Disposal of shares (note 4)		3,300
Income from investments		
Bank interest (note 5)		8,400
		(186,600)
Interest payable (note 6)		(31,200)
Loss before taxation		(217,800)

Notes

1   *Professional fees*

Professional fees are as follows:

	£
Accountancy and audit fee	3,400
Legal fees in connection with the issue of share capital	7,800
Legal fees in connection with the renewal of a ten year property lease	2,900
Legal fees in connection with the issue of debentures (see note 6)	5,800
	19,900

2   *Repairs and renewals*

The figure of £22,800 for repairs and renewals includes £9,700 for constructing a new wall around the company's premises and £3,900 for repairing the wall of an office building after it was damaged by a lorry. The remaining expenses are all fully allowable.

3   *Other expenses*

The figure of £363,000 for other expenses includes £1,360 for entertaining suppliers; £700 for entertaining employees; £370 for counselling services provided to an employee who was made redundant; and a fine of £420 for infringing health and safety regulations. The remaining expenses are all fully allowable.

4   *Profit on disposal of shares*

The profit on the disposal of shares of £3,300 is in respect of a shareholding that was sold on 29 October 2010.

5   *Bank interest received*

The bank interest was received on 31 March 2011. The bank deposits are held for non-trading purposes.

6   *Interest payable*

Sofa Ltd raised a debenture loan on 1 July 2010, and this was used for trading purposes. Interest of £20,800 was paid on 31 December 2010, and £10,400 was accrued at 31 March 2011.

7   *Plant and machinery*

On 1 April 2010 the tax written down values of plant and machinery were as follows:

	£
Main pool	27,800
Expensive motor car (acquired November 2006)	16,400

The following transactions took place during the year ended 31 March 2011:

		Cost/proceeds
		£
12 May 2010	Purchased equipment	1,400
8 June 2010	Sold the expensive motor car	(17,800)
8 June 2010	Purchased motor car (1) CO_2 emissions 175g/km	22,200
2 August 2010	Purchased motor car (2) CO_2 emissions 125 g/km	10,900
19 October 2010	Purchased motor car (3) CO_2 emissions 105 g/km	13,800
8 January 2011	Sold a lorry	(7,600)
18 January 2011	Sold motor car (2)	(8,800)
10 February 2011	Purchased a second-hand freehold office building	280,000

The expensive motor car sold on 8 June 2010 for £17,800 originally cost £26,800. The lorry sold on 8 January 2011 for £7,600 originally cost £24,400.

The cost of the second-hand office building purchased on 10 February 2011 for £280,000 includes fixtures qualifying as plant and machinery (but not as integral features). These fixtures originally cost £44,800, and at the date of sale had a market value of £12,600 and a written down value of £9,400. Sofa Ltd and the vendor of the office building have made a joint election regarding the sale price of the fixtures to enable Sofa Ltd to claim the maximum possible amount of capital allowances in respect of them.

8   *Purchase of factory*

On 1 July 2010 Sofa Ltd purchased a new factory. The factory was constructed at a cost of £558,000 (including £158,000 for the land and £68,000 for a showroom). It was brought into use on 1 July 2010.

Required

Calculate Sofa Ltd's tax adjusted trading loss for the year ended 31 March 2011. Your answer should commence with the loss before taxation figure of £217,800 and should list all of the items in the income statement account indicating by the use of a zero (0) any items that do not require adjustment. You should assume that the company claims the maximum available capital allowances.   **(20 marks)**

(b)   Sofa Ltd has three subsidiary companies:

Settee Ltd

Sofa Ltd owns 100% of the ordinary share capital of Settee Ltd. For the year ended 30 June 2010 Settee Ltd had taxable total profits of £240,000, and for the year ended 30 June 2011 will have taxable total profits of £90,000.

Couch Ltd

Sofa Ltd owns 60% of the ordinary share capital of Couch Ltd. For the year ended 31 March 2011 Couch Ltd had taxable total profits of £64,000.

Futon Ltd

Sofa Ltd owns 80% of the ordinary share capital of Futon Ltd. Futon Ltd commenced trading on 1 January 2011, and for the three-month period ended 31 March 2011 had taxable total profits of £60,000.

Required

Advise Sofa Ltd as to the maximum amount of group relief that can potentially be claimed by each of its three subsidiary companies in respect of its trading loss for the year ended 31 March 2011.

(5 marks)

(Total = 25 marks)

49 Gastron Ltd (TX 06/09)

Gastron Ltd, a United Kingdom resident company, is a luxury food manufacturer. The company's summarised income statement for the year ended 31 March 2011 is as follows:

	Note	£	£
Gross profit			866,660
Operating expenses			
Depreciation		85,660	
Amortisation of leasehold property	1	6,000	
Gifts and donations	2	2,700	
Professional fees	3	18,800	
Other expenses	4	220,400	
			(333,560)
Operating profit			533,100
Income from investments			
Income from property	5	20,600	
Bank interest	6	12,400	
Dividends	7	54,000	
			87,000
Profit from sale of fixed assets			
Disposal of shares	8		80,700
			700,800
Interest payable	9		(60,800)
Profit before taxation			640,000

Note 1 – Leasehold property
On 1 April 2010 Gastron Ltd acquired a leasehold office building, paying a premium of £60,000 for the grant of a new ten-year lease. The office building was used for business purposes by Gastron Ltd throughout the year ended 31 March 2011. No legal costs were incurred by Gastron Ltd in respect of this lease.

Note 2 – Gifts and donations
Gifts and donations are as follows:

	£
Gifts to customers (pens costing £60 each and displaying Gastron Ltd's name)	1,200
Gifts to customers (hampers of food costing £25 each)	1,100
Donation to local charity (Gastron Ltd received free advertising in the charity's magazine)	400
	2,700

Note 3 – Professional fees
Professional fees are as follows:

	£
Legal fees in connection with the renewal of a 45-year property lease in respect of a warehouse	3,600
Legal fees in connection with the issue of debentures (see note 9)	15,200
	18,800

Note 4 – Other expenses
The figure of £220,400 for other expenses includes £1,300 for entertaining suppliers and £900 for entertaining employees.

Note 5 – Income from property
Gastron Ltd lets out the whole of an unfurnished freehold office building that is surplus to requirements. The office building was let from 1 April 2010 to 31 December 2010 at a monthly rent of £1,800, payable in advance. On 31 December 2010 the tenant left owing two months' rent which Gastron Ltd was unable to recover. During January 2011 the company spent £3,700 decorating the property. The office building was then re-let from 1 February 2011 at a monthly rent of £1,950, on which date the new tenant paid six months' rent in advance.

Note 6 – Bank interest received
The bank interest was received on 31 March 2011. The bank deposits are held for non-trading purposes.

Questions 53

Note 7 – Dividends received

During the year ended 31 March 2011 Gastron Ltd received dividends of £36,000 from Tasteless plc, an unconnected UK company, and dividends of £18,000 from Culinary Ltd, a 100% UK subsidiary company (see note 11). Both figures are the actual cash amounts received.

Note 8 – Profit on disposal of shares

The profit on disposal of shares is in respect of a 1% shareholding that was sold on 14 October 2010. The disposal resulted in a chargeable gain of £74,800. This figure is after taking account of indexation.

Note 9 – Interest payable

The interest payable is in respect of the company's 5% debenture loan stock that was issued on 1 April 2010. The proceeds of the issue were used to finance the company's trading activities. Interest of £30,400 was paid on 30 September 2010 and again on 31 March 2011.

Note 10 – Plant and machinery

On 1 April 2010 the tax written down values of plant and machinery were as follows:

	£
Main pool	16,700
Expensive motor car (acquired October 2008)	18,400

The following transactions took place during the year ended 31 March 2011:

		Cost/(Proceeds) £
19 May 2010	Purchased equipment	21,600
12 July 2010	Purchased motor car (1) CO_2 emissions 140 g/km	9,800
11 August 2010	Purchased motor car (2) CO_2 emissions 105 g/km	16,200
5 October 2010	Purchased a lorry	17,200
5 March 2011	Sold equipment	(3,300)

The equipment sold on 5 March 2011 for £3,300 was originally purchased in 2006 for £8,900.

Note 11 – Subsidiary company

Gastron Ltd owns 100% of the ordinary share capital of Culinary Ltd. On 13 February 2011 Culinary Ltd sold a freehold factory and this resulted in a capital loss of £66,000. For the year ended 31 March 2011 Culinary Ltd made no other disposals and paid corporation tax at the small profits rate of 21%.

Required

(a) Calculate Gastron Ltd's tax adjusted trading profit for the year ended 31 March 2011, after deducting capital allowances. Your computation should commence with the profit before taxation figure of £640,000, and should list all of the items referred to in notes (1) to (9) indicating by the use of zero (0) any items that do not require adjustment. **(15 marks)**

(b) Calculate Gastron Ltd's corporation tax liability for the year ended 31 March 2011, on the basis that no election is made between Gastron Ltd and Culinary Ltd in respect of capital gains. **(7 marks)**

(c) State the date by which Gastron Ltd's corporation tax liability for the year ended 31 March 2011 should be paid, and advise the company of the interest that will be due if the liability is not paid until 31 August 2012. **(3 marks)**

(d) Explain the group relationship that must exist in order for two or more companies to form a group for capital gains purposes. **(2 marks)**

(e) State the time limit for Gastron Ltd and Culinary Ltd to make a joint election to transfer the capital gain on Gastron Ltd's disposal of shares (see note 8) to Culinary Ltd, and explain why such an election will be beneficial.

(3 marks)

(Total = 30 marks)

VAT

Questions 50 to 54 cover the VAT rules for both corporate and unincorporated businesses, the subject of Part G of the BPP Study Text for Paper F6.

50 Lithograph Ltd (BTX)   18 mins

Lithograph Ltd runs a printing business, and is registered for VAT. Because its annual taxable turnover is only £250,000, the company uses the annual accounting scheme so that it only has to prepare one VAT return each year. The annual VAT period is the year ended 31 December.

Year ended 31 December 2009

The total amount of VAT payable by Lithograph Ltd for the year ended 31 December 2009 was £10,200.

Year ended 31 December 2010

The following information is available:

(1)   Sales invoices totalling £250,000 were issued to VAT registered customers, of which £160,000 were for standard rated sales and £90,000 were for zero-rated sales.

(2)   Purchase invoices totalling £45,000 were received from VAT registered suppliers, of which £38,000 were for standard rated purchases and £7,000 were for zero-rated purchases.

(3)   Standard rated expenses amounted to £28,000. This includes £3,600 for entertaining customers.

(4)   On 1 January 2010 Lithograph Ltd purchased a motor car costing £18,400 for the use of its managing director. The manager director is provided with free petrol for private mileage, and the cost of this is included in the standard rated expenses in note (3). The relevant annual scale charge is £1,385. Both figures are inclusive of VAT.

(5)   During the year ended 31 December 2010 Lithograph Ltd purchased machinery for £24,000, and sold office equipment for £8,000. Input VAT had been claimed when the office equipment was originally purchased.

(6)   On 31 December 2010 Lithograph Ltd wrote off £4,800 due from a customer as an impairment loss. The debt was in respect of an invoice for a standard rated supply that was due for payment on 31 May 2010.

Unless stated otherwise all of the above figures are exclusive of VAT. Assume that the standard rate of VAT was 17.5% in both 2009 and 2010.

Required

(a)   Calculate the monthly payments on account of VAT that Lithograph Ltd will have made in respect of the year ended 31 December 2010, and state in which months these will have been paid.   **(3 marks)**

(b)   (i)   Calculate the total amount of VAT payable by Lithograph Ltd for the year ended 31 December 2010.
                                                                                              (5 marks)

       (ii)   Based on your answer to part (i) above, calculate the balancing payment that would have been paid with the annual VAT return, and state the date by which this return was due for submission.
                                                                                              (2 marks)

                                                                                     (Total = 10 marks)

51 Tardy Ltd (BTX)

18 mins

Tardy Ltd registered for value added tax (VAT) on 1 July 2008. The company's VAT returns have been submitted as follows:

Quarter ended	Submitted	VAT paid/ (refunded) £
30 September 2008	One month late	18,600
31 December 2008	One month late	32,200
31 March 2009	On time	8,800
30 June 2009	Two months late	3,400
30 September 2009	One month late	(6,500)
31 December 2009	On time	42,100
31 March 2010	On time	(2,900)
30 June 2010	On time	3,900
30 September 2010	On time	18,800
31 December 2010	Two months late	57,300
31 March 2011	On time	9,600

Tardy Ltd always pays any VAT that is due at the same time that the related return is submitted.

During May 2011 Tardy Ltd discovered that a number of errors had been made when completing its VAT return for the quarter ended 31 March 2011. As a result of these errors the company will have to make an additional payment of VAT.

Required

(a) State, giving appropriate reasons, the default surcharge consequences arising from Tardy Ltd's submission of its VAT returns for the quarter ended 30 September 2008 to the quarter ended 31 December 2010 inclusive. **(7 marks)**

(b) Explain how Tardy Ltd can voluntarily disclose the errors relating to the VAT return for the quarter ended 31 March 2011. You are not required to discuss any penalties arising as a result of these errors.

(3 marks)

(Total = 10 marks)

52 Ram-Rom Ltd (BTX)

18 mins

Ram-Rom Ltd commenced trading as a manufacturer of computer equipment on 1 January 2010. The company registered for value added tax (VAT) on 1 September 2010. Its inputs for each of the months from January 2010 to August 2010 are as follows:

		Goods purchased £	Services incurred £	Fixed assets £
2010	January	12,300	1,400	42,000
	February	11,200	5,100	–
	March	12,300	7,400	–
	April	16,400	6,300	14,400
	May	14,500	8,500	–
	June	18,800	9,000	–
	July	18,500	9,200	–
	August	23,400	8,200	66,600

During August 2010 Ram-Rom Ltd sold all of the fixed assets purchased during April 2010 for £12,000.

On 1 September 2010 £92,000 of the goods purchased were still in stock.

The above figures are all exclusive of VAT. Ram-Rom Ltd's sales are all standard rated.

The following is a sample of the new sales invoice that Ram-Rom Ltd is going to issue to its customers:

SALES INVOICE

Ram-Rom Ltd
123 The High Street
London WC1 2AB
Telephone 0207 100 1234

Customer: XYZ Computers plc
Address: 99 The Low Road
Glasgow G1 2CD

Invoice Date and Tax Point: 1 September 2010

Item Description	Quantity	Price £
Hard Drives	5	220.00
Motherboards	2	100.00
Total Amount Payable (Including VAT)		320.00

Directors: Y Ram & Z Rom
Company Number: 1234567
Registered Office: 123 The High Street, London WC1 2AB

Ram-Rom Ltd pays for all of its inputs one month after receiving the purchase invoice. However, many customers are not paying Ram-Rom Ltd until four months after the date of the sales invoice. In addition, several customers have recently defaulted on the payment of their debts. In order to encourage more prompt payment, Ram-Rom Ltd is considering offering all of its customers a 5% discount if they pay within one month of the date of the sales invoice. No discount is currently offered.

Required

(a)   Explain why Ram-Rom Ltd was able to recover input VAT totaling £43,160 in respect of inputs incurred prior to registering for VAT on 1 September 2010.   **(5 marks)**

(b)   State what alterations Ram-Rom Ltd will have to make to its new sales invoices in order for them to be valid for VAT purposes.   **(3 marks)**

(c)   Explain the VAT implications of Ram-Rom Ltd offering all of its customers a 5% discount for prompt payment.   **(2 marks)**

(Total = 10 marks)

53 Sandy Brick (BTX)   18 mins

Sandy Brick has been a self-employed builder since 2005. He registered for value added tax (VAT) on 1 January 2011, and is in the process of completing his VAT return for the quarter ended 31 March 2011. The following information is relevant to the completion of this VAT return:

(1)   There were no transactions prior to 4 January 2011.

(2)   Sales invoices totaling £44,000 were issued to VAT registered customers in respect of standard rated sales. Sandy offers his VAT registered customers a 5% discount for prompt payment.

(3)   Sales invoices totaling £16,920 were issued to customers that were not registered for VAT. Of this figure, £5,170 was in respect of zero-rated sales with the balance being in respect of standard rated sales. Standard rated sales are inclusive of VAT.

(4)   On 10 January 2011 Sandy received a payment on account of £5,000 in respect of a contract that was completed on 28 April 2011. The total value of the contract is £10,000. Both of these figures are inclusive of VAT at the standard rate.

(5)   Standard rated materials amounted to £11,200, of which £800 were used in constructing Sandy's private residence.

(6)   Since February 2010 Sandy has paid £120 on the 15th of each month for the lease of office equipment. This expense is standard rated. The input tax on this supply was £21 per month from February to December 2010 and £24 from January 2011.

(7) During the quarter ended 31 March 2011 £400 was spent on mobile telephone calls, of which 30% relates to private calls. This expense is standard rated.

(8) On 20 February 2011 £920 was spent on repairs to a motor car. The motor car is used by Sandy in his business, although 20% of the mileage is for private journeys. This expense is standard rated.

(9) On 15 March 2011 equipment was purchased for £6,000. The purchase was partly financed by a bank loan of £5,000. This purchase is standard rated.

Unless stated otherwise all of the above figures are exclusive of VAT.

Required

Calculate the amount of VAT payable by Sandy for the quarter ended 31 March 2011.   **(10 marks)**

54 Anne Attire (TX 06/09)   27 mins

Anne Attire runs a retail clothing shop. She is registered for value added tax (VAT) and is in the process of completing her VAT return for the quarter ended 30 November 2010.

The following information is available (all figures are exclusive of VAT):

(1) Cash sales amounted to £42,000, of which £28,000 was in respect of standard rated sales and £14,000 was in respect of zero-rated sales.

(2) Sales invoices totalling £12,000 were issued in respect of credit sales. These sales were all standard rated. Anne offers all of her credit sale customers a 5% discount for payment within one month of the date of the sales invoice, and 90% of the customers pay within this period. The sales figure of £12,000 is stated before any deduction for the 5% discount.

(3) Purchase and expense invoices totalling £19,200 were received from VAT registered suppliers. This figure is made up as follows:

	£
Standard rated purchases and expenses	11,200
Zero rated purchases	6,000
Exempt expenses	2,000
	19,200

Anne pays all of her purchase and expense invoices two months after receiving the invoice.

(4) On 30 November 2010 Anne wrote off two impairment losses that were in respect of standard rated credit sales. The first impairment loss was for £300, and was in respect of a sales invoice due for payment on 15 July 2010. The second impairment loss was for £800, and was in respect of a sales invoice due for payment on 10 April 2010.

Anne does not use the cash accounting scheme.

Anne will soon be 60 years old and is therefore considering retirement. On the cessation of trading Anne can either sell the fixed assets of her business on a piecemeal basis to individual VAT registered purchasers, or she can sell the entire business as a going concern to a single VAT registered purchaser.

Required

(a) Calculate the amount of VAT payable by Anne Attire for the quarter ended 30 November 2010 and state the date by which the VAT return for this period was due for submission.   **(6 marks)**

(b) State the conditions that Anne Attire must satisfy before she will be permitted to use the cash accounting scheme and advise her of the implications of using the scheme.   **(5 marks)**

(c) Advise Anne Attire as to what will happen to her VAT registration, and whether output VAT will be due in respect of the fixed assets, if she ceases trading and then:

   (i) Sells her fixed assets on a piecemeal basis to individual VAT registered purchasers;   **(2 marks)**

   (ii) Sells her entire business as a going concern to a single VAT registered purchaser.   **(2 marks)**

   (Total = 15 marks)

Answers

1 Brad, Lauren, Tom and Sarah

Text references. Chapters 2 and 3.

Top tips. Note that the question asked for the tax liability and not the tax due – the tax liability is **before** deduction of any tax credits such as PAYE.

		Marks
(a)	**Brad**	
	Employment income	½
	Interest	½
	PA	1
	Tax bands	1
	Tax rates	1
	Exempt income	1
	Lauren	
	Interest and treasury stock (gross)	½
	ISA – exempt income	½
	Dividends	½
	PA	½
	Gift Aid – extend BRB	1
	Tax bands	1
	Tax rates	1
		10
(b)	**Tom**	
	Pensions	½
	Building society interest	½
	Gift Aid	1
	PAA	1
	Tax bands	1
	Tax rates	1
		5
(c)	**Sarah**	
	Trade profit	½
	Bank interest	½
	Dividend	½
	Pension premiums	1
	Tax bands	1½
	Tax rates	1
		5
		20

(a)   **Brad: Income Tax Computation 2010/11**

	Non-savings £	Savings £	Total £
Employment income	104,500		
BSI (2,200 × 100/80)		2,750	
Net income	104,500	2,750	107,250
Less PA (W)	(2,850)		(2,850)
Taxable income	101,650	2,750	104,400

Tax

	£
On non savings income	
£37,400 @ 20%	7,480
£64,250 @ 40%	25,700
On savings income	
£2,750 @ 40%	1,100
Income tax liability	34,280

Note. Premium Bond winnings and interest on National Savings & Investments Certificates are exempt income.

Personal allowance

	£	£
PA		6,475
Net income	107,250	
Less limit	(100,000)	
	7,250	
÷ 2		(3,625)
PA		2,850

Lauren: Income Tax Computation 2010/11

	Non-savings £	Savings £	Dividend £	Total £
Employment income	46,000			
BSI (2,200 × 100/80)		2,750		
Treasury stock		2,000		
Dividends (2,250 × 100/90)			2,500	
Net income	46,000	4,750	2,500	53,250
Less PA	(6,475)			(6,475)
Taxable income	39,525	4,750	2,500	46,775

Tax

	£
On Non-savings Income	
£37,400 @ 20%	7,480
£1,250 @ 20% (note)	250
£875 @ 40%	350
On Savings Income	
£4,750 @ 40%	1,900
On Dividend Income	
£2,500 @ 32.5%	813
Income tax liability	10,793

Note. The basic rate limit is extended by the gross amount of the Gift Aid payment. £37,400 + (1,000 × 100/80) = £38,650. Dividends and interest received from an ISA are exempt.

(b) **Tom: Income Tax Computation 2010/11**

	Non-savings income £	Savings income £	Total £
State pension	4,226		
Employment pension	6,390		
BSI (13,520 × 100/80)		16,900	
Net income	10,616	16,900	27,516
Less age allowance (W)	(9,182)		(9,182)
Taxable income	1,434	16,900	18,334

Tax

	£
On Non-savings income	
£1,434 @ 20%	287
On Savings income	
(£2,440 – £1,434) £1,006 @ 10%	101
(£16,900 – £1,006) £15,894 @ 20%	3,179
Income tax liability	3,567

Working

Age enhanced personal allowance

	£	£
PAA > 65		9,490
Net income	27,516	
Less Gift Aid £3,200 × 100/80	(4,000)	
	23,516	
Less limit	(22,900)	
	616	
÷ 2		(308)
PAA		9,182

Note. The grossed up value of the Gift Aid payment is deducted from net income when calculating the age allowance.

(c) **Sarah: Income Tax Computation 2010/11**

	Non-savings £	Savings £	Dividend £	Total £
Trading income	164,000			
BI (8,000 × 100/80)		10,000		
Dividends (4,950 × 100/90)			5,500	
Net/taxable income (no PA)	164,000	10,000	5,500	179,500

Tax

	£
On Non-savings income	
£37,400 @ 20%	7,480
£20,000 @ 20% (note)	4,000
£106,600 @ 40%	42,640
On Savings income	
£6,000 @ 40%	2,400
£4,000 @ 50%	2,000
On Dividend income	
£5,500 @ 42.5%	2,337
Income tax liability	60,857

Note. The basic rate limit and the higher rate limit are extended by the gross amount of the personal pension payments. Basic rate limit £37,400 + (16,000 × 100/80) = £57,400. £150,000 + (16,000 × 100/80) = £170,000.

2 Domingo, Erigo and Fargo

Text references. Chapters 3 and 4 on employees, Chapter 5 on pensions, Chapter 7 on trading income, Chapter 8 on capital allowances and Chapter 17 on self assessment for individuals.

Top tips. Watch out for the starting rate band for savings income where there is little or no non-savings income.

Easy marks. The administrative aspects in parts (b) and (c) were easy marks.

Examiner's comments. In part (a) many candidates did not appreciate that donations to charity not made under gift aid are simply ignored, and some candidates missed the income limit for the age-related personal allowance. The expense claim in respect of the business mileage driven by the employed brother often caused problems. Either it was incorrectly calculated, or it was treated as a benefit. Part (b) was well answered. In part (c) few candidates appreciated that the period of retention differs between taxpayers in business and those not in business. However, virtually all candidates were aware of the £3,000 penalty.

Marking scheme

				Marks
(a)	(i)	*Domingo Gomez*		
		Pensions	1	
		Building society interest	1	
		Interest from savings certificates	½	
		Donations	½	
		Personal allowance	2	
		Income tax	1	
				6
	(ii)	*Erigo Gomez*		
		Salary	½	
		Pension contributions	1	
		Charitable payroll deductions	1	
		Relocation costs	1	
		Mileage allowance	1½	
		Personal allowance	½	
		Income tax	½	
				6
	(iii)	*Fargo Gomez*		
		Trading profit	½	
		Pre-trading expenditure	1	
		Capital allowances	2	
		Personal allowance	½	
		Extension of basic rate band	2	
		Income tax	1	
				7
(b)		Paper returns	2	
		Return filed online	1	
				3
(c)		Domingo and Erigo	1	
		Fargo	1	
		Penalty for not keeping records	1	
				3
				25

(a) (i) **Domingo Gomez – Income tax computation 2010/11**

	Non-savings income £	Savings income £	Total £
State pension	4,500		
Occupational pension	2,300		
BSI £14,400 × 100/80		18,000	
NS&I certificate interest - exempt			
Net income	6,800	18,000	24,800
Less: PAA	(6,800)	(1,740)	(8,540)
Taxable income	-	16,260	16,260

Income tax
£		
2,440 @ 10%		244
13,820 @ 20%		2,764
16,260		
Income tax liability		3,008

Note. No tax relief is available in respect of the donations as they were not made under the Gift Aid scheme.

Working

	£
Net income	24,800
Less income limit	(22,900)
Excess	1,900
PAA (65 - 74)	9,490
Less half excess £2,200 × ½	(950)
Revised PAA	8,540

(ii) **Erigo Gomez – Income tax computation 2010/11**

	Non-savings income £
Salary	36,000
Less: pension contributions £36,000 x 6%	(2,160)
charitable payroll deductions £100 x 12	(1,200)
	32,640
Relocation costs (W1)	3,400
	36,040
Less: mileage allowance (W2)	(2,400)
Net income	33,640
Less: personal allowance	(6,475)
Taxable income	27,165

Income tax
£27,165 @ 20%/ Income tax liability	5,433

Workings

1   Only £8,000 of relocation costs are exempt, and so the taxable benefit is £3,400 (11,400 – 8,000).

2   The mileage allowance received will be tax-free, and Erigo can make the following expense claim:

	£
10,000 miles @ 40p	4,000
8,000 miles @ 25p	2,000
	6,000
Mileage allowance 18,000 @ 20p	(3,600)
	2,400

(iii)   **Fargo Gomez – Income tax computation 2010/11**

	Non-savings income £
Trading profit £(64,800 – 2,600) (N)	62,200
Less: capital allowances (W1)	(1,100)
Net income	61,100
Less: personal allowance	(6,475)
Taxable income	54,625

Income tax

£	
37,400 @ 20%	7,480
8,200 @ 20% (W2)	1,640
9,025 @ 40%	3,610
54,625	
Income tax liability	12,730

Note. The advertising expenditure incurred during May 2010 is pre-trading, and is treated as incurred on 6 July 2010. An adjustment is therefore required.

Workings

1   Fargo's period of account is nine months' long so the capital allowances in respect of his motor car are £11,000 × 20% x 9/12 = 1,650 × 16,000/24,000 = £1,100.

2   Fargo's basic rate tax band is extended by £5,200 in respect of the personal pension contribution and £2,400 × 100/80 = £3,000 in respect of the gift aid donations. The extension to the basic rate band is therefore £(5,200 + 3,000).= £8,200.

(b)   (1)   Unless the return is issued late, the latest date that Domingo and Erigo can file paper self-assessment tax returns for 2010/11 is 31 October 2011.

(2)   If Domingo completes a paper tax return by 31 October 2011 then HM Revenue and Customs will prepare a self-assessment tax computation on his behalf.

(3)   Fargo has until 31 January 2012 to file his self-assessment tax return for 2010/11 online.

(c)   (1)   Domingo and Erigo were not in business during 2010/11, so their records must be retained until one year after 31 January following the tax year, which is 31 January 2013.

(2)   Fargo was in business during 2010/11, so all of his records (both business and non-business) must be retained until five years after 31 January following the tax year, which is 31 January 2017.

(3)   A failure to retain records for 2010/11 could result in a maximum penalty of £3,000.

3 Vigorous plc

Marking scheme

		Marks	
(a)	Earnings limit	1	
	Test – cash and benefits	1	
	Directors	1	
			3
(b)	**Andrea**		
	Car benefit – %	1	
	– contributions	1	
	– calculations	½	
	Fuel benefit	1	
	Living accommodation – annual value	½	
	– additional benefit	2	
	– furniture	1	
	Mobile phone	½	
	Ben		
	Loan – average method	1½	
	– strict method	2	
	Relocation	1	
	Car benefit – %	1	
	– calculation	1	
	Chai		
	Van	1	
	Television – current MV calculation	1	
	– original MV calculation	1½	
	Health club	1	
	Computer	½	
			19
(c)	PAYE code	1	
	Self assessment	1	
	Other collection methods	1	
			3
			25

(a) A P11D employee is one who is an employee earning at least £8,500 per annum or a director (in most cases).

In deciding whether an employee earns £8,500, add together the total earnings and benefits that would be taxable if the employee was a P11D employee.

A director is not a P11D employee if he does not have a material interest in the company (control of more than 5% of the ordinary share capital) and is either a full time working director of the company or the company is non-profit making or is established for charitable purposes only.

(b) **Andrea**

Car benefit

Amount by which CO_2 emissions exceed base line:

$(255 - 130) = 125 \div 5 = 25$

Add to 15% = 40% – but maximum taxable % is 35%

	£
£19,400 × 35%	6,790
Less contribution for private use £150 × 12	(1,800)
Taxable benefit for P11D	4,990

Fuel benefit

£18,000 × 35% = £6,300

Living accommodation

Annual value: £7,000

Additional benefit

	£
Cost of property	130,000
Improvements before 6 April 2010	14,000
	144,000
Less *de minimis*	(75,000)
	69,000

× 4% (official rate of interest) = £2,760

Furniture

20% × £6,000 = £1,200

Mobile phone

Exempt benefit

Ben

Taxable cheap loan

Average method $\dfrac{120,000 + 100,000}{2}$ = £110,000 × 4% × 9/12 =   £3,300

Strict method

	£
1 July – 30 September	
£120,000 × 4% × 3/12	1,200
1 October – 31 March	
£100,000 × 4% × 6/12	2,000
	3,200

Ben should elect for the strict method.

Note. This was the answer that the examiner expected. However, strictly speaking Vigorous plc would enter the average method figure of £3,300 on the P11D and then it would have been up to the employee to elect for the strict method.

Relocation costs

First £8,000 – exempt

Excess is taxable benefit £(9,300 – 8,000) = £1,300

Car benefit

Round down CO_2 emissions to nearest 5 ie 125

Below baseline so the taxable % is 15 + 3% (for diesel car) = 18%

Taxable benefit for P11D

18% × £11,200 × 6/12 = £1,008

Chai

Van benefit

Scale charge

£3,000 × 10/12 = £2,500

Television

		£
Greater of:		
(i)	Current market value	250
	Less price paid by employee	(150)
		100

		£
And		
(ii)	Market value when first provided	800
	Less benefit 2008/09 (20% × £800)	(160)
	benefit 2009/10 (20% × £800)	(160)
		480
	Less price paid	(150)
		330

Taxable benefit for P11D: £330

Health club membership

Cost to employer (marginal cost so limited to direct costs): £150

Computer

Benefit for private use £1,900 × 20% = £380

(c) Income tax on benefits provided for more than one year will usually be collected in future years by adjusting the employee's PAYE code. Alternatively tax will be collected through the self assessment system.

However tax up to £2,000 can be collected by adjusting the PAYE code for the employee.

Tax on minor benefits may be paid by the employer under an employees' PAYE settlement agreement.

4 Bryan Thompson

Text references. Chapter 2 on tax computation. Chapters 3 and 4 on employees. Chapter 6 on property income. Chapter 12 on NIC.

Top tips. Be methodical and work through each item in a separate working. You can then summarise the results in the tax computation.

(a) **Income tax**

	Non-savings £	Savings £	Dividend £
Employment income (W1)	88,108		
Rental income (W4)	4,000		
Dividends (1,800 × 100/90)			2,000
Bank interest (3,200 × 100/80)		4,000	
Net income	92,108	4,000	2,000
Personal allowance	(6,475)		
Taxable income	85,633	4,000	2,000

		£
Income tax		
£37,400 @ 20%		7,480
£48,233 @ 40%		19,293
Savings income		
£4,000 × 40%		1,600
Dividends		
£2,000 @ 32.5%		650
Tax liability		29,023

Workings

1   Employment income

	£
Salary	75,000
Car benefit: £25,000 @ ((150 – 130)/5 + 15%) = 19%	4,750
Fuel £18,000 @ 19%	3,420
Car for wife (note 1) £7,500 @ 15% = 1,125 × 6/12	563
Medical insurance (note 2)	1,200
Trip (W2)	1,125
Removal costs (W3)	9,550
Total	95,608
Less occupational pension contribution (note 3)	
10% × £75,000	(7,500)
Employment income	88,108

2   Trip to Florida

	£	£
Wife's flight		1,000
Hotel charge	100	
Single charge	(75)	
Extra re wife	£25 × 5	125
		1,125

3   Removal expenses

	£
Agents fees	4,500
Removal costs	750
Stamp duty	10,500
Legal fees	1,800
	17,550
Less allowed	(8,000)
Assessable	9,550

4   Rental income

	£	£
Rent		20,000
Caretaker	2,600	
Heat and Light	1,400	
Interest	6,000	
Wear and tear 10% × £20,000	2,000	
		(12,000)
		8,000

£8,000 × ½ = £4,000

Notes

(1) Wife's fuel is not a taxable benefit as she pays for all of her private fuel.

(2) Son's medical costs already covered by Private Medical Insurance which is taxable on Bryan as a taxable benefit.

(3) Bryan's pension contribution is deducted directly from his salary at source. The contribution paid by his employer is not a taxable benefit.

(b) NIC

Bryan will pay Class 1 NICs on his salary only.

					£
(43,875 – 5,715)	=	38,160 @ 11%	=		4,198
(75,000 – 43,875)	=	31,125 @ 1%	=		311
Class 1 NIC due					4,509

5 Sam and Kim White

Text references. Chapters 2, 3, 4, 7 and 8.

Top tips. Allocate your time for each part of the question and ensure you attempt every part.

Easy marks. Adjustment to profit in part (a) and Kim's income tax computation in part (b).

Examiner's comments. This question was very well answered by the majority of candidates. In part (a) the adjustments for use of office, business use of a private telephone and own consumption caused the most problems, with a number of candidates being unsure as to whether adjustments should be added or subtracted in order to arrive at the tax adjusted trading profit. Part (b) was also well answered, with only the expense claim for the business mileage causing any difficulty. This was often treated as a benefit rather than as an expense. Part (c) was answered reasonably well, especially the transfer into the spouse's sole name. Many candidates correctly calculated the amount of income tax saving.

Marking scheme

			Marks
(a)	Net profit	½	
	Depreciation	½	
	Motor expenses	1½	
	Patent royalties	1	
	Professional fees: breach of contract	½	
	Professional fees: professional fees	½	
	Gifts to customers	1	
	Own consumption	1	
	Use of office	1	
	Private telephone	1	
	Capital allowances – Pool	1	
	– Motor car	1½	
			11
(b)	**Sam White**		
	Trading profit	½	
	Building society interest	1	
	Personal allowance	½	
	Income tax	1	

Kim White

	Mark
Salary	½
Beneficial loan	1
Expense claim	2
Building society interest	½
Loan interest	1
Personal allowance	½
Income tax	1½
	10

(c) **Individual savings accounts**

	Mark
Limit	1
Tax saving	1
	2

Transfer to Kim's sole name

	Mark
Tax rates	1
Tax saving	1
	2
	25

(a) **Sam White – Trading profit for the year ended 5 April 2011**

	£	£
Net profit		50,000
Add back: Depreciation	7,600	
Motor expenses £8,800 × 20% (N1)	1,760	
Patent royalties (N2)	0	
Professional fees: breach of contract	0	
Professional fees: accountancy personal CGT advice	320	
Other expenses: gifts to customers £(560 + 420) (N3)	980	
Goods for own consumption	1,480	12,140
		62,140
Less: Use of home £5,120 x 1/8	640	
Private telephone £1,600 × 25%	400	
Capital allowances (W)	6,100	(7,140)
Trading profit		55,000

Working – Capital allowances

	Main pool £	Motor car £	Allowances £
TWDV brought forward	18,500	20,200	
WDA – 20%	(3,700)		3,700
WDA – restricted		(3,000) × 80%	2,400
WDV carried forward	14,800	17,200	6,100

Notes

1   Of the 25,000 miles driven by Sam during the year ended 5 April 2011, 20,000 (5,000 + 15,000 [25,000 – 5,000 = 20,000 × 75%]) were for business journeys. The business proportion is therefore 80% (20,000/25,000 × 100).

2   Patent royalties are allowed as a deduction when calculating the trading profit, so no adjustment is required.

3   Gifts to customers are an allowable deduction if they cost less than £50 per recipient per year, are not of food, drink, tobacco or vouchers for exchangeable goods and carry a conspicuous advertisement for the business making the gift.

(b)   **Sam White – Income tax computation 2010/11**

	Non-savings income £	Savings income £	Total £
Trading income (part (a))	55,000		
Building society interest			
£1,200 × 100/80 = £1,500/2		750	
Net income	55,000	750	55,750
Less: personal allowance	(6,475)		(6,475)
Taxable income	48,525	750	49,275

Income tax

	£
Non-savings income	
£37,400 × 20%	7,480
£11,125 × 40%	4,450
Savings income	
£750 × 40%	300
Income tax liability	12,230

Kim White – Income tax computation 2010/11

		Non-savings income £	Saving income £	Total £
Employment income				
Salary	21,600			
Loans (W1)	400			
	22,000			
Less expense claim (W3)	(4,625)	17,375		
BSI £1,200 x 100/80 = £1,500 ÷2			750	
Total income		17,375	750	18,125
Less deductible interest (W4)		(140)		(140)
Net income		17,235	750	17,985
Less personal allowance		(6,475)		(6,475)
Taxable income		10,760	750	11,510

Income tax

	£
Non-savings income	
£10,760 x 20%	2,152
Savings income	
£750 x 20%	150
Income tax liability	2,302

Workings

(1)   The taxable benefit from the beneficial loan is £12,000 at 4% × 10/12 = £400.

(2)   Ordinary commuting (travel between home and the permanent workplace) does not qualify for relief. The travel to a temporary workplace qualifies as it is for a period lasting less than 24 months.

(3)   Kim can therefore make an expense claim based on 12,500 (11,200 + 1,300) miles as follows:

	£
10,000 miles at 40p	4,000
2,500 miles at 25p	625
	4,625

(4)   The loan interest paid of £140 is eligible for relief since the loan was used by Kim to finance expenditure for a relevant purpose.

(c) **Individual savings accounts**

(1) Both Sam and Kim can invest a maximum of £10,200 each tax year into an ISA of which up to £5,100 can be held as cash.

(2) Interest received from ISAs is exempt from income tax, so Sam will save tax at the rate of 40% whilst Kim will save tax at the rate of 20% each on gross interest of £306 (£1,500 × 5,100/25,000).

Transfer to Kim's sole name

(1) Sam pays Income tax at the rate of 40%, whilst Kim's basic rate tax band is not fully utilised.

(2) Transferring the building society deposit account into Kim's sole name would therefore save tax of £150 (£750 × 20% (40% – 20%)).

6 Edmond Brick

Text references. Chapter 6 deals with property income.

Top tips. Remember that property income is pooled to give a single profit or loss. However, if someone has furnished holiday lettings and other lettings, two sets of accounts have to be drawn up as if there were two separate UK property businesses. This is so that profits and losses treated as trade profits and losses can be identified. The examiner has helpfully structured this question so that you were required to make such separate calculations.

Easy marks. Deduction of expenses such as council tax, insurance and advertising were easy marks.

Examiner's comments. This was a very well answered question. In part (a) some candidates discussed the qualifying conditions for a furnished holiday letting rather than the advantages of a property being so treated. Parts (b) and (c) presented few problems. The only aspects that consistently caused difficulty were the capital allowances for the furnished holiday letting (candidates either claimed wear and tear allowance or deducted the full cost of the capital expenditure) and the furnished room (candidates did not appreciate that rent-a-room relief could be claimed).

Marking scheme

		Marks
(a)	Availability of capital allowances	1
	Trading loss relief	1
	Relevant earnings for pension purposes	1
		3
(b)	Rent receivable	½
	Repairs	1
	Other expenses	½
	Capital allowances	1
		3
(c)	**Property two**	
	Rent receivable	½
	Council tax	½
	Insurance	½
	Wear and tear allowance	1
	Property three	
	Rent receivable	½
	Insurance	½
	Advertising	½
	Impairment loss	½
	Loan interest	½

Property four

Lease premium	1
Rent receivable	½
Insurance	½
Rent paid	½
Room	
Rent received	½
Rent a room relief	1
	9
	15

(a) The income tax advantages of Property one being treated as a trade under the furnished holiday letting rules are:

(i) Capital allowances are available on furniture instead of the 10% wear and tear allowance.

(ii) Loss relief is available against general income instead of just against property business income.

(iii) The income qualifies as relevant earnings for pension relief purposes.

(b) **Property one**

	£
Rent receivable £370 × 18	6,660
Less: repairs	(7,400)
other allowable expenditure	(2,710)
capital allowances	
£5,700 (covered by AIA)	(5,700)
Loss	(9,150)

(c) **Property two**

	£	£
Rent receivable £575 × 12	6,900	
Less: council tax	(1,200)	
insurance	(340)	
wear and tear allowance		
10% × £(6,900 – 1,200)	(570)	
Profit		4,790

Property three

Rent receivable £710 × 7	4,970	
Less: insurance	(290)	
advertising	(670)	
impairment loss £710 × 3	(2,130)	
loan interest	(6,700)	
Loss		(4,820)

Property four

Premium taxable as property business income (W)	13,800	
Rent receivable	4,600	
	18,400	
Less: insurance	(360)	
rent payable	(6,800)	
		11,240
Furnished Room		
Rent receivable	5,040	
Less: rent a room relief (note)	(4,250)	
Profit		790
Property business profit		12,000

Working

	£
Premium paid	15,000
Less: 2% × (5-1) × £15,000	(1,200)
Taxable as property business income	13,800

Note. Claiming rent a room relief in respect of the furnished room £(5,040 – 4,250) = £790 is more beneficial than the normal basis of assessment £(5,040 – 1,140) = £3,900.

7 Peter Chic

Text reference. Employment income and benefits are covered in Chapters 3 and 4. Property income is dealt with in Chapter 6. The computation of taxable income and the income tax liability is covered in Chapter 2. National insurance contributions are dealt with in Chapter 12.

Top tips. Set out the computation of taxable income in the standard three column layout. Use workings to show the details rather than putting them directly into the computation.

Easy marks. The calculation of national insurance contributions should have been easy marks.

Examiner's comments. In part (a) a few candidates did not appreciate that both bonuses were to be treated as earnings, whilst the basis of assessing the second mobile telephone was not always known. Some candidates deducted the gift aid donation rather than extending the basic rate tax band. In part (b) the most common mistake was to include taxable benefits when calculating Class 1 national insurance contributions.

Marking scheme

			Marks
(a)	Salary		½
	Bonus payments		1
	Car benefit	– relevant percentage	1
		– capital contribution	½
		– calculation	½
	Fuel benefit		1
	Living accommodation	– annual value	1
		– additional benefit	2
	Mobile telephone		1
	Health club membership		½
	Overseas allowance		½
	Property business profit	– rent receivable	1
		– irrecoverable rent	½
		– repairs	½
		– advertising	½
		– loan interest	1
		– insurance	1
		– wear and tear allowance	1
	Building society interest		½
	Dividends		½
	Premium bond prize		½
	Personal allowance		½
	Extension of basic rate band		1
	Income tax		1½
	Tax suffered at source		1½
			21

(b) Employee Class 1 NIC 1½
    Employer Class 1 NIC 1½
    Employer Class 1A NIC <u>1</u>
    <u>4</u>
    <u>25</u>

(a) **Income tax computation 2010/11**

	Non-savings income £	Savings income £	Dividend income £	Total £
Employment income (W1)	79,680			
Property income (W5)	3,560			
BSI £1,760 × 100/80		2,200		
Dividends £720 × 100/90			800	
Net income	83,240	2,200	800	86,240
Less: personal allowance	(6,475)			
Taxable income	76,765	2,200	800	79,765

Note. Premium bond prize is exempt from income tax.

	£	£
Tax		
£37,400 × 20%		7,480
£3,000 × 20% (extended band) (W6)		600
£36,365 × 40%		14,546
£2,200 × 40%		880
£800 × 32½%		260
Tax liability		23,766
Less: tax deducted at source		
PAYE	14,670	
BSI £2,200 × 20%	440	
Dividend £800 × 10%	80	(15,190)
Tax payable		8,576

Workings

1 *Employment income*

	£	£
Salary	45,600	
Bonus received 10.4.10	4,300	
Bonus received 25.3.11	3,600	53,500
Car benefit (W2)	7,175	
Fuel benefit (W2)	6,300	
Living accommodation (W3)	12,145	
Mobile phone (W4)	50	
Health club membership	510	
Overseas allowance – exempt up to £10 per night for overseas expenses	nil	26,180
Employment income		79,680

2   *Car benefit*

$$\frac{220 - 130}{5} = 18 + 15 + 3 \text{ (diesel)} = 36\%$$

Maximum % is 35.

	£
List price	22,500
Less: contribution	(2,000)
	20,500
× 35%	7,175

Fuel benefit

£18,000 × 35%	6,300

3   *Living accommodation*

	£	£
Annual benefit		8,225
Additional benefit		
Cost of property	160,000	
Improvements before start of tax year	13,000	
	173,000	
Less: *de minimis*	(75,000)	
	98,000	
Benefit @ 4%		3,920
Total accommodation benefit		12,145

4   *Mobile phone*

One mobile phone is exempt
Second mobile phone is calculated on private use of asset basis ie £250 × 20%   £50

5   *Property income*

	£	£
Property one – rent receivable £500 × 5		2,500
Property two – rent receivable £820 × 8		6,560
		9,060
Irrecoverable rent £500 × 2	1,000	
Repairs to roof	600	
Advertising	875	
Loan interest	1,800	
Insurance £(660 × 3/12 + 1,080 × 9/12)	975	
Wear and tear £2,500 × 10% (N)	250	(5,500)
Property income		3,560

Note. The wear and tear allowance has been calculated as 10% of the gross rents receivable as this is more beneficial than 10% of the rents received.

6   Basic rate band extended by gross Gift Aid donations
£2,400 × 100/80   £3,000

(b)   **National insurance contributions 2010/11**

Primary Class 1 (paid by Peter)

		£
£(43,875 – 5,715) = 38,160 × 11%		4,198
£(53,500 – 43,875) = 9,625 × 1%		96
		4,294

Secondary Class 1 (paid by Haute-Couture Ltd)

£(53,500 – 5,715) = 47,785 × 12.8%		6,116

Class 1A (paid by Haute-Couture Ltd)

£26,180 × 12.8%		3,351

8 Peach, Plum and Pear

Marking scheme

		Marks
Ann Peach		
Taxable income	½	
Extension of basic rate band	1	
Income tax	½	
Amount qualifying for tax relief	1	
		3
Basil Plum		
Tax relief on contribution	1	
Excess contribution charge	1	
		2
Chloe Pear		
Taxable income	½	
Income tax	½	
Amount qualifying for tax relief	1	2
		7

(a) **Ann Peach**

	Non-savings income £
Trading income	49,100
Less: personal allowance	(6,475)
Taxable income	42,625

Maximum personal pension contribution is higher of (1) £3,600 and (2) Relevant earnings £49,100 ie £49,100. The remaining £2,900 is not given tax relief.

Basic rate band is therefore £(37,400 + 49,100)   £86,500

Tax is therefore £42,625 × 20%   £8,525

(b) **Basil Plum**

Basil can make a maximum personal pension contribution of £330,000. Therefore his contribution of £270,000 will be given tax relief.

However, the excess charge applies to the contribution over the annual allowance so some of the tax relief given will be clawed back through this charge.

Tutorial note
The charge for contributions in excess of the annual allowance is not examinable on a computational basis.

(c) **Chloe Pear**

	Non-savings income £
Property income	25,000
Less: personal allowance	(6,475)
Taxable income	18,525

Maximum personal pension contribution is £3,600 since Chloe has no relevant earnings. This will have been given tax relief at source by Chloe paying £3,600 × 80% = £2,880. The remaining £4,600 contribution is not given tax relief.

Tax is therefore £18,525 × 20%   3,705

9 Na Style

Text references. Assessment of trading profits is covered in Chapter 9. Adjustment of trading profit is in Chapter 7. The income tax computation is dealt with in Chapter 2 and administration aspects in Chapter 17.

Top tips. As you deal with each adjustment to profit, tick it off in the question – this method should ensure that you do not miss out any item and thus lose marks.

Easy marks. The administration aspects in part (d) should have been 3 easy marks.

Examiner's comments. This question was very well answered, and there were many high scoring answers. In part (a) some candidates lost marks because they did not show the relevant tax years in which profits were assessable. There were few problems as regards the calculation of the trading profit or the income tax payable, although many candidates did not appreciate that interest from government stocks is received gross and is taxable. As regards the balancing payment and payments on account, candidates were often not aware of the relevant dates. In part (d) many candidates did not appreciate that a 5% penalty would be imposed in addition to the interest charge.

		Marks
(a)	First tax year trading profits	1	
	Second tax year trading profits	1½	
	Third tax year trading profits	½	
	Overlap profits	2	
			5
(b)	Net profit	½	
	Depreciation	½	
	Motor expenses	1	
	Accountancy	½	
	Legal fees	½	
	Property expenses	1	
	Own consumption	1	
	Fine	½	
	Donation to political party	½	
	Trade subscription	½	
	Private telephone	1	
	Capital allowances	½	
			8
(c) (i)	*Income tax computation*		
	Trading profit	½	
	Building society interest	½	
	Individual savings account	½	
	Interest from savings certificates	½	
	Interest from government stocks	1	
	Dividends	½	
	Personal allowance	½	
	Income tax liability	1	
	Income tax suffered at source	1	
			6
(ii)	*Income tax payments*		
	Balancing payment	1½	
	Payments on account	1½	
			3
(d)	Interest	1	
	Calculation	1	
	Surcharge	1	
			3
			25

(a) **Na Style trading profits 2007/08, 2008/09 and 2009/10**

Year	Basis period	Working	Taxable profits £
2007/08	1.01.08 – 5.4.08	£25,200 × 3/6	12,600
2008/09	1.01.08 – 31.12.08 (N)	£25,200 + £21,600 × 6/12	36,000
2009/10	1.7.08 – 30.6.09		21,600

Note. Because the accounting period ending in the second tax year is less than twelve months, the basis period for that year is the first twelve months of trading.

Overlap profits

Overlap period	Working	Overlap profits £
1.01.08 – 5.4.08	£25,200 × 3/6	12,600
1.07.08 – 31.12.08	£21,600 × 6/12	10,800

(b) **Na Style tax adjusted trading profit for year ended 30 June 2010**

	£	£
Net profit		22,000
Add: depreciation	1,300	
motor expenses – private use		
7,000/8,000 × £2,200	1,925	
professional fees – accountancy	0	
professional fees – lease (N)	1,260	
property expenses – private use		
1/3 × £12,900	4,300	
purchases – goods taken for own use (selling price)	450	
other expenses – fine	400	
other expenses – political party donation	80	
other expenses – trade subscription	0	
		9,715
		31,715
Less: telephone – business use 20% × £1,200	240	
capital allowances	810	(1,050)
Tax adjusted trading profit		30,665

Note. Legal expenses relating to the *grant* of a short lease are not allowable.

(c) (i) **Na Style tax payable for 2010/11**

	Non-savings income £	Savings income £	Dividend income £	Total £
Trading income (part (b))	30,665			
BSI £560 × 100/80		700		
ISA interest (exempt)				
NS&I interest (exempt)				
Interest from stocks (gross)		810		
UK dividends £1,080 × 100/90			1,200	
Net income	30,665	1,510	1,200	33,375
Less: personal allowance	(6,475)			
Taxable income	24,190	1,510	1,200	26,900

	£
Income tax	
Non-savings income	
£24,190 × 20%	4,838
Savings income	
£1,510 × 20%	302
Dividend income	
£1,200 × 10%	120
Tax liability	5,260

	£	£
Less: tax suffered		
Tax credit on dividend income £1,200 × 10%	120	
Tax on building society interest £700 × 20%	140	
		(260)
Tax payable		5,000

(ii) **Na Style balancing payment for 2010/11**

	£
Tax payable (part (i))	5,000
Less: payments on account	(3,200)
Balancing payment due 31 January 2012	1,800

First payment on account 2011/12
½ × £5,000 due 31 January 2012 — 2,500
Second payment on account 2011/12
½ × £5,000 due 31 July 2012 — 2,500

(d) **Consequences of not making balancing payment until 31 May 2012**

Interest is charged where a balancing payment is paid late. This will run from 1 February 2012 to 31 May 2012.

The interest charge will be £1,800 × 3% × 4/12 = £18.

In addition, a penalty of £1,800 @ 5% = £90 will be imposed as the balancing payment is made after the penalty date (30 days after the due date) but not more than five months after the penalty date.

10 Simon House

Text references. The badges of trade are discussed in Chapter 7 which also deals with the computation of trading profit. Chapter 2 deals with income tax computation. Chapter 13 covers computation of chargeable gains for individuals.

Top tips. Think carefully about what costs are allowable as part of trading expenses in part (b) and, alternatively, as part of the cost of the asset in part (c). Not all the expenses are allowable in both cases.

Easy marks. The examiner gave you the badges of trade in part (a) so it should have been easy marks to comment on them.

Examiner's comments. This question was very well answered, and often helped marginal candidates to achieve a pass mark. In part (a) a number of candidates failed to score any marks because they did not state what did or did not indicate trading. For example, stating that the 'length of ownership' means how long an item has owned did not score any marks. It was necessary to explain that the sale of property within a short time of its acquisition is an indication of trading. Part (b) presented no problems for most candidates. In this type of question it is always best to produce full computations for each option. This will maximise marks if any mistakes are made. It was pleasing to see that many candidates correctly restricted the Class 2 NIC to 19 weeks' contributions.

			Marks
(a)	Subject matter	½	
	Length of ownership	½	
	Frequency of transactions	½	
	Work done	½	
	Circumstances of realisation	½	
	Profit motive	½	
			3
(b)	Income	½	
	Acquisition of house	½	
	Legal fees on acquisition	½	
	Renovation costs	½	
	Legal fees on sale	½	
	Loan interest	1	
	Personal allowance	½	
	Income tax liability	1	
	Class 4 NICs	1½	
	Class 2 NICs	1½	
			8
(c)	Sale proceeds	½	
	Legal fees on sale	½	
	Cost of house	½	
	Legal fees on acquisition	½	
	Enhancement expenditure	½	
	Loan interest – not allowable	½	
	Annual exempt amount	½	
	Capital gains tax liability	½	
			4
			15

(a) **Badges of trade**

Subject matter

Some assets are commonly held as investments for their intrinsic value, for example an individual may buy shares for dividend income produced by them or may buy a painting to enjoy it as a work of art. A subsequent disposal of an investment asset usually produces a capital gain. Where the subject matter of a transaction is not an investment asset, any profit on resale is usually a trading profit.

Length of ownership

If items purchased are sold soon afterwards, this indicates trading transactions.

Frequency of transactions

Transactions which may, in isolation, be of a capital nature will be interpreted as trading transactions where their frequency indicates the carrying on of a trade.

Work done

When work is done to make an asset more marketable, or steps are taken to find purchasers, this is likely to be indicative of trading.

Length of ownership

If items purchased are sold soon afterwards, this indicates trading.

Circumstances of realisation

A forced sale, for example to realise funds for an emergency, is not likely to be treated as trading.

Motive
The absence of a profit motive will not necessarily preclude a tax charge as trading income, but its presence is a strong indication that a person is trading.

(b) **Simon House income tax and NICs for 2010/11 if trading**

	£	£
Income		260,000
Less: *costs incurred*		
house	127,000	
legal fees on acquisition	1,800	
renovation	50,600	
legal fees on sale	2,600	
loan interest		
£150,000 × 6% × 4/12	3,000	
		(185,000)
Trading income/Net income		75,000
Less: personal allowance		(6,475)
Taxable income		68,525

Income tax		
£37,400 @ 20%		7,480
£31,125 @ 40%		12,450
Income tax liability		19,930

Class 4 NICs		
£(43,875 – 5,715) = £38,160 @ 8%		3,053
£(75,000 – 43,875) = £31,125 @ 1%		311
Total Class 4 NICs		3,364

Class 2 NICs		
£2.40 x 19 weeks (N)		46

Note. Class 2 contributions are paid for complete weeks, running from midnight on Sunday to the following midnight on Saturday, during which self-employed activity takes place for the whole or part of the week. In this case, the first week starts at midnight on Sunday 25 April 2010 and the last week ends on Saturday 4 September 2010, which comprises 19 weeks. Credit should be given by the examiner for any reasonable attempt at this calculation (ie recognising that Class 2 NICs were only due during the period of trading, not for the whole year 2010/11).

(c) **Simon House capital gains tax 2010/11 if not trading**

	£	£
Sale proceeds		260,000
Less: legal fees on sale		(2,600)
Net proceeds of sale		257,400
Less: cost of house	127,000	
legal fees on acquisition	1,800	
renovation	50,600	
loan interest (N)	0	
		(179,400)
Chargeable gain		78,000
Less: annual exempt amount		(10,100)
Taxable gain		67,900

	£	£
Capital gains tax		
£37,400 @ 18%		6,732
£(67,900 – 37,400) = 30,500 @ 28%		8,540
Capital gains tax liability		15,272

Note. The loan interest is a revenue expense and so is not allowable in computing the chargeable gain.

11 Malcolm

Text references. Chapter 10 looks at trading losses.

Top tips. You should not be tempted in a question like this merely to list the various loss reliefs. You need to make an attempt at giving your rationale for the use of the losses. Remember that you will probably get marks for your rationale even if you have not used the loss in the most efficient way.

		Marks
(a)	Trading losses	
	2009/10	2
	2010/11	2
	Offset of loss – carry back against general income 2008/09	1
	– current year general income 2009/10	1
	Order of claims	1
	No claims against general income 2010/11	1
	Why no further claims against general income	2
	Carry forward against future trade profits	2
		12
(b)	Time limit – claim against general income	1
	Time limit – carry forward against trading profits	2
		3
		15

(a) Trading losses are:

	£	£
2009/10 (1.8.09 – 5.4.10)		
(£10,000 + 4/12 × £20,000)		(16,667)
2010/11 (1.12.09 – 30.11.10)		
Loss	20,000	
Less used in 2009/10	(6,667)	
		(13,333)
		(30,000)

Each of these losses can be relieved against the general income of the year of the loss and/or the preceding year.

2009/10 loss

	2008/09	*2009/10*
	£	£
Employment income	8,000	7,500
Interest (£3,040 × $\frac{100}{80}$)	3,800	3,800
Total income	11,800	11,300
Loss relief against general income	(11,800)	(4,867)
Net income	0	6,433

A claim against general income in 2008/09 results in a waste of personal allowances. However, the claim is worthwhile as it leads to a repayment of income tax in respect of the year and the alternative is to carry the loss forward.

A claim against general income in 2009/10 to utilise the balance of the 2009/10 loss obtains tax relief for the loss quickly and it only wastes a small amount of personal allowance.

2010/11 loss

A claim against general income in 2010/11 (ie against interest income) would not be worthwhile as it would merely waste the personal allowance. A claim against general income in 2009/10 would also waste the personal allowance but it would allow a further claim to be made to set the loss against the chargeable gain in 2009/10. However, this would waste the CGT annual exempt amount of £10,100 and save no CGT.

Alternatively, if a claim against general income was not made for the 2009/10 loss in 2008/09, the 2010/11 loss could be carried back against the general income of the previous three years under early years loss relief. £11,800 of the loss would be set off in 2008/09 and the balance in 2009/10 leaving net income in 2009/10 of £9,767. This is clearly less beneficial than the claim against general income for the 2009/10 loss considered above.

A better alternative is to carry the 2010/11 loss forward for relief against trading income of 2011/12:

	2011/12 £
Trading income	17,000
Less carry forward loss relief	(13,333)
	3,667
Building society interest	3,800
	7,467

This leaves enough income in 2011/12 to absorb the personal allowance. Income tax is saved in 2011/12 on the whole of the loss set off.

(b) The claims against general income for the 2009/10 loss must be made by the 31 January which is nearly two years after the end of the tax year of the loss: thus by 31 January 2012.

There is no statutory time limit by which a claim to relieve a loss by carry forward must be made. However, a claim to establish the amount of the loss of 2010/11 to be carried forward must be made 5 April which is four years after the end of the year of the loss: thus by 5 April 2015. Once the loss is established, it will be carried forward and used where possible each year until used up.

12 Robert Sax

Text references. The basis period rules are all dealt with in Chapter 9.

Top tips. Be methodical in your approach. Deal with the opening year rules first, then identify the year of change, and apply the CYB to all other years. Apply the cessation rules to the final year.

		Marks
2003/04	– actual basis	1½
2004/05	– Last 12m of period	2
2005/06	– CYB	1
Overlap profits created		2
2006/07	– CYB	
2007/08	– CYB	1½
2008/09	– CYB	
2009/10	– Identify year of change	1
	– 15 m/e 31.12.09	1
	– Deduct overlap profits	2
2010/11	– Identify year of cessation	1
	– Deduct overlap profits	2
		15

2003/04   1.6.03 – 5.4.04

$$\frac{10}{16} \times £30,000$$ £18,750

2004/05   1.10.03 – 30.9.04

$$\frac{12}{16} \times £30,000$$ £22,500

Overlap profits

= 1.10.03 – 5.4.04 (6 months)

= $\frac{6}{16} \times £30,000$ £11,250

2005//06	Y/e/30.9.05	£40,000
2006/07	Y/e 30.9.06	£50,000
2007/08	Y/e 30.9.07	£60,000
2008/09	Y/e 30.9.08	£55,000

2009/10   "Year of change"

1.10.08 – 31.12.09 (15m)   £75,000

less overlap relief

$$\frac{3}{6} \times £11,250$$ (5,625)

                                                                                £69,375

2010/11   Year of cessation

1.1.10 – 31.3.11

(£40,000 + £12,000)   £52,000

less overlap relief

(£11,250 – £5,625)   (5,625)

                                                                                £46,375

13 Vanessa Serve and Serene Volley

Text references. Chapter 2 deals with taxable income and computation of income tax. Chapter 5 covers pensions. Look in Chapters 7 and 8 for computation of trading income and capital allowances. Chapters 3 and 4 cover employment income. Chapter 12 deals with national insurance contributions. Chapter 17 covers self assessment. Value added tax is dealt with in Chapters 26 and 27.

Top tips. You should use the standard layout for income tax computations, separating out the different types of income. Note that part (b) on VAT could be tackled without reference to part (a) and you might have wanted to start on part (b).

Easy marks. The calculation of the national insurance contributions in part (a)(ii) were easy marks. You should also have known the due dates in part (a)(iii).

Examiner's comments. In part (a) many candidates did not appreciate that it was not necessary to gross up the interest received from an investment account at the National Savings & Investment Bank, nor that interest from savings certificates is exempt from tax. The contribution to the occupational pension scheme was often used to extend the basic rate tax band rather than being deducted in calculating employment income. Many candidates wasted time in calculating a fuel benefit despite the question clearly stating that no fuel was provided for private journeys. The one aspect of the question that consistently caused problems was the calculation of the balancing payments and the payments on account, and this section was often not answered at all. It was disappointing that many candidates were not aware of the relevant due dates. The VAT aspects in part (b) were well answered, although far too many candidates incorrectly deducted input VAT when calculating the amount of VAT payable using the flat rate scheme.

Marking scheme

				Marks
(a)	(i)	*Vanessa Serve*		
		Trading profit	½	
		Capital allowances	1½	
		NS&I bank interest	1	
		Personal allowance	½	
		Extension of basic rate band	1	
		Income tax payable	1	
		Serene Volley		
		Salary	½	
		Pension contribution	1	
		Car benefit	1½	
		NS&I certificate interest – exempt	½	
		Personal allowance	½	
		Income tax liability	1	
		Income tax suffered at source	½	
				11
	(ii)	*Vanessa Serve*		
		Class 2 NICs	1	
		Class 4 NICs	1½	
		Serene Volley		
		Class 1 NICs	1½	
				4

(iii)   *Vanessa Serve*

Balancing payment	1
Due date	½
Payments on account	1
Due dates	½
Serene Volley	
Balancing payment	½
Due date	½
No payment on account required	1
	5

(b)   (i)   *Output tax*

Sales	½
Input tax	
Telephone	1
Car purchase	½
Car repairs	1
Equipment	1
Other expenses	1
	5

(ii)

Fixed percentage scheme limit	1
Simplified administration	2
VAT saving	2
	5
	30

(a)   (i)   **Vanessa Serve – income tax**

	Non-savings income £	Savings income £	Total £
Trading profit	52,400		
Less: capital allowance (W1)	(1,820)		
Taxable trading income	50,580		
NS&I bank interest (gross)		1,100	
Net income	50,580	1,100	51,680
Less: personal allowance	(6,475)		
Taxable income	44,105	1,100	45,205

Tax

	£
£37,400 × 20%	7,480
£6,400 × 20% (extended band for pension)	1,280
£305 × 40%	122
£1,100 × 40%	440
Income tax liability/payable	9,322

Working 1

	Ca £	Allowance £
TWDV b/f	13,000	
Less WDA @ 20%	(2,600)	1,820
	× 14/20	
TWDV c/f	10,400	

Serene Volley – income tax

	Non-savings Income £
Salary	26,400
Less: pension contribution	(1,320)
	25,080
Car benefit (W2)	4,100
Net income	29,180
Less: personal allowance	(6,475)
Taxable income	22,705

Working 2

Car benefit percentage
180 – 130 = 50 ÷ 5 = 10 +15 = 25%

£16,400 × 25%   £4,100

Note. The interest on the NS&I savings certificates is exempt from income tax.
Tax

	£
£22,705 × 20% / Income tax liability	4,541
Less: PAYE	(4,490)
Income tax payable	51

(ii) **Vanessa Serve – national insurance contributions**

	£	£
Class 2 NICs		
52 × £2.40		125
Class 4 NICs		
£(43,875 – 5,715) = 38,160 × 8%	3,053	
£(50,580 – 43,875) = 6,705 × 1%	67	3,120
Total NICs		3,245

Serene Volley – national insurance contributions

	£
Class 1 NICs	
£(26,400 – 5,715) = 20,685 × 11%	£2,275

(iii) **Vanessa Serve – balancing payment and payments on account**
Balancing payment 2010/11

	£
Income tax and Class 4 payable £(9,322 + 3,120)	12,442
Less: payments on account	(8,460)
Income tax due on 31 January 2012	3,982

Payments on account 2011/12

Due 31 January 2012 £12,442 ÷ 2	£6,221
Due 31 July 2012 £12,442 ÷ 2	£6,221

Serene Volley – balancing payment and payments on account

Balancing payment 2010/11

Income tax due 31 January 2012	£51

Payments on account 2011/12

No payment on account required for as income tax due for previous tax year is below £1,000 *de minimis* limit.

(b)   (i)   **Vanessa Serve – value added tax payable**

		£	£
Output tax			
Sales:	£18,000 × 20%		3,600
Input tax			
Telephone:	£600 × 20% × 60% (note 1)	72	
Car purchase (note 2)		0	
Car repairs:	£987 × 20/120 (note 3)	164	
Equipment:	£1,760 × 20% (note 4)	352	
Other expenses:	£(2,200 – 400) × 20% (note 5)	360	(948)
VAT payable for quarter ending 31 March 2011			2,652

Notes

1   Only the business element of telephone use is recoverable.

2   No input tax can be recovered on a car not exclusively used for business purposes.

3   The whole of the input tax on the car repairs is recoverable because there is some business use of the car.

4   The input tax on the equipment is recoverable in this VAT period because the actual tax point is 29 March 2011 when payment was made.

5   No input tax is recoverable on business entertaining.

(ii)   To join the flat rate scheme, Vanessa's business must have a tax exclusive annual taxable turnover of up to £150,000.

The main advantage of using the scheme is the simplification of VAT administration. Since Vanessa does not have VAT registered customers, she would not have to issue VAT invoices. Also she would not have to record purchase invoices.

There may also be a VAT saving by using the flat rate scheme. For example, if Vanessa had used the scheme in the quarter to 31 March 2011, her VAT liability would have been:

Output tax

£(18,000 + 3,600) = £21,600 × 8.5%   £1,836

This is a saving of £(2,652 – 1,836)   £816

14 Samantha Fabrique

Text references. Chapter 10 deals with trading losses.

Top tips. You should use the standard layout for losses: set up the columns and lines required and then slot in the numbers. A loss memorandum is also useful as a double check that you have used the losses correctly.

Easy marks. There were easy marks for setting out the trading income and gains stated in the question and using the personal allowance and annual exempt amount.

Examiner's comments. In part (a) many candidates explained the loss reliefs that were available rather than the factors that must be taken into account when deciding which loss reliefs to actually claim. In part (b) many candidates claimed loss relief against the total income for the year of the loss despite this income clearly being covered by the personal allowance. Very few candidates, even if they showed the capital gains separately, claimed loss relief against capital gains.

		Marks
(a)	Rate of tax	1
	Timing of relief	1
	Waste of personal allowance/annual exempt amount	1
		3
(b)	Trading income	½
	Trading loss relief carried forward	1
	Building society interest	½
	Trading loss relief against general income	1
	Personal allowance	½
	Gains	½
	Capital loss relief carried forward	1
	Trading loss relief against gains	1
	Annual exempt amount	1
		7
		10

(a) Factors that will influence an individual's choice of loss relief claim are:

(i) The rate of income tax or capital gains tax at which relief will be obtained, with preference being given to income charged at the additional rate of 50%, then the higher rate of 40%.

(ii) The timing of the relief obtained, with a claim against general income/capital gains of the current year or preceding year resulting in earlier relief than a carry forward claim against future trading profits.

(iii) The extent to which the income tax personal allowance and the capital gains tax annual exempt amount will be wasted by using a claim against general income/capital gains.

(b) **Samantha Fabrique – taxable income**

	2008/09	2009/10	2010/11	2011/12
	£	£	£	£
Trading income	6,290	51,600	0	12,390
Less: trading loss relief carried forward	(0)	(0)	(0)	(7,000)
	6,290	51,600	0	5,390
Building society interest	0	2,100	3,800	1,500
	6,290	53,700	3,800	6,890
Less: trading loss relief against general income (N)	(0)	(53,700)	(0)	(0)
Net income	6,290	0	3,800	6,890
Less: personal allowance	(6,290)	(0)	(3,800)	(6,475)
Taxable income	0	0	0	415

Samantha Fabrique – taxable gains

	2008/09	2009/10	2010/11	2011/12
	£	£	£	£
Gains	20,100	23,300	0	13,500
Less: trading loss relief against gains (note)	(0)	(23,300)	(0)	(0)
	20,100	0	0	13,500
Less: capital loss carried forward	(0)	(0)	(0)	(3,400)
	20,100	0	0	10,100
Less: annual exempt amount	(10,100)	(0)	(0)	(10,100)
Taxable gains	10,000	0	0	0

Note. Loss relief has been claimed against general income and gains for 2009/10 since this gives relief at the earliest date and at the highest rates of tax. No claim should be made to set the loss against general income in 2010/11 since this is already covered by the personal allowance for that year.

Trading loss memorandum

	£
Loss 2010/11	84,000
Less: used 2009/10 (income)	(53,700)
used 2009/10 (gains)	(23,300)
Available for c/f	7,000
Less: used 2011/12	(7,000)
Loss unused	0

15 Wright and Wong

Text references. Chapter 5 on pensions and Chapter 11 on partnerships.

Top tips. There is no limit on the total amount of contributions that can be made, but there is a limit on the amount qualifying for tax relief.

Easy marks. Explaining the method of obtaining tax relief.

(a) **Maximum contributions**

Geoff and Sam can contribute any amount to their personal pension regardless of the level of their earnings. However tax relief will only be given for contributions up to their earnings for the tax year.

The partnership profits of £175,000 split 4:1 gives Geoff £140,000 profit and Sam £35,000. Therefore, Geoff should contribute a maximum of £140,000 and Sam £35,000 to ensure that they receive tax relief on their contributions.

(b) **Tax relief**

Basic rate tax relief is given through the pension holder paying contributions net of 20%. This means that they pay only 80% of the gross payment into the pension. The government pays the extra 20% on their behalf to the pension provider.

Geoff will pay £112,000 (£140,000 × 80%) and Sam will pay £28,000 (£35,000 × 80%).

In addition Geoff will be entitled to higher rate relief. This is given by extending the basic rate band for the year by the amount of the gross contribution.

Tax relief is only available for the year in which the contribution is made.

Sam's tax liability

	£
Trading profit	35,000
Personal allowance	(6,475)
Taxable income	28,525
£28,525 at 20%	£5,705

Geoff's tax liability

	£
Trading profit	140,000
Personal allowance (N1)	(6,475)
Taxable income	133,525
£133,525 at 20% (N2))	£26,705
Tax liability	

Notes

1   Geoff's net adjusted income is £(140,000 – 140,000) = nil. This means that he will be entitled to the personal allowance in full.

2   Higher rate tax relief will be given by extending Geoff's basic rate tax band for 2010/11 to £(37,400 + 140,000) = £177,400.

(c)   **No earnings**

There is no need for the individual to have earnings. A contribution of up to £3,600 per tax year may be made into a pension regardless of the level of earnings.

16 Amy Bwalya

Text references. Chapter 9 for sole trader basis period rules. Chapter 11 for partnerships.

Top tips. It is easier to get marks if you set out the rules as well as the dates – that way if you make a silly mistake the examiner can see that you know the rules.

			Marks
(a)	2008/09	1	
	2009/10	2	
	2010/11	1	
	Overlap profits	1	
			5
(b)	6.4.10 – 31.12.10		
	Interest	1	
	Salary	1	
	Split balance	1	
	1.1.11 – 5.4.11		
	Interest	½	
	Salary	½	
	Split balance	½	
	Totals for each partner	½	
			5
(c)	2008/09	1	
	2009/10 year of change		
	9m to 30.6.09	½	
	Add 3m from prior year	1	
	2010/11 year of cessation		
	Profits not yet taxed	1½	
	Less: overlap from start	½	
	Less: overlap from change of accounting date	½	
			5
			15

(a) **Amy's trading profits**

	£	£
2008/09		
1 August 2008 – 5 April 2009		
$^8/_{10}$ × £38,500		30,800
2009/10		
<12m so tax 1st 12 months of trade		
1 August 2008 – 31 July 2009		
10m to 31 May 2009	38,500	
+ $^2/_{12}$ × £52,800	8,800	
		47,300
2010/11		
CYB y/e 31 May 2010		52,800
Overlap profits		
1 August 2008 – 5 April 2009	30,800	
1 June 2009 – 31 July 2009	8,800	
10 months		39,600

(b) **Cedric, Eli & Gordon's trading profits**

	Total £	C £	E £	G £
6 April 2010 – 31 December 2010				
Interest: $^9/_{12}$ × capital @ 10%	8,250	3,000	5,250	
Salary: $^9/_{12}$ × 6,000	4,500		4,500	
Balance: 60:40	54,750	32,850	21,900	
Total: $^9/_{12}$ × 90,000	67,500	35,850	31,650	
1 January 2011 – 5 April 2011				
Interest: $^3/_{12}$ × capital @ 10%	2,250		1,750	500
Salary: $^3/_{12}$ × 6,000	1,500		1,500	
Balance: 70:30	18,750		13,125	5,625
Total: $^3/_{12}$ × 90,000	22,500		16,375	6,125
Total	90,000	35,850	48,025	6,125

Trading income assessments:

Cedric	£35,850
Eli	£48,025
Gordon	£6,125

(c) **Ivan's trading profits**

	£	£
2008/09		
CYB y/e 30 September 2008		36,000
2009/10		
Year of change (Tax 12m to new accounting date)		
9m to 30 June 2009	23,400	
+ 3m from previous yr: 3/12 × 36,000	9,000	
Total 12m		32,400
2010/11		
Year of cessation of trade		
Tax everything not already taxed		
Y/e 30 June 2010	28,800	
6m to 31 December 2010	10,800	
Less: overlap		
(i) From start of business	(4,500)	
(ii) From change of accounting date	(9,000)	
		26,100

17 Ae, Bee, Cae, Dee and Eu

Text references. Partnerships are covered in Chapter 11. Assessable trading income is dealt with in Chapter 9 and capital allowances are covered in Chapter 8.

Top tips. You must attempt each part of a multi-part question like this one to ensure you have a good chance of passing the exam.

Easy marks. Obtaining relief for overlap profits in part (c) was an easy mark.

Examiner's comments. This question was extremely well answered by the majority of candidates, many of whom scored maximum marks. One of the main problems in the answers of poorer candidates was not showing the appropriate tax years, thus losing a lot of marks throughout. The only common mistake was that in part (b) for the year of change, candidates often used an actual basis rather than the 12 months to the new accounting date.

				Marks
(a)	2008/09			1½
	2009/10			1
	2010/11	– Ae and Bee		1
		– Cae		1½
				5
(b)	(i)	2008/09		1
		2009/10		2
		2010/11		1
				4
	(ii)	Overlap profits		1
(c)	2009/10	– Assessment		1
		– Capital allowances		½
	2010/11	– Assessment		1
		– Capital allowances		1½
		– Relief for overlap profits		1
				5
				15

(a)   **Division of partnership profits for A, B and C**

	Total	A	B	C
	£	£	£	£
y/e 30.6.09	54,000	27,000	27,000	–
y/e 30.6.10	66,000	33,000	33,000	–
y/e 30.6.11	87,000	29,000	29,000	29,000

Then allocate to tax years:
2008/09
A and B – First year
Actual basis 1.7.08 – 5.4.09

	A	B	C
9/12 x £27,000	20,250	20,250	–

2009/10
A and B – Second year
First 12 months y/e 30.6.09

	A	B	C
	27,000	27,000	–

2010/11
A and B – Third year
CYB y/e 30.6.10

	A	B
	33,000	33,000

C – First year
Actual basis 1.7.10 – 5.4.11

	C
9/12 x £29,000	21,750

(b)   (i)   **Change of accounting date for D**

		£	£
2008/09			
CYB y/e 5.4.09			32,880
2009/10 (year of change)			
Basis period is 12 months to new a/cting date – 31.7.09			
1.8.08 – 5.4.09			
8/12 × £32,880		21,920	
6.4.09 - 31.07.09		16,240	38,160
2010/11			
CYB y/e 31.7.10			54,120

(ii)   Overlap profits
        1.8.08 – 5.4.09
        8/12 × £32,880   21,920

(c)   **Cessation for E**

	£	£
2009/10		
CYB y/e 30.6.09 Trading income	62,775	
Less: CAs (W)	(1,575)	61,200
2010/11		
Cessation y/e 30.6.10 and p/e 30.09.10	72,000	
Trading income £(57,600 + 14,400)		
Less: CAs £(1,260 + 3,140)(W)	(4,400)	
Overlap profits	(19,800)	47,800

Working

	Main pool	Allowances
	£	£
y/e 30.6.09		
TWDV b/f	7,875	
WDA @ 20%	(1,575)	1,575
TWDV c/f	6,300	
y/e 30.6.10		
WDA @ 20%	(1,260)	1,260
TWDV c/f	5,040	
p/e 30.9.10		
Addition	2,400	
Disposal	(4,300)	
BA	3,140	3,140

18 Auy Man and Bim Men

Text references. Residence is dealt with in Chapter 2. Adjustment of profit is covered in Chapter 7 and capital allowances in Chapter 8. Assessable trading income is dealt with in Chapter 9 and partnerships in Chapter 11. National insurance contributions are the subject of Chapter 12. VAT is covered in Chapters 26 and 27.

Top tips. Remember that rules for capital allowances on cars changed from April 2009 so you need to look carefully to see when each car was acquired. CO_2 emissions are only relevant for cars acquired from April 2009.

Easy marks. There were easy marks for the adjustment of profit in part (b) provided that you followed the instructions in the question to start with the profit before taxation figure and indicated with a zero any items which did not require adjustment.

Examiner's comments. This question was well answered, especially parts (b) and (c). In part (a) several candidates simply repeated the information contained within the question rather than explaining the 183 day rule and the substantial visits rule. There were generally no problems with part (b) although a number of candidates did not appreciate that they had to deduct the salary and interest on capital before allocating the balance of profits. Most candidates scored maximum marks for part (c). In part (d) the tax point was explained reasonably well, although some candidates wasted time by also giving details for the supply of goods. Some students struggled with the VAT calculation, assuming this to be much more complicated than it actually was. For 2 marks, all that was required was to select the output VAT of £21,600 and input VAT of £140 and £180 from the text, and then calculate the amount payable of £21,280. It was not necessary to calculate any VAT figures and therefore the fact that the period spanned the date when the VAT rate changed was irrelevant. The main problem as regards the VAT calculation using the flat rate scheme was that candidates incorrectly deducted input VAT.

Marking scheme

			Marks
(a)	Auy Man	1	
	Bim Men	1	
			2
(b)	**Trading profit**		
	Depreciation	½	
	Input VAT	½	
	Motor expenses	1	
	Entertaining employees	½	
	Appropriation of profit	½	
	Excessive salary	½	
	Deduction of capital allowances	½	
	Capital allowances - Main pool	2	
	- Motor car [1]	1½	
	- Motor car [2]	2	
	- Special rate pool	1½	
	- First year allowance	1½	
	Trading income assessments		
	Salary	½	
	Interest on capital	1	
	Balance of profits	1	
			15
(c)	Auy Man	2	
	Bim Man	1	
			3

			Marks
(d)	**(i)**	**Tax point**	
		Basic tax point	1
		Payment received or invoice issued	1
		Issue of invoice within 14 days	1
			3
	(ii)	**VAT paid**	
		Output VAT and input VAT	1
		Calculation	1
			2
	(iii)	**Flat rate scheme**	
		Joining the scheme	1
		Continuing to use the scheme	1½
		VAT payable	2
		VAT saving	½
			5
			30

(a) **Residence status**

Auy will be treated as resident in the United Kingdom for 2010/11 as she was present in the United Kingdom for 183 days or more.

Bim will be treated as resident in the United Kingdom for 2010/11 as she has made substantial visits to the United Kingdom. Her visits have averaged 91 days or more over four consecutive tax years.

(b) **Adjusted trading profit for y/e 5 April 2011**

		£	£
Profit before taxation			82,000
Add:	depreciation	3,400	
	input VAT	0	
	motor expenses £2,600 × 30%	780	
	entertaining employees	0	
	appropriation of profit: salary for Bim	4,000	
	appropriation of profit: excessive salary for Auy's husband £(15,000 – 10,000)	5,000	
			13,180
			95,180
Less:	capital allowances (W)		(15,180)
Tax adjusted trading profit			80,000

Working

Capital allowances y/e 5 April 2011

	Main pool £	Motor car [1] £	Motor car [2] £	Special rate pool £	Allow-ances £
TWDV b/f	3,100	18,000	14,000		
Additions					
Motor car [4]	14,200				
Motor car [5]				8,700	
	17,300				
Disposal					
Motor car [2]			(13,100)		
BA			(900) x 70%		630
WDA @ 20%	(3,460)				3,460
WDA - max		(3,000) x 70%			2,100
WDA @ 10%				(870)	870

		Main pool £	Motor car [1] £	Motor car [2] £	Special rate pool £	Allow- ances £
Addition						
Motor car [3]	11,600					
FYA @ 100%	(11,600) x 70%					8,120
	0					
TWDV c/f		13,840	15,000		7,830	
Allowances						15,180

Tutorial notes

Motor car [1] was owned at 6 April 2009 and therefore continues to qualify for writing down allowance at the rate of 20% subject to a maximum of £3,000.

Motor car [3] has CO_2 emissions of less than 110 grams per kilometre and therefore qualifies for the 100% first year allowance.

Motor car [4] has CO_2 emissions between 111 and 160 grams per kilometre, and therefore qualifies for writing down allowances at the rate of 20%.

Motor car [5] has CO_2 emissions over 160 grams per kilometre and therefore qualifies for writing down allowances at the rate of 10%.

Trading income assessments 2010/11

	Total £	Auy Man £	Bim Men £
Salary	4,000	0	4,000
Interest £56,000/34,000 @ 5%	4,500	2,800	1,700
Balance (80:20)	71,500	57,200	14,300
	80,000	60,000	20,000

(c)   **Auy Man and Bim Men – national insurance contributions 2010/11**

Auy Man

	£
Main rate: £(43,875 – 5,715) = 38,160 @ 8%	3,053
Additional rate: £(60,000 – 43,875) = 16,125 @ 1%	161
	3,214

Bim Men

	£
Main rate only: £ (20,000 – 5,715) = 14,285 @ 8%	£1,143

(d)   (i)   **Tax point**

The basic tax point is the date when services are completed.

If an invoice is issued or payment received before the basic tax point, then this becomes the actual tax point.

If an invoice is issued within 14 days of the basic tax point, the invoice date will usually be the actual tax point.

(ii)   **VAT paid for the year ended 5 April 2011**

The partnership's output VAT is £21,600 and its total input VAT is £(180 + 140) = £320.

Therefore VAT of £21,280 (21,600 – 320) will have been paid to HM Revenue & Customs during the year ended 5 April 2011.

(iii)   **Flat rate scheme**

The partnership can join the flat rate scheme if its expected taxable turnover (excluding VAT) for the next 12 months does not exceed £150,000.

The partnership can continue to use the scheme until its total turnover (including VAT, but excluding sales of capital assets) for the previous year exceeds £230,000.

If the partnership had used the flat rate scheme throughout the year ended 5 April 2011 then it would have paid VAT of £(142,200 + 21,600) = £163,800 @ 11% = £18,018.

This is a saving of £(21,280 – 18,018) = £3,262 for the year.

19 Pi Casso

Text references. Chapter 17 covers self assessment and payment by individuals.

Top tips. Take care to start with the correct tax year. You need to realise that if you are paying tax for 2010/11 that the payments on account will be based on the previous year 2009/10. Take care when stating payment dates. Take the time to start correctly and then be methodical.

Easy marks. Parts (c) and (d) required you to write out the rules for filing returns and enquiries. These should be easy marks.

Examiner's comments. Part (a) caused the most problems, with the vast majority of candidates not being able to demonstrate how payments are calculated and paid under the self-assessment system. Class 2 national insurance contributions were often incorrectly included, whilst few candidates appreciated that a claim to reduce payments on account was possible. In part (b) most candidates appreciated that interest would be due, but very few mentioned the potential penalty that could be charged. It was disappointing that the self-assessment tax return submission dates were often not known in part (c). The same comment applies to part (d). Candidates often gave a long list of reasons why HMRC could enquire into a return, but failed to mention that an enquiry might be on a completely random basis.

Marking scheme

			Marks
(a)	Second payment on account for 2009/10	2	
	Balancing payment for 2009/10	2	
	Claim to reduce payments on account	1	
	Payments on account for 2010/11	1	
	Balancing payment for 2010/11	1	
	First payment on account for 2011/12	1	
			8
(b)	Interest	1	
	Penalty	1	
			2
(c)	Paper based return	1	
	Return filed online	1	
			2
(d)	Notification date	1	
	Random bases	1	
	Income/Deductions	1	
			3
			15

(a)

Due date	Tax year	Payment	£
31 July 2010	2009/10	Second payment on account (N1)	2,240
31 January 2011	2009/10	Balancing payment (N2)	5,490
31 January 2011	2010/11	First payment on account (N3)	1,860
31 July 2011	2010/11	Second payment on account	1,860
31 January 2012	2010/11	Balancing payment (N4)	Nil
31 January 2012	2011/12	First payment on account (N5)	1,860

Notes

(1)   The second payment on account for 2009/10 is based on Pi's income tax and Class 4 NIC liability for 2008/09. It is therefore £2,240 (3,240 + 1,240 = 4,480 × 50%).

(2)   The balancing payment for 2009/10 is £5,490 (4,100 + 990 + 4,880) = £9,970 less the payments on account of £4,480 (£2,240 × 2)).

(3)   Pi will make a claim to reduce her total payments on account for 2010/11 to £3,720 (2,730 + 990), so each payment will be £1,860 (3,720 × 50%).

(4)   The balancing payment for 2010/11 is £Nil (3,720 less the payments on account of 3,720 (1,860 × 2)).

(5)   The first payment on account for 2011/12 is based on Pi's income tax and Class 4 NIC liability for 2010/11. It is therefore £1,860 (2,730 + 990 = 3,720 × 50%).

(b)   (1)   If Pi's payments on account for 2010/11 were reduced to nil, then she would be charged interest on the payments due of £1,860 from the relevant due date to the date of payment.

(2)   A penalty of the difference between the reduced payment on account and the correct payment on account may be charged if the claim to reduce the payments on account to nil was made fraudulently or negligently.

(c)   (1)   Unless the return is issued after 31 July 2011, the latest date that Pi can submit a paper based self-assessment tax return for 2010/11 is 31 October 2011.

(2)   Alternatively, Pi has until 31 January 2012 to file her self-assessment tax return for 2010/11 online.

(d)   (1)   If HMRC intend to enquire into Pi's 2010/11 tax return they will have to notify her within twelve months of the actual filing date if the return was delivered on or before the due date.

(2)   HMRC have the right to enquire into the completeness and accuracy of any return and such an enquiry may be made on a completely random basis.

(3)   However, enquiries are generally made because of a suspicion that income has been undeclared or because deductions have been incorrectly claimed.

20 Ernest Vader

Marking scheme

				Marks
(a)	Tax evasion		1	
	Tax avoidance		1	
	Non-disclosure of disposal		1	
				3
(b)	Professional judgement: standard of conduct		1	
	Advise disclosure		1	
	Obligation to report for money laundering		½	
	Cease to act and inform HMRC		½	
				3
(c)	Written information notice			1
(d)	Lack of sufficient information		1	
	Time limits		1	
				2
(e)	(i)	Interest period	1	
		Calculation	1	
				2
	(ii)	Maximum penalty	1	
		Link to behaviour	1	
		Actual penalty	1	
		Disclosure	1	
				4
				15

(a)   **Tax evasion and tax avoidance**

Tax evasion is illegal and involves the reduction of tax liabilities by not providing information to which HMRC is entitled or providing HMRC with deliberately false information.

In contrast, tax avoidance involves the minimisation of tax liabilities by the use of any lawful means, although certain tax avoidance schemes must be disclosed to HMRC.

If Ernest makes no disclosure of the capital gain then this will be viewed as tax evasion as his tax liability for 2010/11 will be understated by £18,000.

(b)   **Ethics**

The matter is one of professional judgement. A trainee Chartered Certified Accountant would be expected to act honestly and with integrity.

Ernest should therefore be advised to disclose details of the capital gain to HMRC.

If such disclosure is not made you would be obliged to report under the money laundering regulations and you should also consider ceasing to act for Ernest. In these circumstances you would be advised to notify HMRC that you no longer act for him although you would not need to provide any reason for this.

(c)   **Obtaining information from taxpayer**

HMRC can request information from Ernest by issuing a written information notice.

(d)   **Discovery assessment**

A discovery assessment can be raised because Ernest's self-assessment tax return did not contain sufficient information to make HMRC aware of the capital gain.

The normal time limit for making a discovery assessment is 4 years after the end of the tax year, but this is extended to 6 years if there has been careless understatement and 20 years if there has been deliberate understatement.

(e)   (i)   **Interest**

Interest will run from the due date of 31 January 2012 to the payment date of 31 July 2012.

The interest charge will therefore be £18,000 × 3.0% × 6/12 = £270.

(ii)   **Penalties**

The amount of penalty is based on the tax due but unpaid as a result of the failure to notify and the maximum penalty is 100% of that tax due.

However, the actual penalty will be linked to Ernest's behaviour.

Since Ernest would appear to have deliberately failed to notify HMRC of his capital gain, the actual penalty is likely to be 70% of the tax unpaid which is £18,000 x 70% = £12,600. This assumes that there is no attempt at concealment.

The penalty would have been substantially reduced if Ernest had disclosed the capital gain, especially if the disclosure had been unprompted by HMRC prior to discovery. The maximum reduction would be to 20% of the tax unpaid.

21 Jack Chan

Text references. Chapters 13 to 16 on CGT.

Marking scheme

		Marks
(a)	**Goodwill**	
	Gift relief	2
	Office	
	Gift relief	2
	Warehouse	
	Gain	½
	No gift relief	1
	Shares	
	Bonus issue	1
	Gain	½
	Plot of land	
	Part disposal	1
	Gain	½
	Set off loss	½
	Annual exempt amount	½
	CGT	1
	Due date	½
		11
(b)	Goodwill	½
	Office	½
	Gains on remaining assets (from (a))	½
	Set off loss and annual exempt amount	1
	CGT	1½
		4
		15

(a)   **Total gains**

	£
Goodwill (W1)	50,000
Office (W2)	–
Warehouse (W3)	45,000
Shares (W4)	8,000
Land (W5)	26,317
	129,317
Less loss brought forward	(6,100)
Total gains	123,217
Less annual exempt amount	(10,100)
Taxable gains	113,117

CGT	£
£(38,900 – 24,000) = 14,900 × 18% (W6)	2,682
£(113,117 – 14,900) = 98,217 × 28%	27,501
CGT liability 2010/11	30,183
CGT due on 31 January 2012	

1 *Goodwill*

	£
Market value	60,000
Less cost	(Nil)
	60,000
Less gift relief	(10,000)
Gain immediately chargeable	50,000

The amount paid for the goodwill exceeds allowable cost by £50,000, so £50,000 is immediately chargeable.

2 *Office*

	£
Market value	130,000
Less cost	(110,000)
	20,000
Less gift relief	(20,000)
Gain immediately chargeable	–

As the amount paid for the office was less than the allowable cost, gift relief is available to defer the whole gain arising.

3 *Warehouse*

	£
Market value	140,000
Less cost	(95,000)
Gain chargeable	45,000

Gift relief is not available to defer a gain on a non-business asset.

4 *Shares*

	Number	Cost £
Purchase January 2004	10,000	8,000
Bonus issue: 1 for 5	2,000	–
	12,000	8,000

	£
Proceeds	16,000
Less cost	(8,000)
Gain chargeable	8,000

A bonus issue is an issue of free shares in proportion to an existing shareholding. As they are free shares, there is no cost – instead the original cost is allocated to all of the shares held.

5 *Land*

	£
Proceeds	45,600
Less cost £125,000 × $\dfrac{45,600}{45,600+250,000}$	(19,283)
Gain chargeable	26,317

Where there is a part disposal of an asset the original cost must be apportioned between the part being sold and the remainder.

6 *Basic rate band*

The basic rate band will be extended by the gross amount of the Gift Aid donation to £37,400 + (1,200 × 100/80) = £38,900.

(b) **Gains on assets eligible for entrepreneurs' relief**

	£
Goodwill	60,000
Office	20,000
Taxable gains	80,000
Other gains (as before)	
Warehouse	45,000
Shares	8,000
Land	26,317
	79,317
Less loss brought forward (best use)	(6,100)
	73,217
Less annual exempt amount (best use)	(10,100)
Taxable gains	63,117

CGT	£
£80,000 × 10%	8,000
£63,117 × 28%	17,673
CGT	25,673

The gains qualifying for entrepreneurs' relief use the basic rate band in priority to those not qualifying for the relief. This means that all of the basic rate band is used the gains qualifying for entrepreneurs' relief and the remaining gains are all taxable at 28%.

Jack has used £80,000 of his £5,000,000 lifetime allowance for entrepreneurs' relief.

22 Peter Shaw

Text references. Chapters 13 to 16 on CGT.

		Marks
(a)	**Building**	
	Gain	1	
	Takeover	
	Gain on cash received	2	
	No gain on shares	1	
	Shares	
	Share pool	2	
	Gain	1	
	Summary	
	Set off loss brought forward	1	
	Annual exempt amount	1	
	CGT liability	2	
			11
(b)	Conditions for entrepreneurs' relief	2	
	Annual exempt amount used against gain on painting	1	
	CGT payable	1	
			4
			15

(a) **Summary of gains:**

		£
Building (W1)		400,000
Forum Follies plc (W2)		5,000
Dassau plc (W3)		7,100
Less losses b/f		(6,400)
Total gains		405,700
Less annual exempt amount		(10,100)
Taxable gain		395,600

CGT

	£
£(37,400 – 15,000) = 22,400 @ 18%	4,032
£(395,600 - 22,400) = 373,200 @ 28%	104,496
CGT liability 2010/11	108,528

CGT due 31 January 2012

Workings

1 *Building*

	£
Proceeds	600,000
Less cost	(200,000)
Gain	400,000

2 *The takeover of Forum Follies plc*

The elements in the takeover consideration have the following values:

	£
Ordinary shares (30,000 × £3.00)	90,000
Cash	10,000
Total consideration received	100,000

A gain only arises on the date of the takeover in respect of the cash element of the takeover consideration. The gain in respect of the shares received is deferred until those shares are sold.

	£
Cash received (above)	10,000
Cost £50,000 × 10,000/110,000	(5,000)
Gain	5,000

3 *Dassau plc shares*

(i) Share pool

	Shares	Cost £
December 1985	1,000	2,000
Rights issue April 2001 1:2 @ £2	500	1,000
	1,500	3,000
Disposal November 2010	(1,200)	(2,400)
	300	600

(ii)

	£
Proceeds	9,500
Less cost	(2,400)
Gain	7,100

(b) The sale of shares may be eligible for entrepreneurs' relief. In order to qualify Janet needed to have a 5% shareholding/voting rights and to have been an officer or employer of Dot Ltd which must be a trading company. All these conditions must be met for at least one year prior to the disposal.

Janet has met the conditions and the capital gains tax on the gain on sale will be as follows:

	£
Gain (AE will be used against gain on painting)	900,000
CGT	
£900,000 × 10%	90,000

23 David and Angela Brook

> **Text references.** Chapter 13 deals with general computation of chargeable gains. Chattels and Principal Private Residence relief are in Chapter 14. Shares are covered in Chapter 16.
>
> **Top tips.** Work through the disposals in order and then bring them together in a summary for each taxpayer. Don't forget that you need to compute the capital gains tax liabilities, not just state the taxable gains.
>
> **Easy marks.** The calculation of the gains before applying reliefs should have gained easy marks. Use of the annual exempt amount and calculation of the tax payable were also straightforward.
>
> **Examiner's comments.** Although there were some very good answers to this question from well prepared candidates, it caused problems for many and was often the reason that they failed to achieve a pass mark. One particular problem was that a lot of time was often spent performing unnecessary calculations for the exempt assets, and then not having sufficient time to deal with the chargeable assets. Many candidates therefore did a lot of work for this question but scored few marks. The jointly owned property caused particular difficulty. Only a few candidates correctly calculated the principal private residence exemption. Some candidates did not allocate the resulting chargeable gain between the couple but instead deducted an annual allowance and calculated a separate tax liability.

		Marks
Jointly owned property		
Car – exempt		½
House:	Proceeds	½
	Cost	½
	PPR exemption period	2½
	Calculation of exemption	1
David Brook		
Antique table – exempt		1
Bend Ltd – no gain, no loss disposal		½
Galatico plc:	Deemed proceeds	1
	Cost	2
	Rights issue	1
Half share in house		½
Annual exempt amount		½
Capital gains tax		½
Angela Brook		
Antique clock – marginal relief		2
Bend Ltd:	Proceeds	½
	Cost	1
Business	– shop	1
	– goodwill	1
Half share in house		½
Annual exempt amount		½
Capital gains tax		1½
		20

Jointly owned property

Car
Exempt asset

House

	£
Proceeds	393,900
Less: cost	(86,000)
	307,900
Less: PPR relief (W1)	
$£307,900 \times \dfrac{219}{252}$	(267,580)
Gain	40,320

Workings

1

		Exempt months	Chargeable Months
1.10.89 – 31.3.93	Actual occupation	42	
1.4.93 – 31.12.96	Up to 4 years working elsewhere	45	
1.1.97 – 31.12.04	Actual occupation	96	
1.1.05 – 30.9.07	Not occupied		33
1.10.07 – 30.9.10	Last 3 years	36	
Total months		219	33

David Brook – capital gains tax payable

Antique table
Exempt gain – non-wasting chattel sold for £6,000 or less

Bend Ltd
No gain, no loss transfer to spouse
Base cost for Angela £48,000

Galatico plc shares

Share pool

	Number	Cost
		£
15.6.07 Purchase	8,000	17,600
24.8.07 Purchase	12,000	21,600
	20,000	39,200
10.7.08 Rights issue 1:4 @ £2	5,000	10,000
	25,000	49,200
14.2.11 Disposal	(15,000)	(29,520)
c/f	10,000	19,680

	£
Market value 15,000 × £2.95 (W2)	44,250
Less: cost	(29,520)
Gain	14,730

Note. The shares in Galatico plc cannot qualify for entrepreneurs' relief because the company is not David's personal company.

2 Quoted share valuation

£2.90 + ¼ £(3.10 – 2.90)   £2.95

	£
½ share in house	20,160
Galatico plc	14,730
	34,890
Less: annual exempt amount	(10,100)
Taxable gains	24,790

Capital gains tax for David

£24,790 × 28%   6,941

Angela Brook – capital gains tax payable

Antique clock

Non-wasting chattel subject to marginal relief

	£
Proceeds	7,200
Less: cost	(3,700)
Gain	3,500

Gain cannot exceed £(7,200 – 6,000) = £1,200 × 5/3   2,000

Bend Ltd shares

	£
Proceeds	62,400
Less: cost	
$£48,000 \times \dfrac{15,000}{20,000}$	(36,000)
Gain	26,400

Note. The shares in Bend Ltd cannot qualify for entrepreneurs' relief because they are in an investment company.

Business

	£	£
Shop		
Proceeds	180,000	
Less: cost	(102,000)	
		78,000
Goodwill		
Proceeds	40,000	
Less: cost	–	
		40,000
Chargeable gains		118,000

Summary

	£
Bend Ltd shares	26,400
½ share in house	20,160
Antique clock	2,000
Chargeable gains	48,560
Less: annual exempt amount (best use)	(10,100)
Taxable gains not qualifying for entrepreneurs' relief	38,460
Taxable gains qualifying for entrepreneurs' relief	118,000

Capital gains tax for Angela	£
£118,000 × 10%	11,800
£38,460 × 28%	10,769
CGT liability 2010/11	22,569

24 Wilson Biazma

Text references. Chapters 13 to 16 deal with the computation of chargeable gains.

Top tips. This question tests several different CGT reliefs. Remember to calculate the gain first, before considering the availability of any reliefs.

Easy marks. The calculation of the five gains were easy marks. Part (a) required the statement of the residence rules. These also should have been easy marks.

Examiner's comments. Part (a) was reasonably well answered, although only a few candidates appreciated that ordinary residence is a matter of where a person habitually resides. Many candidates missed an easy mark by not stating that people who are resident or ordinarily resident will be liable to capital gains tax. Part (b) was also reasonably well answered. The disposal that caused the most problems was the incorporation of the business, with many candidates not appreciating that the gain was simply based on the value of the goodwill transferred.

Marking scheme

			Marks
(a)	183 day rule	1	
	91 day rule	1	
	Ordinary residence	1	
	Liability to CGT	1	
			4
(b)	Taxable gains and calculation of CGT for Wilson	2	
	Office building		
	Proceeds		
	Cost	½	
	Rollover relief	1	
	Entrepreneurs' relief	½	
	Incorporation		
	Proceeds	½	
	Cost	½	
	Incorporation relief	1½	
	Entrepreneurs' relief	½	
	Ordinary shares in Gandua Ltd		
	Proceeds	½	
	Cost	½	
	Gift relief	1½	
	Entrepreneurs' relief	½	
	Antique vase		
	Proceeds	½	
	Cost	½	
	Compensation relief	1	
	Land		
	Proceeds	½	
	Cost	2	
	Ordinary shares in WJD Ltd		
	Proceeds	½	
	Cost	½	

(a) (1) A person will be resident in the UK during a tax year if they are present in the UK for 183 days or more.

(2) A person will also be treated as resident if they visit the UK regularly, with visits averaging 91 days or more a tax year over a period of four or more consecutive tax years.

(3) Ordinary residence is not precisely defined, but a person will normally be ordinarily resident in the UK if this is where they habitually reside.

(4) A person is liable to capital gains tax (CGT) on the disposal of assets during any tax year in which they are either resident or ordinarily resident in the UK.

(b) **Wilson Biazma – Chargeable gains 2010/11**

	£
Gains qualifying for entrepreneurs' relief	
Incorporation (W2)	12,000
Ordinary shares in WJD Ltd (W6)	72,000
Chargeable gains qualifying for entrepreneurs' relief	84,000
Gains not qualifying for entrepreneurs' relief	
Office building (W1)	102,000
Ordinary shares in Gandua Ltd (W3)	8,000
Antique vase (W4)	Nil
Land (W5)	17,000
Chargeable gains	127,000
Less annual exempt amount (v. gains not qualifying for entrepreneurs' relief 1st)	(10,100)
Taxable gains	116,900

	£
CGT on £84,000 @ 10%	8,400
CGT on £116,900 @ 28%	32,732
CGT liability 2010/11	41,132

Note
The gains on the assets qualifying for entrepreneurs' relief are treated as the lowest part of the gains and so use up the basic rate band.

Workings

1 *Office building*

	£
Disposal proceeds	246,000
Less cost	(144,000)
Gain	102,000

Rollover relief is not available because the amount not reinvested of £110,000 (246,000 – 136,000) is greater than the capital gain of £102,000. Entrepreneur's relief does not apply because this is not the sale of the whole or part of the business, merely an asset of the business.

2 *Incorporation*

	£
Proceeds (goodwill)	40,000
Less cost	(Nil)
Gain	40,000
Less incorporation relief £40,000 × $\dfrac{70,000}{70,000+30,000}$	(28,000)
Gain left in charge	12,000

Entrepreneurs' relief is available on the gain left in charge as Wilson owned the retail business for at least one year before disposal to the company and is disposing of the whole of it to the company.

3   *Ordinary shares in Gandua Ltd*

	£
Proceeds (MV)	160,000
Less cost	(112,000)
Gain	48,000
Less gift relief £48,000 × $\frac{150,000}{180,000}$	(40,000)
Gain left in charge	8,000

Entrepreneurs' relief is not available on the gain left in charge as Wilson has not owned the shares for one year prior to the disposal.

4   *Antique vase*

	£
Proceeds (compensation)	68,000
Less cost	(49,000)
Gain	19,000
Less relief for reinvestment (all proceeds reinvested)	(19,000)
Gain left in charge	Nil

5   *Land*

	£
Proceeds	85,000
Less cost £120,000 × $\frac{85,000}{85,000 + 65,000}$	(68,000)
Gain	17,000

6   *Ordinary shares in WJD Ltd*

	£
Disposal proceeds 6,000 × £13	78,000
Less cost 6,000 × £1	(6,000)
Gain	72,000

The disposal is eligible for entrepreneurs' relief as Wilson owned at least 5% of the shares in WJD Ltd (a trading company) and had worked for WJD Ltd and all the conditions have been satisfied for at least one year before the disposal.

25 Nim and Mae

Text references. Chapters 13 to 16 deal with the computation of chargeable gains.

Top tips. Questions may be set about spouses or civil partners. Transfers between these are on a no gain/ no loss basis.

Easy marks. Remembering to deduct the annual exempt amount for each taxpayer and applying the rate of tax should have been 2 easy marks.

Examiner's comments. For the husband, quite a few candidates surprisingly had problems with the valuation rules for quoted shares. It was also not always appreciated that the transfer between spouses and the sale of the UK Government securities were respectively at no gain, no loss, and exempt. Candidates thus wasted time performing unnecessary calculations. Many candidates had difficulty with the cost of the quoted shares disposed of, and they incorrectly included the purchase within the following 30 days as part of the share pool. The restriction of the brought forward capital losses so that chargeable gains were reduced to the amount of the annual exempt amount was often missed. For the wife, many candidates treated the private portion of the principal private residence as taxable rather than the business portion. The investment property included within the disposal of the business was sometimes treated as exempt from CGT and sometimes entrepreneurs' relief was claimed in respect of it. Only a minority of candidates correctly calculate the cost of the wasting asset.

			Marks
Nim Lom			
Kapook plc	Deemed proceeds		2
	Cost		1
	Share pool		2
Jooba Ltd			1
Antique table			1½
UK Government securities			½
Capital losses brought forward			1
Annual exempt amount			½
Capital losses carried forward			½
Mae Lom			
Jooba Ltd	Proceeds		½
	Cost		1
House	Proceeds		½
	Cost		½
	Exemption		1
Business	Goodwill		½
	Office building		½
	Investment property		½
Copyright	Proceeds		½
	Cost		1½
Capital losses brought forward			½
Annual exempt amount			½
Capital gains tax			2
			20

Nim Lom – CGT liability 2010/11

	£	£
Ordinary shares in Kapook plc		
Deemed proceeds (10,000 × £3.70) (W1)	37,000	
Less: cost (W2)	(23,400)	
		13,600
Ordinary shares in Jooba Ltd (no gain, no loss transfer between spouses)		–
Antique table (W3)		3,500
UK Government securities (exempt)		–
Chargeable gains		17,100
Less: losses b/f (W4)		(7,000)
Net chargeable gains		10,100
Less: annual exempt amount		(10,100)
Taxable gains		Nil

Nim therefore has a nil liability to capital gains tax in 2010/11 and capital losses carried forward of £(16,700 – 7,000) = £9,700.

Workings

1   The shares in Kapook plc are valued at the lower of:

   (a) $370 + \frac{1}{4} \times (390 - 370) = 375$;

   (b) $\dfrac{360 + 380}{2} = 370$

   ie 370.

2   The disposal is first matched against the purchase on 24 July 2010 (this is within the following 30 days) and then against the shares in the share pool. The cost of the shares disposed of is, therefore, £23,400 (5,800 + 17,600).

Share pool	*No. of shares*	*Cost*
	£	£
Purchase 19 February 2001	8,000	16,200
Purchase 6 June 2006	6,000	14,600
	14,000	30,800
Disposal 20 July 2010		
£30,800 × 8,000/14,000	(8,000)	(17,600)
Balance c/f	6,000	13,200

3   The antique table is a non-wasting chattel.

	£
Proceeds	8,700
Less cost	(5,200)
Gain	3,500

The maximum gain is $5/3 \times £(8,700 - 6,000) = £4,500$

The chargeable gain is the lower of £3,500 and £4,500, so it is £3,500.

4   The set off of the brought forward capital losses is restricted to £7,000 (17,100 – 10,100) so that chargeable gains are reduced to the amount of the annual exempt amount.

Mae Lom – CGT liability 2010/11

		Gains qualifying for entrepreneurs' relief	Gains not qualifying for entrepreneurs' relief
	£	£	£
Ordinary shares in Jooba Ltd			
Disposal proceeds	30,400		
Less: cost £16,000 × 2,000/5,000 (N1)	(6,400)		
			24,000
House			
Disposal proceeds	186,000		
Less: cost	(122,000)		
	64,000		
Less: principal private residence exemption (W)	(56,000)		
			8,000
Business			
Goodwill	80,000		
Freehold office building	136,000		
	216,000	216,000	
Investment property (N2)			34,000

	£	Gains qualifying for entrepreneurs' relief £	Gains not qualifying for entrepreneurs' relief £
Copyright			
Disposal proceeds	9,600		
Less: cost £10,000 × 15/20 (N3)	(7,500)		
			2,100
Chargeable gains			68,100
Less: losses b/f (best use)			(8,500)
Net chargeable gains			59,600
Less: annual exempt amount (best use)		....	(10,100)
Taxable gains		216,000	49,500
Capital gains tax @ 10%/28% (N4)		21,600	3,860
Capital gains tax liability 2010/11 £(21,600 + 13,860)			35,460

Working

One of the eight rooms in Mae's house was always used exclusively for business purposes, so the principal private residence exemption is restricted to £(64,000 × 7/8) = £56,000.

Notes

1   Nim's original cost is used in calculating the capital gain on the disposal of the shares in Jooba Ltd because the transfer between the spouses was on a no gain/no loss basis.

2   The investment property does not qualify for entrepreneurs' relief because it was never used for business purposes.

3   The copyright is a wasting asset. The cost of £10,000 must therefore be depreciated based on an unexpired life of 20 years at the date of acquisition and an unexpired life of 15 years at the date of disposal.

4   Mae's taxable income plus the gains qualifying for entrepreneurs' relief use up her basic rate band, so the gains not qualifying for entrepreneurs' relief are taxable at 28%.

26 Amanda, Bo and Charles

Text references. The calculation of chargeable gains for individuals is covered in Chapter 13. Business reliefs are in Chapter 15 and principal private residence relief is in Chapter 14.

Top tips. You were asked to state the chargeable gain for each taxpayer – this is the gain before the annual exempt amount and so you should not have wasted time by deducting the exempt amount. Also note that in the first two parts of the question, entrepreneurs' relief was to be ignored.

Easy marks. There were easy marks to be gained by calculating the gains before reliefs were applied.

Examiner's comments. This question was not as well answered as would have been expected given that it was effectively three short separate questions on reasonably straightforward areas of capital gains tax. Base costs were often not shown despite these being required in parts (a) and (b). In part (a) far too many candidates treated this as one disposal rather than dealing with each asset separately. In the second section only a few candidates appreciated that incorporation relief was restricted according to the proportion of cash consideration to total consideration. Part (b) was reasonably well answered, although few candidates could correctly calculate the revised base cost following the restriction of holdover relief in the second section. Although there were some very good answers to part (c), far too many candidates had problems calculating the principal private residence exemption, and often lost marks by not showing detailed workings. Even when the correct exemption was calculated this was often shown as the amount chargeable rather than the exempt amount. In the second section it was not always appreciated that letting relief was available.

					Marks
(a)	(i)	Goodwill gain		1	
		Freehold shop gain		1	
		Incorporation relief		1	
		Base cost of shares		<u>1</u>	
					4
	(ii)	Gain chargeable	– explanation	1	
			– calculation	1	
		Base cost of shares		<u>1</u>	
					3
(b)	(i)	Gain		1	
		Gift relief		1	
		Base cost of shares		<u>1</u>	
					3
	(ii)	Gain chargeable		1	
		Base cost of shares		<u>1</u>	
					2
(c)	(i)	Gain		1	
		Period of exemption		3	
		PPR relief		<u>1</u>	
					5
	(ii)	Letting relief exemption		2	
		Revised gain		<u>1</u>	
					<u>3</u>
					<u>20</u>

(a) (i) **Amanda Moon: full incorporation relief**

	£	£
Proceeds of goodwill	90,000	
Less: cost	<u>(nil)</u>	90,000
Proceeds of shop	165,000	
Less: cost	<u>(120,000)</u>	<u>45,000</u>
Gains		<u>135,000</u>

Note. The net current assets are not chargeable assets and therefore are not part of the computation.

Incorporation relief will apply to the whole of the gains because:
- the business is transferred as a going concern
- all its assets (other than cash) are transferred
- the consideration is wholly in shares.

Therefore Amanda will not have any chargeable gains in 2010/11.

The base cost of her 300,000 £1 shares will be £(300,000 − 135,000) = <u>£165,000</u>.

(ii)   **Amanda Moon: partial incorporation relief**

If Amanda takes 200,000 £1 shares and £100,000 in cash, the following partial incorporation relief will apply:

$$\text{Gain} \times \frac{\text{Value of shares received from the company}}{\text{Total value of consideration from the company}}$$

$$£135,000 \times \frac{£200,000}{£300,000} = £90,000$$

Amanda's chargeable gains in 2010/11 will therefore be £(135,000 – 90,000) = £45,000.

The base cost of her 200,000 £1 shares will be £(200,000 – 90,000) = £110,000.

(b) (i)   **Bo Neptune: full gift relief**

	£
MV of shares	210,000
Less: cost	(94,000)
Gain	116,000

Gift relief will apply to the whole of the gain because the shares are qualifying business assets (unquoted trading company shares) and there is no consideration paid for the disposal.

Therefore Bo will not have a chargeable gain in 2010/11.

The base cost of the shares for Bo's son will be £(210,000 – 116,000) = £94,000.

(ii)   **Bo Neptune: partial gift relief**

If Bo's son paid £160,000 for the shares, this is a sale at an undervalue and partial gift will be available. The part of the gain equal to the excess of actual consideration over actual cost is chargeable immediately and only the balance of the gain is deferred.

Bo's chargeable gain in 2010/11 will therefore be £(160,000 – 94,000) = £66,000. The remainder of the gain of £(116,000 – 66,000) = £50,000 will be deferred by gift relief.

The base cost of the shares for Bo's son will be £(210,000 – 50,000) = £160,000.

(c) (i)   **Charles Orion: principal private residence relief**

	£
Sale proceeds	282,000
Less: cost	(110,000)
Gain	172,000
Less: PPR relief (W)	
$\frac{90}{144} \times £172,000$	(107,500)
Chargeable gain	64,500

Working

Period	Total months	Exempt months	Chargeable months
1.10.98 – 31.3.00 (occupied)	18	18	0
1.4.00 – 31.3.03 (see below)	36	36	0
1.4.03 – 30.9.07 (absent)	54	0	54
1.10.07 – 30.9.10 (last 36 months)	36	36	0
	144	90	54

During the period 1.4.00 and 31.3.03 (three years' absence for any reason), Charles is deemed to be resident in the property because he actually occupies the property both before and after the period of absence.

(ii) **Charles Orion: principal private residence relief and letting relief**

If Charles had rented out the house between 1 April 2000 and 31 December 2008, he would be entitled to letting relief in respect of the period of letting not covered by the main principal private resident relief (ie 54 months). This is the lowest of:

Gain exempt under PPR rules: $\dfrac{90}{144} \times £172,000$ £107,500

Gain attributable to letting: $\dfrac{54}{144} \times £172,000$ £64,500

£40,000 (maximum)   £40,000

The letting relief is therefore £40,000 and the chargeable gain is:

	£
Gain	172,000
Less: PPR relief	(107,500)
Less: letting relief	(40,000)
Chargeable gain	24,500

27 Naomi

Text references. Chapter 18 covers the inheritance tax examinable in F6.

Top tips. Deal with each transfer of value in date order. The question helpfully sets out how you should examine the transfers ie looking at the IHT implications during the donor's lifetime and then re-examining the effect of the donor's death.

Easy marks. There were easy marks for explaining the annual exemption and the spouse exemption.

Marking scheme

	Marks
(a) *6 May each year*	
Annual exemptions	1
15 August 2002	
Transfer of value	½
Chargeable lifetime transfer	½
Nil rate band available	½
IHT on balance @ 20%	½
12 September 2007	
Transfer of value	1
Potentially exempt transfer	½
14 February 2009	
Transfer of value	½
Chargeable lifetime transfer	½
Nil rate band available	½
IHT on balance @ 20/80	½
Gross transfer	½
	7

(b)   *6 May each year*
      Remains exempt   ½
      15 August 2002
      Death more than 7 years of transfer - no additional tax chargeable   ½
      No repayment of lifetime IHT   ½
      12 September 2007
      Transfer of value at date of gift   ½

      Potentially exempt transfer becomes chargeable   ½
      Nil rate band available   ½
      IHT on balance @ 40%   ½
      Taper relief   ½
      14 February 2009
      Transfer of value at date of gift   ½
      Nil rate band available   ½
      IHT on balance @ 40%   ½
      Deduct lifetime tax   ½
                                                                                                      6

(c)   Spouse exemption   ½
      Residue chargeable   ½
      Nil rate band available   ½
      IHT @ 40%   ½
                                                                                                      2
                                                                                                     15

(a)   **IHT implications of lifetime gifts by Naomi**

      6 May each year

      The gift of quoted shares worth £3,000 on 6 May each year will use the annual exemption for the tax year
      starting on 6 April in that year.

      15 August 2002

      There is a transfer of value for inheritance tax of £300,000 as a gift is a gratuitous disposition which results in a
      diminution in the value of the donor's estate of this amount.

      This is a chargeable lifetime transfer because it is not an exempt transfer and not a transfer to another
      individual.

      The nil rate band available is £250,000 because the donor did not make any chargeable transfers in the seven
      years before 15 August 2002 (transfers after 15 August 1995).

      The inheritance tax payable on this transfer is calculated as follows:

				£
Gross transfer of value				300,000
				£
IHT	£250,000	× 0% =		Nil
	£ 50,000	× 20% =		10,000
	£300,000			10,000

      12 September 2007

      There is a transfer of value for inheritance tax as a gift is a gratuitous disposition which results in a diminution
      in the value of the donor's estate. This diminution is:

	£
Value of shares held before gift	50,000
Value of shares held after gift	(4,000)
Transfer of value	46,000

This is potentially exempt transfer because it is not an exempt transfer but it is a transfer to another individual. A potentially exempt transfer is exempt during the lifetime of the donor so there is no lifetime tax payable.

14 February 2009

There is a transfer of value for inheritance tax as a gift is a gratuitous disposition which results in a diminution in the value of the donor's estate. The diminution in value is the value of the house plus the lifetime inheritance tax that Naomi agrees to pay.

This is a chargeable lifetime transfer because it is not an exempt transfer and not a transfer to another individual.

There was a lifetime transfer of value of £300,000 in seven years before 14 February 2009 (transfers after 14 February 2002) so the nil rate band available was £(312,000 – 300,000) = £12,000.

The inheritance tax payable on this transfer is calculated as follows:

			£
Net transfer of value			90,000
			£
IHT	£12,000	× 0% =	Nil
	£ 78,000	× 20/80 =	19,500
	£90,000		19,500

The gross transfer is £(90,000 + 19,500) = £109,500.

Check

IHT	£12,000	× 0% =	Nil
	£ 97,500	× 20% =	19,500
	£109,500		19,500

(b) **IHT implications of Naomi's death on lifetime gifts**

6 May each year

These transfers remain exempt and there are no implications of Naomi's death on them.

15 August 2002

There is no additional tax charge on this transfer because the donor died more than seven years from making it.

There is no repayment of lifetime inheritance tax.

12 September 2007

This potentially exempt transfer becomes chargeable because of the donor's death within seven years of making it.

The transfer of value is £46,000 which was the diminution in value of the donor's estate at the date of the transfer. The subsequent sale does not affect this value.

There was a lifetime transfer of value of £300,000 in seven years before 12 September 2007 (transfers after 12 September 2000) so the nil rate band available is £(325,000 – 300,000) = £25,000.

The inheritance tax payable on this transfer is calculated as follows:

			£
Gross transfer of value			46,000
			£
IHT	£25,000	× 0% =	Nil
	£ 21,000	× 40% =	8,400
	£46,000		8,400
	Less taper relief @ 20% (death between 3 and 4 years after transfer)		(1,680)
	IHT payable		6,720

14 February 2009

Additional tax is payable on this chargeable lifetime transfer because the donor died within seven years of making it.

The gross transfer of value is £109,500. The increase in value of the house at the date of the donor's death is not subject to inheritance tax.

There were lifetime transfers of value of £300,000 and £46,000 in seven years before 14 February 2009 (transfers after 14 February 2002) so the nil rate band of £325,000 is completely used up.

The inheritance tax payable on this transfer is calculated as follows:

		£
Gross transfer of value		109,500
IHT	£109,500 × 40% =	43,800
	Less: lifetime tax paid	(19,500)
Additional death tax		24,300

There is no taper relief because the donor died within three years of making the transfer.

(c) **Inheritance tax implications of the terms of Naomi's Will**

There is no inheritance tax on legacy of £250,000 given to Robert under Naomi's Will because of the spouse exemption.

The residue of the estate is chargeable to IHT as it a transfer of value to another individual.

There were lifetime transfers of value of £46,000 and £109,500 in seven years before 12 October 2010 (transfers after 12 October 2003) so the nil rate band available is £(325,000 − 46,000 − 109,500) = £169,500.

The inheritance tax payable on this transfer is calculated as follows:

			£
Gross transfer of value £(550,000 − 250,000)			300,000
IHT	£169,500	× 0% =	Nil
	£130,500	× 40% =	52,200
	£300,000		52,200

28 Malakai and Moira

Text references. Chapter 18 covers the inheritance tax examinable in F6.

Top tips. Use the pro forma for the death estate to compute the amount chargeable to inheritance tax. It is a good idea to tick off each item in the question as you enter it on the pro forma – this ensures that you do not lose any marks by missing out an item.

Easy marks. There were easy marks for the deduction of liabilities in calculating the death estate.

Marks

(a) Quoted shares ½
House 1
Chattels ½
Cash in ISA ½
Car ½
Credit card ½
Bank overdraft ½
Council tax ½
Gambling debt 1
Funeral expenses ½
Spouse exemption ½
Effect of lifetime transfer 1
IHT on death estate ½
Payment of IHT by Ezra 1
Due date for payment of IHT by Ezra <u>1</u>
10

(b) Stuart's nil rate band unused ½
Transfer to Moira 1
Potentially exempt transfer now chargeable 1
IHT on death estate 1½
Due date for payment of IHT on death estate <u>1</u>
<u>5</u>
<u>15</u>

(a) **Malakai's death estate**

	£	£
Quoted shares		210,000
House (N1)		325,000
Chattels		10,000
Cash in ISA (N2)		11,500
Car		<u>15,000</u>
		571,500
Less: credit card	7,000	
bank overdraft	4,500	
council tax	800	
gambling debt (N3)	0	
funeral expenses	<u>5,600</u>	
		(17,900)
		553,600
Less: spouse exemption		(100,000)
Chargeable death estate		453,600

Notes

1 The endowment mortgage is repaid upon death by the life assurance element of the mortgage so there is no liability to be deducted from the value of the house.

2 There is no IHT exemption for assets held in an ISA.

3 The gambling debt to Joe is not deductible because it was not incurred for consideration.

The gift to Malakai's brother was a potentially exempt transfer which became chargeable because Malakai died within 7 years of making it.

The transfer of value was:

	£
Gift	256,000
Less: annual exemption 2008/09	(3,000)
annual exemption 2007/08 b/f	(3,000)
Potentially exempt transfer now chargeable	250,000

This is covered by the nil rate band at death of £325,000.

The nil rate band available on the death estate is £(325,000 – 250,000) = £75,000.

The IHT on the death estate is therefore (£453,600 – 75,000) = £378,600 @ 40% = £151,440.

This was payable by Ezra, as Malakai's executor, on 20 February 2011 when he submitted the IHT account.

(b) **IHT implications of Moira's death**

Stuart used 90% of his nil rate band so the remaining 10% was unused.

Moira's personal representatives can claim to transfer this unused nil rate band to Moira. The proportion of the nil rate band transferred at Moira's death is £325,000 x 10% = £32,500.

The total nil rate band available to set against Moira's lifetime transfer and her death estate is therefore £(32,500 + 325,000) = £357,500.

The gift to Moira's brother was a potentially exempt transfer which became chargeable because Moira died within seven years of making it.

The transfer of value was:

	£
Gift	340,000
Less: annual exemption 2009/10	(3,000)
annual exemption 2008/09 b/f	(3,000)
Potentially exempt transfer now chargeable	334,000

This is covered by the nil rate band of £357,500 available on Moira's death. The remaining nil rate band is £(357,500 – 334,000) = £23,500.

The IHT on the death estate is therefore £(600,000 – 23,500) = £576,500 @ 40% = £230,600.

The IHT is due on the death estate is the earlier of the date on which the personal representatives submit their account or 31 July 2011

29 Artem

> **Text references.** Chapter 18 covers the inheritance tax examinable in F6.
>
> **Top tips.** Remember that potentially exempt transfers are treated as exempt during the donor's lifetime and will be exempt if the donor survives 7 years from making the gift.
>
> **Easy marks.** There were easy marks for spotting the annual exemption, the small gifts exemption and the marriage exemption.

Marks

(a)   *10 December 2002*

Annual exemptions x 2   ½

Potentially exempt transfer   ½

17 January 2007

Annual exemptions x 2   ½

Chargeable lifetime transfer   ½

Nil rate band available   ½

IHT on balance @ 20/80   ½

Gross transfer   ½

15 February 2007

Small gift exemption   ½

18 August 2007

Annual exemption   ½

Potentially exempt transfer   ½

17 June 2008

Annual exemption   ½

Chargeable lifetime transfer   ½

Nil rate band available   ½

IHT on balance @ 20%   ½

1 August 2009

Marriage exemption   ½

Annual exemption   ½

Potentially exempt transfer   ½

5 September 2009

Spouse exemption   ½

                                                                        9

(b)   *10 December 2002*

Exempt as more than 7 years before death   ½

17 January 2007

Within nil rate band at death   ½

18 August 2007

Potentially exempt transfer now chargeable   ½

Nil rate band available   ½

IHT on balance @ 40%   ½

Taper relief   ½

17 June 2008

Nil rate band exceeded   ½

IHT @ 40%   ½

Lifetime tax deducted   ½

1 August 2009

Potentially exempt transfer now chargeable   ½

Nil rate band exceeded   ½

IHT @ 40%   ½

                                                                        <u>6</u>
                                                                        <u>15</u>

(a)   **Lifetime inheritance tax implications**

10 December 2002

The first £6,000 of this transfer is an exempt transfer because of the annual exemptions for 2002/03 and 2001/02.

Answers 129

The remaining £(65,000 – 6,000) = £59,000 is a potentially exempt transfer as it is a gift to an individual. This is treated as an exempt transfer during Artem's life.

17 January 2007

The first £6,000 of this transfer is an exempt transfer because of the annual exemptions for 2006/07 and 2005/06.

The remaining £(296,000 – 6,000) = £290,000 is a chargeable lifetime transfer because it is not a transfer to another individual.

This is the first chargeable transfer that Artem makes and so the nil rate band is available in full.

The inheritance tax on this transfer is:

			£
Net transfer of value (Artem pays IHT)			290,000
			£
IHT	£285,000	× 0% =	Nil
	£ 5,000	× 20/80 =	1,250
	£290,000		1,250

The gross transfer of value for accumulation is £(290,000 + 1,250) = £291,250.

Check

IHT	£285,000	× 0% =	Nil
	£ 6,250	× 20% =	1,250
	£ 291,250		1,250

15 February 2007

The gift to the nephew is exempt as a small gift.

18 August 2007

The first £3,000 of this transfer is an exempt transfer because of the annual exemption for 2007/08.

The remaining £(46,000 – 3,000) = £43,000 is a potentially exempt transfer as it is a gift to an individual. This is treated as an exempt transfer during Artem's life.

17 June 2008

The first £3,000 of this transfer is an exempt transfer because of the annual exemption for 2008/09.

The remaining £(103,000 – 3,000) = £100,000 is a chargeable lifetime transfer because it is not a transfer to another individual.

There was a lifetime transfer of value of £291,250 in seven years before 17 June 2008 (transfers after 17 June 2001) so the nil rate band available was £(312,000 – 291,250) = £20,750.

The inheritance tax on this transfer is:

			£
Gross transfer of value (Trustees pay tax)			100,000
			£
IHT	£20,750	× 0% =	Nil
	£ 79,250	× 20% =	15,850
	£100,000		15,850

1 August 2009

The first £2,500 of this gift is exempt under the marriage exemption as a transfer from a remoter ancestor. The next £3,000 of this transfer is an exempt transfer because of the annual exemption for 2009/10.

The remaining £(66,000 – 2,500 – 3,000) = £60,500 is a potentially exempt transfer as it is a gift to an individual. This is treated as an exempt transfer during Artem's life.

5 September 2009

The gift to Artem's wife is an exempt transfer under the spouse exemption.

(b) **Death inheritance tax implications**

10 December 2002

The potentially exempt transfer of £59,000 is exempt because Artem died more than 7 years after making it.

17 January 2007

The gross chargeable lifetime transfer of £291,250 was made within 7 years before Artem's death and so additional inheritance tax might be payable.

However, the transfer is now covered by the nil rate band at the date of Artem's death of £325,000.

18 August 2007

The potentially exempt transfer of £43,000 is chargeable transfer because it was made within the 7 years before Artem's death.

There was a lifetime transfer of value of £291,250 in seven years before 18 August 2007 (transfers after 18 August 2000) so the nil rate band available is £(325,000 – 291,250) = £33,750.

The inheritance tax on this transfer is:

				£
Gross transfer of value				43,000
				£
IHT	£33,750	× 0% =		Nil
	£ 9,250	× 40% =		3,700
	£43,000			3,700
Less: taper relief (3 to 4 years) @ 20%				(740)
Death tax payable				2,960

17 June 2008

The chargeable transfer of £100,000 was made within 7 years before Artem's death and so additional inheritance tax might be payable.

Lifetime transfers of value of £291,250 and £43,000 were made in seven years before 17 June 2008 (transfers after 17 June 2001) which exceed the nil rate band on death of £325,000.

The inheritance tax on this transfer is:

			£
Gross transfer of value			100,000
			£
IHT	£100,000	× 40% =	40,000
Less: lifetime IHT paid			(15,850)
Death tax payable			24,150

There is no taper relief as Artem died within 3 years of making this transfer.

1 August 2009

The potentially exempt transfer of £60,500 is chargeable transfer because it was made within the 7 years before Artem's death.

Lifetime transfers of value of £291,250, £43,000 and £100,000 were made in seven years before 1 August 2009 (transfers after 1 August 2002). These exceed the nil rate band on death of £325,000.

The inheritance tax on this transfer is:

			£
Gross transfer of value			60,500
			£
IHT £60,500 × 40% =			24,200

There is no taper relief as Artem died within 3 years of making this transfer.

30 IHT transfers

Text references. Chapter 18 covers the inheritance tax examinable in F6.

Top tips. Where a question is divided into discrete parts such as this one, it is important to attempt ALL of the parts of the question to achieve a reasonable mark.

Easy marks. There were easy marks for explaining common exemptions such as the annual exemption, the marriage exemption and the small gifts exemption.

Marking scheme

			Marks
(a)	Gift is transfer of value	½	
	Annual exemptions	1	
	Marriage exemption	½	
	Potentially exempt transfer	1	
			3
(b)	Small gifts exemption		1
(c)	Sale at undervalue so diminution in estate	1	
	Transfer of value definition	1	
	No gratuitous intent so not transfer of value	1	
			3
(d)	Diminution in estate	1	
	Chargeable lifetime transfer	½	
	Nil rate band	½	
	Cumulation for seven years	1	
			3
(e)	Transfer of value but exempt	½	
	Out of income	½	
	Habitual	½	
	Maintains usual standard of living	½	
			2
(f)	Potentially exempt transfer	1	
	Chargeable on death within 7 years	½	
	Value of transfer	½	
	Better to give shares than cash	½	
	Taper relief	½	
			3
			15

(a)   **Bilal**

The gift of £20,000 is a transfer of value for inheritance tax.

Bilal can use his £3,000 annual exemptions for 2010/11 and 2009/10 and also the marriage exemption which is £5,000 for a gift to the donor's child.

The remaining transfer of value is £(20,000 – 3,000 – 3,000 – 5,000) = £9,000. This is a potentially exempt transfer as it is a transfer to another individual. It will become a chargeable transfer if Bilal dies within seven years of making it but will be covered by his nil rate band.

(b)   **Sammy**

Gifts up to £250 per person in any one tax year are exempt under the small gifts exemption.

(c)   **Terry**

There has been a sale at an undervalue and Terry's estate has been reduced in value by £(20,000 – 1,000) = £19,000.

However, a transfer of value for IHT requires the diminution to be as a result of a gratuitous disposition. Since Terry thought that he was obtaining a market value for the value, his bad business deal is not a transfer of value as he had no gratuitous intent.

(d)   **Lucas**

There is a transfer of value as the gift is a gratuitous disposition which results in a diminution in the value of the donor's estate. This diminution is:

	£
Value of shares held before gift (8,000 × £37.50)	300,000
Value of shares held after gift (6,000 × £18.75)	(112,500)
Transfer of value	187,500

This is chargeable lifetime transfer as it is a transfer to trustees. However there is no lifetime tax payable because the transfer is within the available nil rate band of £325,000.

The transfer will be cumulated with any further transfers in the next seven years, including the death estate, if Lucas dies within this time.

(e)   **Donald**

There is a transfer of value of £1,000 each month. The transfers will be exempt under the normal expenditure out of income exemption because the transfer is:

*   made out of income; and
*   part of the normal expenditure of the donor (habitual); and
*   leaves the donor with sufficient income to maintain his usual standard of living.

(f)   **Jas**

If either cash or shares are given, the transfer of value will be a potentially exempt transfer so the transfer will be treated as exempt while Jas is alive.

If Jas dies within seven years of making the transfer it will become a chargeable transfer and will be subject to death rates at the date of death. However, in either case, the transfer of value will be £100,000 as any increase in value of the shares is not be subject to inheritance tax. On purely IHT terms, Jas should therefore make a gift of the shares rather than cash.

If Jas dies between three and seven years of making the transfer, taper relief will reduce the death tax.

31 Wireless Ltd

Marking scheme

				Marks
(a)	(i)	End of preceding accounting period	1	
		Commencement of trading	1	2
	(ii)	Trading profit	½	
		Director's remuneration	1	
		Employer's Class 1 NIC	1	
		P&M – Pool	1	
		– AIA	2	
		– WDA	1	
		IBA – Land	½	
		– General offices	1	
		– Eligible expenditure	1	
		– Allowance	1½	
		Loan interest	½	
		Gift aid donation	1	
				12
(b)	(i)	Registration limit	1	
		February 2011	1	
		Notification	1	
		Date of registration	1	
				4
	(ii)	**Goods**		
		Business purposes/Not sold or consumed	1½	
		Four year limit	1	
		Services		
		Business purposes	½	
		Six month limit	1	
				4

(iii) Output VAT   1
Revenue   1
Input VAT   1

 3

(iv) ½ for each point made   3

 28

(a) (i) (1) An accounting period will normally start immediately after the end of the preceding accounting period.

          (2) An accounting period will also start when a company commences to trade or when its profits otherwise become liable to corporation tax.

  (ii) **Wireless Ltd – Taxable total profits for the period ended 31 March 2011**

	£	£
Trading profit		75,788
Less: Director's remuneration £(23,000 + 2,212) (N)	25,212	
Capital allowances P&M (W1)	19,360	
IBA (W2)	980	
		(45,552)
		30,236
Loan interest		1,110
Total profits		31,346
Gift aid donation		(1,800)
Taxable total profits		29,546

Note. The director's remuneration can be deducted as it was paid within nine months of the end of the period of account. The employer's Class 1 NIC will be £2,212 (23,000 – 5,715 = 17,285 × 12.8%).

Workings

1 **Plant and machinery**

	AIA £	Main pool £	Allowances £
Additions qualifying for AIA			
20.9.10 Office equipment (treated as 1.10.10)	3,400		
5.10.10 Machinery	10,200		
11.10.10 Alterations	4,700		
	18,300		
AIA (£100,000 x 6/12 = £50,000 max)	(18,300)		18,300
Addition not qualifying for AIA			
18.2.11 Car		10,600	
WDA @ 20% × 6/12		(1,060)	1,060
TWDV c/f		9,540	
Allowances			19,360

2 **Industrial buildings allowance**

	£
Site preparation	8,000
Canteen for employees	22,000
Factory	68,000
Eligible expenditure	98,000
WDA £98,000 × 1%	980

Note. The general offices do not qualify as they are more than 25% of the cost.

(b) (i) (1) Wireless Ltd would have been liable to compulsory VAT registration when its taxable supplies during any 12-month period exceeded £70,000.

   (2) This happened on 28 February 2011 when taxable supplies amounted to £87,100.

   (3) Wireless Ltd would have had to notify HMRC by 30 March 2011, being 30 days after the end of the period.

   (4) The company will have been registered from 1 April 2011 or from an agreed earlier date.

(ii) Input VAT on goods purchased prior to registration

   (1) The goods must have been acquired for business purposes and not be sold or consumed prior to registration.

   (2) The goods were acquired in the four years prior to VAT registration.

   Input VAT on services supplied prior to registration

   (1) The services must have been supplied for business purposes.

   (2) The services were supplied in the six months prior to VAT registration.

(iii) (1) Wireless Ltd's sales are all to VAT registered businesses, so output VAT can be passed on to customers.

   (2) The company's revenue would therefore not have altered if it had registered for VAT on 1 October 2010.

   (3) However, registering for VAT on 1 October 2010 would have allowed input VAT incurred from that date to be recovered.

(iv) The following information is required:

   (1) The supplier's name, address and registration number.
   (2) The date of issue, tax point and an invoice number.
   (3) The name and address of the customer.
   (4) Description of goods, including quantity, unit price, rate of VAT and VAT exclusive cost.
   (5) Total invoice price excluding VAT.
   (6) Each VAT rate and total VAT

32 Crash-Bash Ltd

Text references. Capital allowances are covered in Chapter 8. Computing taxable total profits is in Chapter 19 and the computation of corporation tax in Chapter 20. Overseas matters for companies is covered in Chapter 24. VAT is dealt with in Chapters 26 and 27.

Top tips. You could start with part (b) if you are confident about VAT since you were told that it was independent of part (a).

Easy marks. Registration for VAT is often examined so you should have been able to gain easy marks in part (b)(i).

Examiner's comments. In the first section of part (a) most candidates were not aware that the essential point regarding residence is where a company's central management and control is exercised. Most candidates had little difficulty with the corporation tax computation, and there were many perfect answers to this part of the question. However, the overseas income was often treated as franked investment income or simply ignored. The double taxation relief was sometimes used to reduce the overseas income rather than the corporation tax liability. As regards transfer pricing, very few candidates gave detailed enough answers to score more than one or two marks. It was surprising that very few candidates even appreciated that the pricing policy would result in the company's UK corporation tax liability being reduced.

In part (b) the VAT aspects of the question were not so well answered. Many candidates incorrectly stated that VAT registration was necessary because the company had exceeded the registration limit over the previous 12 months. They even gave the wrong date of registration despite this being given in the question. A number of candidates prepared the company's VAT return showing output VAT and input VAT, rather than calculating the amount of pre-registration input VAT. Very few candidates were aware of when default interest is charged.

				Marks
(a)	(i)	Central control and management in the UK	1	
		Board meetings held in the UK	<u>1</u>	
				2
	(ii)	UK trading profit	½	
		Advertising expenditure	1	
		Plant and machinery – AIA	1	
		– FYA @ 100%	1	
		– disposal	½	
		– WDA	1	
		Industrial building – eligible expenditure	1	
		– allowance	1	
		Overseas income	1	
		Overseas dividend	1	
		FII	1	
		Corporation tax	2	
		Double taxation relief	<u>2</u>	
				14
	(iii)	Reduction in UK corporation tax	1	
		Use of market value	1	
		Definition of market value	1	
		Adjustment under self assessment	<u>1</u>	
				4
(b)	(i)	Registration limit	1	
		Taxable supplies for September 2010	1	
		Notification	<u>1</u>	
				3
	(ii)	Stock – explanation	1	
		– calculation	½	
		Services – explanation	1	
		– calculation	1	
		Total VAT recovery	<u>½</u>	
				4
	(iii)	Net errors less than limit	1	
		Net errors exceeding limit	1	
		Default interest	<u>1</u>	
				<u>3</u>
				<u><u>30</u></u>

(a) (i) **Residence of Crash-Bash Ltd in the United Kingdom**

Companies that are incorporated overseas are only treated as being resident in the UK if their central management and control is exercised in the UK.

Since the directors are UK based and hold their board meetings in the UK, this would indicate that Crash-Bash Ltd is managed and controlled from the UK and therefore it is resident in the UK.

(ii) **Crash-Bash Ltd corporation tax liability for nine months ended 31 March 2011**

	£
UK trading profit (W1)	340,000
Overseas income	20,000
Taxable total profits	360,000
FII £36,000 × 100/90 (N)	40,000
Augmented profits	400,000

	£
Corporation tax (W4)	
FY 2010	
£360,000 × 28%	100,800
Less: 7/400 × (562,500 − 400,000) × (360,000/400,000)	(2,559)
	98,241
Less: DTR (W5)	(5,458)
CT liability	92,783

Note. The dividend from Safety Inc is not FII because it is received from a 51% group company. It is exempt from UK corporation tax.

Workings

1 *UK trading profit*

	£
Tax adjusted trading profit	445,900
Less: pre-trading advertising expenditure (N)	(12,840)
capital allowances (W2)	(91,410)
IBAs (W3)	(1,650)
	340,000

Note. The advertising expenditure incurred in June 2010 is pre-trading expenditure within seven years prior to the commencement of trading and is treated as incurred on the first day of trading (1 July 2010).

2 *Plant and machinery*

	AIA £	FYA @ 100% £	Main pool £	Allowances £
Additions qualifying for AIA%				
2.10.10	100,000			
AIA £100,000 × 9/12	(75,000)			75,000
	25,000			
Transfer balance to pool	(25,000)		25,000	
Additions qualifying for FYA @ 100%				
28.11.10 Car		13,200		
FYA @ 100%		(13,200)		13,200
Disposal				
12.2.11			(3,600)	
			21,400	
WDA @ 20% × 9/12			(3,210)	3,210
TWDV c/f			18,190	
Allowances				91,410

Note. The annual investment allowance is reduced to £75,000 (100,000 × 9/12) because Crash–Bash Ltd's accounting period is nine months long. The writing down allowance is similarly restricted to 9/12.

3   IBAs

	£
Eligible cost	
Total expenditure	320,000
Less: land	(100,000)
Eligible cost	220,000

IBA: 1% × £220,000 × 9/12 = £1,650

The IBA is restricted to 9/12 because the accounting period is nine months long.

4   Corporation tax limits

	FY 2010 9 months to 31 March 2011 £
Augmented profits	400,000
Lower limit	
£300,000 × 9/12 × ½	112,500
Upper limit	
£1,500,000 × 9/12 × ½	562,500

There is one associated company (Safety Inc) so the limits are one-half of the usual limits. Marginal relief applies because augmented profits fall between the lower and upper limits.

5   Double taxation relief

Lower of:

(i)   UK corporation tax on overseas trading income:

$\dfrac{20,000}{360,000}$ × £98,241 =   £5,458

(ii)   Overseas tax £20,000 @28.75% = £5,750

ie £5,458

(iii) **Crash-Bash Ltd and Safety Inc transfer pricing**

Invoicing for the exported crash helmets at less than the market price will reduce the UK trading profits of Crash-Bash Ltd and therefore its UK corporation tax.

A true market price will therefore have to be substituted for the transfer price. This will be the 'arms length' price that would be charged if the parties to the transaction were independent of each other.

Crash-Bash Ltd will be required to make the adjustment in its corporation tax self-assessment tax return.

(b) (i) **Crash-Bash Ltd compulsory VAT registration**

Traders must register for VAT if at any time they expect their taxable supplies for the following 30-day period to exceed £70,000.

Crash–Bash Ltd realised that its taxable supplies for September 2010 were going to be at least £100,000. The company was therefore liable to register from 1 September 2010 (the start of the 30-day period).

Crash–Bash Ltd had to notify HMRC by 30 September 2010 (the end of the 30-day period).

(ii) **Crash-Bash Ltd pre-registration VAT**

VAT incurred before registration can be treated as input tax and recovered from HMRC subject to certain conditions.

If the claim is for input tax suffered on goods purchased prior to registration then the following conditions must be satisfied.

- The goods were acquired for the purpose of the business which either was carried on or was to be carried on by the trader at the time of supply.

- The goods have not been supplied onwards or consumed before the date of registration.

- The VAT must have been incurred in the four years prior to the effective date of registration.

Crash-Bash Ltd can therefore recover the input VAT paid on the stock held at 1 September 2010. The input VAT on the stock recoverable is £108,600 x 17.5% = £19,005.

If the claim is for input tax suffered on the supply of services prior to registration then the following conditions must be satisfied.

- The services were supplied for the purposes of a business which either was carried on or was to be carried on by the trader at the time of supply.

- The services were supplied within the six months prior to the date of registration.

Crash-Bash Ltd can therefore recover the input VAT paid on the services incurred in July and August 2010. The input VAT on the services recoverable is £(22,300 + 32,700) = £55,000 x 17.5% = £9,625. The total input VAT recovery is therefore £(19,005 + 9,625) = £28,630.

(iii) **Crash-Bash Ltd VAT errors**

If the errors on a VAT return for the period ending 30 November 2010 did not exceed the greater of:

- £10,000 (net under-declaration minus over-declaration); or
- 1% x net VAT turnover for return period ended 30 November 2010 (maximum £50,000);

then the errors can be corrected on the return for the quarter ended 28 February 2011.

Errors in excess of the limit should be notified to HMRC in writing eg by letter.

Default interest will only be charged where the limit for notifying errors in the next return is exceeded.

33 Mice Ltd

Text references. Property business income is dealt with in Chapters 6 and 19. Losses for companies are in Chapter 22 and group relief in Chapter 23. Capital allowances are covered in Chapter 8. Calculation of income tax is in Chapter 2 and national insurance contributions in Chapter 12.

Top tips. You should use the loss relief pro-forma in part (a)(ii).

Easy marks. The calculation of property business profit in part (a) was straightforward and should have been easy marks.

Examiner's comments. This question was generally very well answered, especially the calculation of the property business profit in part (a) where most candidates scored virtually maximum marks. In part (b) several candidates explained whether or not group relief would be available rather than calculating the amount of relief. In part (c) most candidates were aware of what capital allowances were available, although some candidates incorrectly stated that the ventilation system would qualify for industrial buildings allowance. Many candidates complicated part (d) by performing long calculations, making this much more time consuming than necessary for 3 marks. However, they should have appreciated that this was additional remuneration so the calculations were simply £40,000 × 40%, £40,000 × 1% and £40,000 × 12.8% for the 3 marks.

Marks

(a)	(i)	Lease premium received	1½	
		Rent receivable - Property 1	1	
		- Property 2	½	
		- Property 3	½	
		Business rates	½	
		Repairs	1	
		Rent paid	½	
		Advertising	½	
		Insurance	1½	
		Loan interest	½	
				8
	(ii)	**Year ended 31 March 2011**		
		Property business profit	½	
		Loan interest	1½	
		Overseas income	1	
		Chargeable gain	½	
		Loss relief	1	
		Other periods		
		Trading profit	½	
		Property business profit	½	
		Loss relief	1	
		Gift Aid donations	½	
				7
(b)		Period ending 30 June 2010	1½	
		Year ended 30 June 2011	1½	
				3
(c)		Equipment	2	
		Ventilation system	2	
				4
(d)		Income tax	1	
		Employee's NIC	1	
		Employer's NIC	1	
				3
				25

(a) (i) **Mice Ltd – property business profit y/e 31 March 2011**

	£	£
2 Premium received for sub-lease	18,000	
Less: £18,000 × 2% × (8 – 1)	(2,520)	
Amount taxable as property business income		15,480
Property 1 rent accrued £3,200 × 4		12,800
Property 2 rent accrued		6,000
Property 3 rent accrued		0
Gross income accrued		34,280
Less: expenses accrued		
1 business rates	2,200	
1 repairs (N1)	1,060	
2 rent paid	7,800	
3 advertising 1 2 3	680	
insurance £(460 + 310 + (480 × 3/12))	890	
3 loan interest (N2)	-	
		(12,630)
Property business profit		21,650

Notes

1 The enlargement of the car park is capital expenditure which cannot be deducted when calculating the property business profit.

2 Interest paid in respect of a loan to purchase property is set off under the loan relationship rules.

(ii) **Mice Ltd – taxable total profits y/e 31 March 2011**

	£	£
Property business profit		21,650
Loan interest		
Received 31 December 2010	6,400	
Accrued 31 March 2011	3,200	
Paid on property 3 loan - 1 January 2011 to		
31 March 2011	(1,800)	
		7,800
Overseas income (N)		0
Chargeable gain		10,550
Total profits		40,000
Less: current period loss relief		(40,000)
Taxable total profits		0

Note. The overseas dividend income is exempt. However, it is franked investment income and would be relevant when calculating the rate of corporation tax (not relevant here because there are no taxable total profits).

Mice Ltd – total taxable profits for periods ending 31 March 2008, 2009 and 2010

	p/e 31.3.08	y/e 31.3.09	y/e 31.3.10
	£	£	£
Trading profit	83,200	24,700	51,200
Property business profit	2,800	7,100	12,200
Total profits	86,000	31,800	63,400
Less: carry back loss relief	(0)	(0)	(63,400)
	86,000	31,800	0
Less: Gift Aid donation	(1,000)	(1,500)	(0)
Taxable total profits	85,000	30,300	0

There is no loss relief in the period to 31 March 2008 or the year ended 31 March 2009 because loss relief for a continuing business is restricted to 12 months before the loss making period.

(b)   **Mice Ltd and Web-Cam Ltd – group relief**

For the three-month period ended 30 June 2010 group relief is restricted to the profit of £28,000, as this is lower than the loss of £180,000 x 3/12 = £45,000 for the corresponding period.

For the year ended 30 June 2011, group relief is restricted to the loss of £180,000 × 9/12 = £135,000 for the corresponding period, as this is lower than the corresponding profit of £224,000 × 9/12 = £168,000.

(c)   **Mice Ltd – capital allowance**

Equipment

The first £100,000 of expenditure will qualify for the annual investment allowance at the rate of 100%. The remainder of the expenditure will be added to the main pool and therefore will be eligible for writing down allowance at the rate of 20%.

Capital allowances for the year ended 31 March 2011 will therefore be £100,000 + (£25,000 × 20%) = £105,000.

Ventilation system

The annual investment allowance will be available as above. The ventilation system will be integral to the factory, and so the balance of expenditure will only qualify for writing down allowances at the rate of 10%.

Capital allowances for the year ended 31 March 2011 will therefore be £100,000 + (£25,000 × 10%) = £102,500.

(d)   **Director's income tax and national insurance contributions**

The managing director's additional income tax liability for 2010/11 will be £40,000 @ 40% = £16,000.

The additional employee's Class 1 NIC will be £40,000 @ 1% = £400.

The additional employer's Class 1 NIC will be £40,000 @ 12.8% = £5,120.

34 Do-Not-Panic Ltd

Text references. Chapters 19 and 20 cover computing taxable total profits and the corporation tax liability.

Top tips. Split out the long period correctly into the two accounting periods. Remember it is always the first twelve months and then the balance (in this case three months).

Easy marks. Allocating the figures between the two accounting periods should be straightforward.

Examiner's comments. Depending on whether candidates appreciated that the period of account needed to be split into a twelve-month period and a three-month period, this question was either answered very well or quite badly. Invariably many of the less well prepared candidates calculated corporation tax based on a fifteen-month period. The due dates were often omitted or incorrect.

		Marks
Trading profit		1
Capital allowances	– period ended 31 March 2011	1
Interest income	– period ended 31 March 2011	1
Capital gains		1½
Franked investment income		1
Corporation tax	– year ended 31 December 2010	1½
	– period ended 31 March 2011	2
Due dates		1
		10

Do-Not-Panic Ltd – Corporation tax liabilities for the fifteen-month period ended 31 March 2011

	Year ended 31 December 2010 £	Period ended 31 March 2011 £
Trading profit (12:3)	228,000	57,000
Capital allowances (W)	–	(8,000)
	228,000	49,000
Interest income (accruals basis)	–	7,500
Capital gains (42,000 – 4,250)	–	37,750
Total taxable profits	228,000	94,250
Franked investment income	–	25,000
Augmented profits	228,000	119,250

	FY 2009/FY2010	FY2010
y/e 31.12.10	£	
Rates for FY2009 and FY2010 are same so can be dealt with together		
Total taxable profits/augmented profits	228,000	
Lower limit £300,000		
Small profits rate applies		
FY 2009 and FY2010		
£228,000 × 21%	47,880	

y/e 31.3.11
FY 2010
Lower limit
    £300,000 × 3/12 = £75,000
Upper limit
    £1,500,000 × 3/12 = £375,000

		£
Marginal relief applies		
£94,250 × 28%		26,390
Less: $\dfrac{7}{400}$ × £(375,000 − 119,250) × $\dfrac{94,250}{119,250}$		(3,537)
CT for p/e 31.3.11		22,853
Due dates	1 October 2011	1 January 2012

Working

Period ended 31 March 2011

	AIA £	Main pool £	Allowances £
Equipment	8,000		
AIA £100,000 x 3/12 = £25,000 maximum	(8,000)		8,000
TWDV carried forward		–	

35 Quagmire plc

Marking scheme

			Marks
(a)	Large company	1	
	Associated company	1	
	No exception	1	
			3
(b)	Corporation tax liability	1	
	Instalments	1	
	Due dates	1	
			3
(c)	Augmented profit	1	
	No longer a large company	½	
	Due date	1	
	Corporation tax	1½	
			4
			10

(a) **Quagmire plc – payment of corporation tax**

Large companies have to make quarterly instalment payments in respect of their corporation tax liability. A large company is one paying corporation tax at the main rate.

Quagmire plc has one associated company, so the upper limit is reduced to £750,000 (1,500,000/2). Corporation tax will therefore be at the main rate for the year ended 31 January 2011.

There is an exception for the first year that a company is large, provided augmented profits do not exceed £10 million. No exception applies because Quagmire plc was also a large company for the year ended 31 January 2010.

(b) **Quagmire plc –corporation tax liability**

Quagmire plc's corporation tax liability for the year ended 31 January 2011 is £1,200,000 @ 28% = £336,000.

The company will have paid this in four quarterly instalments of £336,000/4 = £84,000.

The instalments will have been due on 14 August 2010, 14 November 2010, 14 February 2011 and 14 May 2011.

(c) **Effect of no associated company**

Quagmire plc's augmented profits for the year ended 31 January 2011 are £1,200,000 plus franked investment income of £200,000 = £1,400,000.

Quagmire plc is no longer a large company since its augmented profits are below the upper limit of £1,500,000. The corporation tax liability will therefore be due in one amount on 1 November 2011.

The corporation tax liability will be £334,500 calculated as follows:

	£
£1,200,000@ 28%	336,000
Less marginal relief	
$£(1,500,000 - 1,400,000) \times (1,200,000/1,400,000) \times \dfrac{7}{400}$	(1,500)
Corporation tax liability	334,500

36 Thai Curry Ltd

> **Text references.** Chapters 19 and 20 for calculation of augmented profits and taxable total profits. Chapter 8 covers capital allowances. Chapter 25 for corporation tax administration.
>
> **Top tips.** It is essential to set out your capital allowances proforma in the correct layout to achieve maximum marks. Ensure that you state all of your assumptions so that you do not miss out on any method marks.
>
> You cannot avoid administration questions in the exam so make sure you know due dates for returns and tax payments.

Marking scheme

		Marks
(a)	Capital allowances	
	TWDV b/f	½
	AIA	2
	Disposals	2
	Balancing allowances	2
	WDA	½
	FYA @ 100%	1
	IBAs	
	Land	1
	Allowance	1
	Trading loss	½
	Deduct allowances	½
		11

					Marks
(b)	Trading profit nil			½	
	Property income				
		Property 1	– rent	1	
			– expense	½	
			– bad debt	1	
		Property 2	– rent	½	
			– lease premium	1½	
	Interest			1	
	Chargeable gain			½	
	Deduct CY loss			1	
	FII			½	
	CT limits			1	
	CT @ 28%			½	
	Marginal relief			1½	
					11
(c)	(i)	Return deadline		1	
		Fixed penalty		1	
		Tax geared penalty		1	
					3
	(ii)	9 months 1 day		1	
		Late payment interest		1	
		Interest calculation		1	
					3
					28

(a) **Thai Curry's adjusted trading loss y/e 31 March 2011**

	£
Trading loss	(35,700)
Less: Capital allowances (W1)	(51,330)
Less: IBAs (W2)	(2,900)
Allowable trading loss	(89,930)

Workings

1   *Capital allowances*

	AIA	FYA @ 100%	Main pool	Exp car	SLA	Allowances
	£	£	£	£	£	£
TWDV b/f			10,600	16,400	2,900	
Additions qualifying for AIA						
8.7.10 Equipment	7,360					
20.9.10 Office (N1)	22,750					
	30,110					
AIA	(30,110)					30,110

	AIA	FYA @ 100%	Main pool	Exp car	SLA	Allowances
	£	£	£	£	£	£
Additions not qualifying for AIA						
26.8.10 Car			15,800			
Disposals						
1.5.10 Equipment			(12,800)			
			13,600			
WDA @ 20%			(2,720)			2,720
15.6.10 SLA (N2)					(800)	
BA					2,100	2,100
14.7.10 Car				(9,700)		
BA				6,700		6,700
Addition qualifying for FYA						
19.11.10 Car	9,700					
100% FYA	(9,700)					9,700
TWDV c/f			10,880			
Allowances						51,330

Notes

(1) The items included within the cost of the office building purchased on 20 March 2011 will qualify for plant and machinery capital allowances. All of the expenditure is covered by the AIA so it is not necessary to distinguish between main pool and special rate pool expenditure.

(2) It has been assumed that the SLA has had fewer than 5 WDAs claimed on it up to this date and that therefore a balancing allowance arises.

2   IBAs

	£
Cost	360,000
Less: land	(70,000)
	290,000
Thus IBA available is £290,000 × 1%	2,900

(b) **Corporation tax liability y/e 31 March 2011**

	£
Trading profit	Nil
Property income (W1)	72,800
Interest (W3)	11,500
Chargeable gain	152,300
Total profits	236,600
Less: current year loss relief	(89,930)
Taxable total profits	146,670
Add: gross dividends: £36,000 × 100/90	40,000
Augmented profits	186,670

	£
CT liability (W4)	
FY 2010: £146,670 × 28%	41,068
Less 7/400 (375,000 – 186,670) × (146,670/186,670)	(2,590)
CT liability	38,478

Workings

1   *Property income*

Property 1

	£	£
8m × £2,200	17,600	
Less: redecoration costs	(8,800)	
Less: rent not recoverable: 2m × £2,200	(4,400)	
Property income		4,400

Property 2

	£	£
8/12 × £18,000	12,000	
Premium taxable as income (W2)	56,400	
Property income		68,400
Total property income		72,800

2   *Lease premium*

	£
Premium (P)	60,000
Less: 2% × (n-1) × P	
2% × (4-1) × 60,000	(3,600)
Taxable as income	56,400

3   *Loan interest*

	£
Received at 30.9.10	8,000
Accrued at 31.3.11	3,500
Total amount (accruals basis)	11,500

4

	FY 2010 12 months to 31.3.11
Taxable total profits	146,670
Augmented profits	186,670
Lower limit	
£300,000/4	75,000
Upper limit	
£1,500,000/4	375,000

Therefore marginal relief applies.

(c)   (i)   **Date for return submission and penalties**

The CT return must be submitted one year after the end of the period of account ie by 31 March 2012.

If the return is not submitted until 30 November 2012 it will be 8 months late. If the return is up to 3 months late there is a fixed penalty of £100. If it more than 3 months late, as it is here, the fixed penalty increases to £200.

As the return is more than 6 months late there is also a tax geared penalty of 10% × unpaid tax, ie 10% × £38,478 = £3,848.

(ii)   **Date for CT payment & interest**

As the company is not large it must pay its corporation tax by 9 months and 1 day after the accounting period, ie by 1 January 2012.

If the tax is not paid until 30 November 2012 it will be 11 months late and interest will be charged from the due date. (in practice, interest is calculated on a daily basis.)

The rate of interest on unpaid tax is 3% and therefore the amount that will be charged is:

3% × 11/12 × £38,478 = £1,058.

37 Hawk Ltd

Marking scheme

				Marks
(a)	**Office building**			
	Disposal proceeds		½	
	Costs of disposal		½	
	Cost		½	
	Costs of acquisition		½	
	Enhancement expenditure		½	
	Indexation	– Cost	1	
		– Enhancement	1	
	Albatross plc			
	Proceeds		½	
	Cost		2	
	Cuckoo plc			
	Proceeds		½	
	Value of shares	– Ordinary shares	1	
		– Preference shares	1	
	Cost		1½	
	Land			
	Proceeds		½	
	Costs		2	
	Corporation tax liability			
	Net chargeable gains		1	
	Calculation		1½	
				16
(b)	(i)	Qualifying disposal	1	
		Amount of reinvestment	1	2
	(ii)	Period of reinvestment		1
	(iii)	Corporation tax savings		1
				20

(a) **Corporation tax liability y/e 31 March 2011**

Net chargeable gains

	£
Office building (W1)	70,937
Albatross Ltd Shares (W2)	25,000
Cuckoo Ltd preference shares (W3)	17,000
Land (W4)	(12,000)
Net chargeable gains	100,937

Workings

1   *Office building*

		£
Proceeds		260,000
Less: disposal costs		(5,726)
Net proceeds of sale		254,274
Less: original costs £(81,000 + 3,200)		(84,200)
enhancement expenditure		(43,000)
Unindexed gain		127,074
Less: indexation allowance		
on original cost		
(222.8 - 140.6)/140.6 (0.585) × £84,200		(49,257)
on enhancement		
(222.8 - 192.0)/192.0 (0.160) × £43,000		(6,880)
Indexed gain		70,937

2   *Albatross Ltd shares*

FA 1985 pool

	No. of shares	*Cost*
		£
1.8.10 Acquisition	6,000	18,600
17.8.10 Acquisition	2,000	9,400
	8,000	28,000
29.8.10 Disposal	(5,000)	(17,500)
c/f	3,000	10,500

	£
Proceeds	42,500
Less: cost	(17,500)
Gain (no indexation allowance)	25,000

3   *Cuckoo Ltd preference shares*

Reorganisation

	MV	*Cost*
	£	£
15,000 Ordinary shares (5,000 × 3) × £4.50	67,500	45,000
10,000 Preference shares (5,000 × 2) × £2.25	22,500	15,000
	90,000	60,000

	£
Proceeds	32,000
Less: cost	(15,000)
Gain (no indexation allowance)	17,000

4   *Land*

	£
Proceeds	120,000
Less: costs £203,500 × $\dfrac{120,000}{120,000 + 65,000}$	(132,000)
Loss	(12,000)

Corporation tax liability

	£
Trading income	125,000
Net chargeable gains	100,937
Taxable total profits	225,937

Hawk Ltd is a small profits company
£225,937 × 21%   47,447

(b) (i) The only disposal that qualifies for rollover relief is the sale of the freehold office building. Shares do not qualify and the land has not been used for business purposes.

The office building was sold for £260,000, and this is therefore the amount that Hawk Ltd will have to reinvest in order to claim the maximum possible amount of rollover relief.

Tutorial note. It would also have been acceptable to state that the net disposal proceeds (£254,274) had to be reinvested to claim the maximum possible of rollover relief.

(ii) The reinvestment will have to take place between 1 May 2009 and 30 April 2013, which is the period starting one year before and ending three years after the date of disposal.

(iii) Corporation tax of £14,897 (£70,937 × 21%) will be saved if the maximum possible amount of rollover relief is claimed.

38 Problematic Ltd

Text references. Chargeable gains for companies are covered in Chapter 21. Taxable total profits are defined in Chapter 20.

Top tips. Make sure you use the three column pro-forma for the FA 1985 pool.

Easy marks. The calculations of taxable total profits simply required the gains calculated to be added together with the figure for trading profit.

Examiner's comments. It was pleasing to see that this question was well answered. On an overall note, it does not create a very good impression when candidates deduct the annual exempt amount when dealing with a company. The only aspect that consistently caused problems in part (a) was the restoration of the asset. Despite the question telling candidates that a claim to defer the gain had been made, many insisted that such a claim was not possible and instead calculated a capital loss. Many candidates did not even attempt part (b) despite the fact that this section generally just required them to provide figures already calculated in part (a).

Marking scheme

		Marks
(a)	**Easy plc**	
	FA 1985 pool - Purchase	½
	- Rights issue	1½
	- Indexation	2
	- Disposal	1
	Chargeable gain	1½
	Office building	
	Proceeds fully reinvested	1
	No disposal on receipt of proceeds	1
	Freehold factory	
	Disposal proceeds	½
	Indexed cost	½
	Rollover relief	2

		Marks
Land		
Proceeds	½	
Incidental costs of disposal	1	
Cost	2	
Taxable total profits		
Chargeable gains	½	
Calculation	½	
		16
(b) Ordinary shares in Easy plc	½	
Office building	1½	
Leasehold factory	1	
Land	1	
		4
		20

(a)   **Problematic plc –taxable total profits for y/e 31 March 2011**

	£
Easy plc shares (W1)	29,741
Office building (W2)	0
Freehold factory (W3)	16,200
Land (W4)	45,550
Trading profit	108,509
Taxable total profits	200,000

Workings

(1)   *Easy plc shares*

FA85 pool

	No. of shares	Cost £	Indexed cost £
Purchase 26.6.95	15,000	12,600	12,600
Index to September 2007			
(208.0 – 149.8)/149.8 × £12,600			4,895
Rights issue 1 for 3 @ £2.20	5,000	11,000	11,000
	20,000	23,600	28,495
Index to June 2010			
(225.0 - 208.0)/208.0 × £28,495			2,329
			30,824
Sale	(16,000)	(18,880)	(24,659)
C/f	4,000	4,720	6,165

Gain	£
Proceeds	54,400
Less: cost	(18,880)
	35,520
Less: indexation £ (24,659 – 18,880)	(5,779)
Chargeable gain	29,741

(2)   *Office building*

The insurance proceeds of £36,000 received by Problematic Ltd have been fully applied in restoring the office building.

There is therefore no disposal on the receipt of the insurance proceeds.

(3)   *Freehold factory*

	£
Proceeds	171,000
Less: indexed cost	(127,000)
	44,000
Less: gain deferred on purchase of leasehold factory £(44,000 – 16,200)	(27,800)
Chargeable gain (amount not reinvested £(171,000 – 154,800)	16,200

(4)   *Land*

	£
Proceeds	130,000
Less: disposal costs	(3,200)
Net disposal proceeds	126,800
Less: indexed cost	
$\dfrac{130,000}{130,000 + 350,000} \times £300,000$	(81,250)
Chargeable gain	45,550

(b)   **Carried forward indexed base costs**

The 4,000 £1 ordinary shares in Easy plc have an indexed base cost of £6,165.

The indexed base cost of the office building is £(169,000 – 36,000 + 41,000) = £174,000.

The leasehold factory is a depreciating asset, so there is no adjustment to the base cost of £154,800.

The indexed base cost of the remaining three acres of land is £(300,000 – 81,250) = £218,750.

Tutorial note. When a replacement asset is a depreciating asset then the gain is not rolled over by reducing the cost of the replacement asset. Instead, the gain is deferred until it crystallises on the earliest of:

–   The disposal of the replacement asset.

–   The date the replacement asset is no longer used in the business.

–   Ten years after the acquisition of the replacement asset which in this case is 10 December 2020.

39 Spacious Ltd

Text references. Chapters 19 and 20 for taxable total profits and corporation tax calculations. Chapter 21 for chargeable gains. CT loss relief covered in Chapter 22.

Top tips. Use a loss proforma when apportioning losses to accounting periods. Use a proforma when calculating capital allowances. Proformas improve the layout of an answer and are liked by the examiner as they help with marking an answer.

Make sure you follow closely the question requirements. Part (b) asks you to consider a loss claim against total profits (and no other loss relief). Don't waste time and effort doing anything extra or different. Part (c) then allows you to discuss carrying the loss forward. Only discuss that option in this section.

Easy marks. The adjustment of the loss was fairly straightforward. Adjustment of a profit/loss is something that you should expect to see in nearly every exam. Calculating capital allowances is another topic which appears regularly in the exam and provides easy marks for the knowledgeable student.

Examiner's comments. A number of candidates achieved maximum marks. In part (b) some candidates carried back all of the loss to the previous period. Part (c) was reasonably well answered if candidates appreciated that the main benefit of carrying the loss forward was that relief was obtained at a higher rate.

		Marks
(a)	Loss before tax	½
	Depreciation	½
	Patent	½
	Professional fees (½ each)	2½
	Repairs/renewals (½ each)	1
	Other expenses (½ each)	1½
	Office building	½
	Bank interest receivable	½
	Interest payable	½
	IBA – land	½
	– general offices	2
	– eligible expenditure	1
	– allowance	½
	Long life asset	1
	P&M – main pool	2
	– AIA	1
	– car sold	1
	– special rate pool	1
	– WDA	1
		19
(b)	Trading income	1
	Interest income	1
	Gain	2
	Capital loss	1
	Loss relief	2
	Gift aid	1
		8
(c)	Year ended 31 March 2011	1
	Period ended 31 March 2010	1
	Carry forward	1
		3
		30

(a) **Trading loss**

	£	£
Loss before taxation		(86,875)
Depreciation	54,690	
Patent royalties (N1)	0	
Accountancy and audit	0	
Legal fees – share capital (N2)	8,800	
Legal fees – debentures (N2)	0	
Legal fees – defence of trade	0	
Legal fees – court action (N2)	900	
Repairs and renewals: new wall (N3)	9,700	
Repairs and renewals: roof repair (N3)	0	
Other expenses: entertaining customers	4,215	
Other expenses: entertaining employees	0	
Other expenses: gift aid	1,000	79,305

	£	£
Office building profit		(7,570)
Bank interest		(54,400)
Interest payable (N4)		(7,000)
		0
Capital allowances – IBAs (W1)	1,635	
– P&M (W2)	118,800	
Trading loss		(120,435)
		(189,405)

Notes

1   No adjustment needed for patent royalties as treated as part of trading expenses.

2   Costs relating to share capital need to be added back as they relate to a capital expense. However, the fees relating to the debentures are a loan relationship expense and thus deductible as a trading expense because the debenture is for trade purposes. Legal fees in relation to fine are not deductible as the fine is a payment contrary to public policy.

3   The cost of the new wall has been added back as a capital expense but the cost of the roof is allowable as it is a repair and therefore a revenue expense.

4   No adjustment is needed for the interest because it relates to a trade purpose loan.

Workings

1   *IBAs*

	£
Drawing office	54,000
Factory £(360,000 – 135,000 – 61,500 – 54,000)	109,500
Allowable cost	163,500

WDA @ 1% = 1,635

Note. General offices cost more than 25% of £(360,000 – 135,000) = £225,000. This means that the expenditure on the general office is not eligible for IBAs.

2   *Plant and machinery*

	AIA	Main pool	Special rate pool	Exp. Car	Allowances
	£	£	£	£	£
TWDV b/f		28,400		14,800	
Additions qualifying for AIA					
1.9.10 Crane	110,000				
AIA (best use)	(100,000)				100,000
	10,000				
Transfer balance to pool	(10,000)		10,000		
10.4.10 Equipment		30,200			
Additions not qualifying for AIA					
5.2.11 Car			27,200		
31.3.11 Car		9,400			
Disposals					
5.2.10 Car				(9,800)	
BA				5,000	5,000
20.3.11 Lorry		(17,600)			
		50,400	37,200		
WDA @ 20%		(10,080)			10,080
WDA @ 10%			(3,720)		3,720
TWDVs c/f		40,320	33,480		
Allowances					118,800

Note. The private use of the car by the employee is not relevant for capital allowance purposes.
No adjustment is ever made to a company's capital allowances to reflect the private use of an asset.

The AIA is allocated against the expenditure which will get the lowest rate of WDAs.

(b)

	Period ended 31 March 2010 £	Year ended 31 March 2011 £
Trading income	218,200	0
Interest income	5,200	7,000
Capital gain (W)	0	15,100
Total profits	223,400	22,100
Less: carry back/current year loss relief	(167,305)	(22,100)
	56,095	0
Less: Gift Aid payment	(800)	0
Taxable total profits	55,295	0

Working

Gain on building

	£
Proceeds	380,000
Less indexed cost	(345,400)
Indexed gain	34,600
Less rollover relief £34,600 – (380,000 – 360,000)	(14,600)
	20,000
Less loss b/f	(4,900)
Capital gain	15,100

(c)   Using the loss in the year to 31 March 2011, Spacious Ltd has saved tax as follows:
£22,100 @ 21% = £4,641

Using the rest of the loss in the period to 31 March 2010, Spacious Ltd has saved 21% × £167,305 = £35,134.

Total tax saved is therefore £39,775.

However, if the loss of £189,405 had been carried forward to year ended 31 March 2012, it would have saved tax of £189,405 × 29.75% = £56,348.

40 Volatile Ltd

Text references. Corporation tax losses are covered in Chapter 22.

Top tips. Don't forget to set up a loss memorandum for each loss so that you can see how the loss is utilised.

Easy marks. You should have been able to state at least 2 of the principles of claiming loss relief in part (a).

Examiner's comments. This question was not particularly well answered. In part (a) far too many candidates explained the loss reliefs available rather than the factors influencing the choice of claims. In part (b) many candidates approached this on a year by year basis, rather than one computation with a column for each of the four periods. This not only wasted time in having to write out four computations, but also made it very difficult to calculate the correct loss relief claims. Other common mistakes included treating the chargeable gains separately (rather than as part of the taxable total profits), and deducting gift aid donations from trading profits rather than total profits after loss relief.

Marks

(a) Rate of tax   1
Timing of relief   1
Gift Aid donations not relieved   <u>1</u>

     3

(b) Trading income   ½
Property business income   ½
Chargeable gains   ½
Loss relief – y/e 31 December 2007   2
Loss relief – y/e 30 September 2010   2½
Gift Aid donations   ½
Unrelieved losses   <u>½</u>

     <u>7</u>
     <u>10</u>

(a) **Choice of loss relief**

The three factors that will influence a company's choice of loss relief claims are:

- The rate at which relief will be obtained:
  - 29.75% if marginal relief applies (best use)
  - 28% at the main rate (second best use)
  - 21% at the small profits rate (third best use)

- How quickly relief will be obtained: loss relief against total profits is quicker than carry forward loss relief.

- The extent to which relief for gift aid donations might be lost.

(b) **Volatile Ltd**

	P/e 31.12.06	Y/e 31.12.07	Y/e 31.12.08	P/e 30.09.09
	£	£	£	£
Trading income	44,000	0	95,200	78,700
Less: carry forward loss relief	(0)	(0)	(8,700)	(0)
	44,000	0	86,500	78,700
Property business income	9,400	6,600	6,500	0
Chargeable gains	5,100	0	0	9,700
Total profits	58,500	6,600	93,000	88,400
Less: current period loss relief	(0)	(6,600)	(0)	(0)
Less: carry back loss relief	(58,500)		(23,250)	(88,400)
	0	0	69,750	0
Less: Gift Aid donations	(0)	(0)	(1,200)	(0)
Taxable total profits	0	0	68,550	0

Loss memorandum

	£
Loss in y/e 31.12.07	73,800
Less: used y/e 31.12.07	(6,600)
Less: used p/e 31.12.06	(58,500)
Less: used y/e 31.12.08	(8,700)
Loss remaining unrelieved	0

	£
Loss in y/e 30.9.10	186,800
Less: used p/e 30.9.09	(88,400)
Less: used y/e 31.12.08	
3 months to 31.12.08	
£93,000 × 3/12	(23,250)
Loss remaining unrelieved	75,150

The loss of y/e 30.9.10 can be carried back against total profits of the previous 12 months ie against the 9 month period ending 30.9.09 and 3 months of the y/e 31.12.08.

41 Jogger Ltd

Text references. Capital allowances are dealt with in Chapter 8. Corporation tax is dealt with in Chapters 19 and 20. Self assessment and payment of tax by companies is covered in Chapter 25. VAT is dealt with in Chapters 26 and 27.

Top tips. You could start with the VAT part of the question as only brief explanations were required for the marks available. You could then have gone back to part (a) which required fairly complex computations which it would have been easy to spend a lot of time preparing.

Easy marks. Stating the due date for payment of corporation tax was an easy mark.

(a) (i) **Trading loss y/e 31.3.11**

		£
Operating loss		(9,140)
Add: depreciation		58,840
		49,700
Less: capital allowances		
P&M (W1)		(103,060)
IBA (W2)		(2,500)
Adjusted trading loss		(55,860)

Workings

1   *Plant and machinery*

	AIA £	Main pool £	Exp. car £	Allowances £
TWDV b/f		21,600	8,800	
Additions qualifying for AIA/FYA				
30.9.10 Machinery	105,000			
AIA	(100,000)			100,000
	5,000			
Transfer balance to pool	(5,000)	5,000		
Additions not qualifying for AIA				
31.7.10 Car		11,800		
Disposals				
20.7.10 Expensive car			(11,700)	
BC			(2,900)	(2,900)
14.3.11 Lorry		(8,600)		
		29,800		
WDA @ 20%		(5,960)		5,960
TWDV c/f		23,840		
Allowances				103,060

2   *IBAs*

	£
£250,000 × 1%	2,500

(ii) **Jogger Ltd – corporation tax computation y/e 31.3.11**

	£
Interest income (W1)	33,060
Property income (W2)	126,000
Chargeable gain	98,300
Total profits	257,360
Less: loss relief	(55,860)
Taxable total profits	201,500
Add: FII £45,000 × 100/90	50,000
Augmented profits	251,500

Corporation tax

	£
Upper limit £1,500,000 / 3 associated companies	500,000
Lower limit £300,000 / 3 associated companies	100,000

	£
Marginal relief applies	
£201,500 × 28%	56,420
Less: 7/400 × £(500,000 – 251,500) × 201,500/251,500	(3,484)
Corporation tax payable	52,936

Workings

1   *Interest income*

		£
Bank interest receivable		8,460
Loan interest – received 31.12.10		16,400
– accrued 31.3.11		8,200
		33,060

2   *Property income*

		£
Premium received		100,000
Less: 2% × (10 – 1) x £100,000		(18,000)
Taxable as property income		82,000
Add: rental income accrued		44,000
		126,000

(iii)   Jogger Ltd's self-assessment tax return for the year ended 31 March 2011 must be submitted by 31 March 2012.

If the company submits its self-assessment tax return eight months late, then there will be an automatic fixed penalty of £200, since the return is more than three months late.

There will also be an additional corporation tax geared penalty of £5,294 (£52,936 x 10%) which is 10% of the tax unpaid six months after the return was due (since it is stated in the question that the corporation tax liability is paid at the same time the self-assessment tax return is submitted which is eight months late) as the total delay is up to 12 months.

(b)   (i)   The late submission of the VAT return for the quarter ended 30 September 2009 will have resulted in HM Revenue and Customs (HMRC) issuing a surcharge liability notice specifying a surcharge period running to 30 September 2010.

The late payment of VAT for the quarter ended 31 March 2010 will have resulted in a surcharge of £778 (£38,900 x 2%) because this is the first default in the surcharge period. The surcharge period will also have been extended to 31 March 2011.

The late payment of VAT for the quarter ended 31 March 2011 will therefore have resulted in a surcharge of £4,455 (£89,100 x 5%) because this is the second default in the surcharge period. The surcharge period will also have been extended to 31 March 2012.

(ii)   **Annual accounting scheme**

The reduced administration from only having to submit one VAT return each year should mean that default surcharges are avoided in respect of the late submission of VAT returns.

In addition, making payments on account based on the previous year's VAT liability will improve both budgeting and possibly cash flow if Jogger Ltd's business is expanding.

Jogger Ltd can apply to use the annual accounting scheme if its expected taxable turnover for the next 12 months does not exceed £1,350,000 exclusive of VAT.

However, the company must be up to date with its VAT returns before it is allowed to use the scheme.

42 B Ltd

Marking scheme

	Marks
Trading income	½
Capital gains	½
Overseas income	1
Interest income	½
Gift Aid payment	1
FII	1
Profit limits	½
Tax calculation	2
DTR – UK profits	½
Overseas income	½
Average rate of CT	1
DTR set off	1
	10

Corporation tax

	£
Trading income	296,000
Capital gains	30,000
Overseas trading income (× 100/80)	2,000
Interest income	8,000
Total profits	336,000
Less Gift Aid donation	(18,000)
Taxable total profits	318,000
FII	32,000
Augmented profits	350,000

FY 2010

Lower limit = £300,000/ 2 = 150,000
Upper limit = £1,500,000/2 = 750,000

Note. Although B Ltd and W Ltd have only been associated for part of the accounting period, they are deemed to have been associated for the *whole* of the period for the purpose of determining the profit limits. Since there are two associated companies, the upper and lower limits must be divided by two.

Marginal relief applies.

	£
£318,000 × 28%	89,040
Less 7/400 (750,000 − 350,000) × $\dfrac{318,000}{350,000}$	(6,360)
	82,680
Less DTR (W1)	(400)
Corporation tax	82,280

Working: Double tax relief

	UK profits £	Overseas income £	Total £
Total profits	334,000	2,000	336,000
Less Gift Aid	(18,000)	–	(18,000)
Total taxable profits	316,000	2,000	318,000

$$CT \ \frac{82,680}{318,000} = 26\%$$

	UK profits £	Overseas income £	Total £
	82,160	520	82,680

Less DTR
  lower of:
  (i)   UK tax (£520)
  (ii)   Overseas tax (£400)

	UK profits £	Overseas income £	Total £
		(400)	(400)
	82,160	120	82,280

43 Sirius Ltd

Text references. Chapter 20 for corporation tax calculation. Chapter 8 for capital allowances and IBAs. Chapter 22 for CT losses and Chapter 24 for overseas aspects of CT.

Easy marks. You should have been able to get a couple of the points in part (b) and calculate the tax on the permanent establishment for easy marks.

Examiner's comments. This question was quite well answered by many of the candidates. Part (a) caused few problems, and many candidates achieved full marks. When dealing with the branch in part (b), the main problem was only including the profits remitted.

Marking scheme

				Marks
(a)	(i)	Depreciation	½	
		Loss on disposals	½	
		Gift Aid	½	
		Dividends paid/ received	½	
		Capital allowances	4	
		Chargeable gain	1½	
		Capital loss	½	
		Use of trading loss	1	
		CT rate	1	
				10
	(ii)	Tax due dates	1	
		Return submission date	1	
				2
	(iii)	Prior year	1	
		Carry forward	1	
		Best use	1	
				3

<table>
<tr><td>(b)</td><td>CT on branch profits</td><td>1</td><td>Marks</td></tr>
<tr><td></td><td>No CT on dividends received from subsidiary</td><td>1</td><td></td></tr>
<tr><td></td><td>Losses</td><td>1</td><td></td></tr>
<tr><td></td><td>Capital allowances</td><td>1</td><td></td></tr>
<tr><td></td><td>Associated companies</td><td>1</td><td></td></tr>
<tr><td></td><td></td><td></td><td>5</td></tr>
<tr><td>(c)</td><td>Branch</td><td></td><td></td></tr>
<tr><td></td><td>Trading income</td><td>½</td><td></td></tr>
<tr><td></td><td>Overseas income</td><td>1</td><td></td></tr>
<tr><td></td><td>CT</td><td>1½</td><td></td></tr>
<tr><td></td><td>DTR</td><td>1</td><td></td></tr>
<tr><td></td><td></td><td></td><td>4</td></tr>
<tr><td></td><td></td><td></td><td>24</td></tr>
</table>

(a) (i) **Corporation tax computation – year ended 31 March 2011**

	£
Taxable trading profit (W1)	Nil
Net chargeable gain (W3)	1,600,730
Total profits	1,600,730
Less current year loss relief (W1)	(57,520)
	1,543,210
Less Gift Aid donation	(25,000)
Taxable total profits	1,518,210
Add: FII (£180,000 × 100/90)	200,000
Augmented profits	1,718,210

Corporation tax payable (W4)

£1,518,210 × 28% = £425,099

Workings

1 *Taxable trading profits*

	£	£
Loss per accounts		(125,000)
Add depreciation	42,750	
loss on disposal of computer equipment	5,260	
loss on sale of factory	39,500	
gift aid donation paid	25,000	
dividends paid	21,000	
		133,510
Less dividends received		(18,000)
		(9,490)
Less capital allowances (W2)		(48,030)
Adjusted trading loss		(57,520)
Taxable trading profits		Nil

If loss relief is claimed as early as possible, the loss will be set off against total profits of the current period of the year ended 31 March 2011.

2   Capital allowances – year ended 31 March 2011

	AIA £	Main pool £	Expensive car £	SLA £	CAs £
TWDV b/f		42,000	13,000	3,600	
Additions eligible for AIA					
Computer (N1)	12,000				
Van	21,680				
	33,680				
AIA	(33,680)				33,680
Disposal (N2)				(250)	
BA				3,350	3,350
WDA @ 20% (N3)		(8,400)	(2,600)		11,000
TWDV c/f		33,600	10,400		
Total allowances					48,030

Notes

(1)   The computer system is eligible for the AIA in the year of purchase. This means that allowances equal to the full cost are received in this first accounting period. There is no benefit to be obtained by treating it as a SLA.

(2)   The lower of original cost and disposal proceeds is used in the capital allowances computation.

(3)   The private use of the car by the director does not affect the company's allowances, which are given in full. Instead the director will be taxable on the benefit of using the car.

3   Disposal of factory – Net chargeable gain

	£
Proceeds	1,750,000
Less: Cost	(85,000)
Unindexed gain	1,665,000
Less: Indexation allowance	
(226.4 - 171.7)/171.7 = 0.319 × £85,000	(27,115)
Chargeable gain	1,637,885
Capital loss b/f	(37,155)
Net chargeable gain	1,600,730

4   Corporation tax rate

FY 2010 Upper limit = £1,500,000

Augmented profits > £1,500,000, therefore Sirius Ltd is a main rate company for corporation tax purposes.

(ii)   **Due dates**

CT payment

The Corporation tax must be paid in four equal instalments of £106,275 (25%) due on the following dates:

- 14 October 2010
- 14 January 2011
- 14 April 2011 and
- 14 July 2011

Tax return

The return must be submitted by 31 March 2012.

(iii) **Use of trading loss**

Sirius Ltd has two options available for its trading loss:

(1)   Carry forward to set off against the first available future trade profits only; and

(2)   Set off against total profits of the current accounting period (as above).

Sirius Ltd cannot carry back the loss to the previous period as there is not enough loss to carry back. A carry back claim can only be made if the current year's taxable total profits has been fully relieved first.

The anticipated profits for the next year are below the corporation tax limit of £300,000 ignoring the possible foreign subsidiary (or £150,000 if a foreign subsidiary is set up). Sirius Ltd would therefore only save tax at 21% and the relief would be obtained at a later date.

The best solution is therefore a current year claim as above, which saves tax at 28%.

(b)   The profits of the branch will be subject to UK corporation tax on an arising basis. Double taxation relief will be available.

A UK company may receive dividends from its non UK subsidiary. The dividends will be exempt from corporation tax.

If the overseas operation trades at a loss, UK tax relief will only be available if it is a branch, not a subsidiary.

Capital allowances will only be available to a branch, not to a subsidiary.

In the case of a subsidiary, it will be an associated company and so will reduce the corporation tax limits.

(c)   **Sirius Ltd's UK corporation tax liability for y/e 31 March 2012 if overseas operation is set up as branch**

	£
Trading income	105,000
Overseas income	200,000
Taxable total profits	305,000
CT @ 28%	85,400
Less marginal relief	
£(1,500,000 – 305,000) × 7/400	(20,913)
	64,487
Less DTR lower of:	
(1) $\dfrac{200,000}{305,000}$ × £64,487= £42,287	
(2) £40,000, ie	(40,000)
Corporation tax liability	24,487

44 A Ltd

Marking scheme

		Marks
(a)	Trading income	½
	Property business income	½
	Interest income	½
	Gift aid	1
	Group relief	3
	FII	½
	CT calculation	2
		8
(b)	Payment date	1
(c)	Filing date	1
		10

(a) **Corporation Tax computation 9 m/e 31 December 2010**

	£	£
Trading income		342,000
Property income		10,000
Interest income		16,000
Total profits		368,000
Less: Gift Aid donation		(17,000)
		351,000
Less: group relief (W1)		(34,000)
Taxable total profits		317,000
Add: Franked Investment Income		1,000
Augmented profits		318,000

	£
Corporation tax	
FY 2010	
£317,000 × 28%	88,760
Less marginal relief	
7/400 (£562,500 – 318,000) × $\frac{317,000}{318,000}$	(4,265)
Corporation tax payable	84,495

Note. It is assumed that the loan interest arose on a non-trading loan and is therefore taxable as interest income.

Workings

1   B Ltd joined the group with A Ltd on 1 July 2010 so for A Ltd's profit making accounting period to 31 December 2010 there are 6 months in common with B Ltd's loss making period.

Thus

A Ltd   6/9 × £351,000 = £234,000
B Ltd   6/12 × (£68,000) = £34,000

Maximum group relief available is lower of two, ie £34,000.

2   The 9 months to 31 December 2010 falls into FY 2010.

      Augmented profits are between the upper and lower limits of £1,500,000 × 9/12 ÷ 2 = £562,500 and
      £300,000 × 9/12 ÷ 2 = £112,500, so marginal relief applies.

(b)   The corporation tax of £84,495 for the nine-month period ended 31 December 2010 must be paid by
      <u>1 October 2011</u>.

(c)   The corporation tax return for the nine-month period ended 31 December 2010 must be filed by
      <u>31 December 2011</u>.

45 Gold Ltd

Text references. Chapters 19 and 20 for corporation tax computation and Chapter 8 for capital allowances. Group relief is dealt with in Chapter 23.

Top tips. You may want to draw a simple diagram showing the accounting periods of each company and how they overlap.

Easy marks. Part (c) required a list of the allocation of group relief which did not need to be related to the facts of the question and therefore should have been answerable even if the figure work in the other parts of the question was not correct.

Drawing a diagram matching profits of the corresponding periods is a good way to ensure you answer the question correctly and gain all the marks. Such a drawing is a perfectly acceptable part of your workings and should be handed in as part of your answer to the examiner.

Examiner's comments. In part (b) many candidates had problems in calculating the group relief for non-coterminous periods. Part (c) was well answered by most candidates. In part (d), the majority of candidates did not appreciate that group relief should be restricted to bring the holding company's profits down to the small profits lower limit.

Marking scheme

			Marks
(a)	Depreciation	½	
	Dividends	½	
	Deduct CAs/ IBAs	1	
	P&M – Main pool	3	
	– Car sold	1	
	– SLA	2	
	– Special rate pool	1½	
	WDAs	2	
	IBA – land	1	
	– offices	1½	
	– WDA	<u>1</u>	
			15
(b)	Trading income	½	
	Property business income/capital gain	½	
	Gift aid donation	1	
	Group relief – year ended 31 December 2009	1½	
	– year ended 31 December 2010	1½	
	Associated company	1	
	Corporation tax	<u>2</u>	
			8

					Marks
(c)	Marginal rate			1	
	Main rate			½	
	Small profits rate			½	
	Loss of Gift Aid relief			1	
	Other considerations			1	
					4
(d)	Year ended 31 December 2009 (Gold Ltd)			1	
	Year ended 31 December 2010 (Gold Ltd)			1	
	Year ended 30 June 2009 (Silver Ltd)			1	
					3
					30

(a) **Trade loss year ended 30 June 2010**

	£	£
Loss before taxation		(50,950)
Add depreciation		35,160
		(15,790)
Less dividend income	116,514	
capital allowances (W1)	6,400	
IBAs (W2)	1,473	
		(124,387)
Trade loss		(140,177)

Workings

1 *Capital allowances*

	Main pool £	Exp car (1) £	SLA £	Special rate pool £	Allowances £
TWDV b/f	46,650	11,750	2,700		
Additions not qualifying for AIA					
31 August 2009 car (2)				23,250	
12 November 2009 car (3)	9,500				
Disposals					
5 July 2009 car (1)		(18,700)			
7 October 2009 van (restrict to cost)	(11,750)				
16 April 2010 SLA			(555)		
	44,400				
BC		(6,950)			(6,950)
BA			2,145		2,145
WDA @ 20%	(8,880)				8,880
WDA @ 10%				(2,325)	2,325
TWDV c/f	35,520			20,925	
Allowances					6,400

2   *Industrial buildings allowance*

		£
Total cost		295,000
Less land		(85,000)
Cost of building		210,000

Offices represent $\dfrac{£62,750}{£210,000}$ = 29.88% of the cost of the building. As this is greater than 25% IBAs

can only be claimed on £147,250 (£210,000 – £62,750).

IBA = £147,250 × 1% = £1,473

(b)   **Gold Ltd – Corporation tax computation**

	Year ended 31 December	
	2009	*2010*
	£	£
Trading income	177,000	90,000
Property business income	5,000	–
Capital gain	–	12,000
Total profits	182,000	102,000
Less Gift Aid donation	(2,000)	(2,000)
	180,000	100,000
Less group relief (W1)	(70,089)	(50,000)
Taxable total profits	109,911	50,000
CT (FYs 08,09,10)		
Small profits rate applies @ 21%	23,081	10,500

Working

Gold Ltd

Loss making period

For year ended 31 December 2009 profits of the corresponding period (1 July 2009 to 31 December 2009) are £180,000 × 6/12 = £90,000 and the corresponding loss is £140,177 × 6/12 = £70,089.

Therefore maximum group relief is £70,089.

For year ended 31 December 2010, profits of the corresponding period (1 January 2010 to 30 June 2010) are £100,000 × 6/12 = £50,000 and the corresponding loss is £70,089.

Therefore maximum group relief is £50,000.

(c)   Group relief should be allocated in the following order:

(1)   To companies in the small profits marginal relief band to bring them down to the small profits rate limit.

(2)   To companies paying the main rate.

(3)   To companies paying the small profits rate.

Consideration should also be given to the loss of Gift Aid relief.

Subject to the above considerations, loss relief should be claimed as early as possible.

(d)   The group relief claim should be restricted to £30,000 for the year ended 31 December 2009 to bring the taxable total profits to the lower limit of £150,000. No claim should be made for year ended 31 December 2010 since the taxable total profits is already below £150,000. Instead the remainder of the loss £(140,177 – 30,000) = £110,177 should be carried back against Silver Ltd's own profit for year ended 30 June 2009 which is mostly taxable at the marginal rate.

46 Apple Ltd

Text references. Corporation tax computations are covered in Chapter 20. Chargeable gains for companies are dealt with in Chapters 21. Group relief is covered in Chapter 23.

Top tips. When using losses, consider the marginal rates of tax of each company.

			Marks
(a)	*Taxable total profits*		
	Apple – Trading profits	1	
	– Capital gains	1	
	Bramley Ltd's Loss	1	
	Cox Ltd's loss	1	
	Delicious Ltd's loss	1	
			5
(b)	*Corporation tax saving*		
	Capital loss – use in Apple Ltd	2	
	Rollover relief	1	
	Proceeds not reinvested still chargeable	1	
	Corporation tax saving	1	
	Use of Bramley Ltd's loss	2	
	Use of Cox Ltd's loss	2	
	Delicious Ltd's loss – not advantageous to transfer	1	
			10
			15

(a)   **Apple Ltd**

	Years ended 31 March		
	2010	2011	2012
	£	£	£
Trading profits	620,000	250,000	585,000
Capital gain	–	120,000	80,000
Taxable total profits	620,000	370,000	665,000

Bramley Ltd

	Years ended 31 March		
	2010	2011	2012
	£	£	£
Trading profits/total profits	–	52,000	70,000
Less: carry forward loss relief	–	(52,000)	(12,000)
Taxable total profits	–	–	58,000

Cox Ltd

	Years ended 31 March		
	2010	*2011*	*2012*
	£	£	£
Trading profits/total profits	83,000	–	40,000
Less: carry back loss relief	(58,000)	–	–
Taxable total profits	25,000	–	40,000

Delicious Ltd

	Years ended 31 March		
	2010	*2011*	*2012*
	£	£	£
Trading profits/total profits	–	90,000	–
Less: carry back loss relief	–	(15,000)	–
Taxable total profits	–	75,000	–

(b) **Apple Ltd**

	Years ended 31 March		
	2010	*2011*	*2012*
	£	£	£
Trading profits	620,000	250,000	585,000
Chargeable gain	–	20,000	36,000
Total profits	620,000	270,000	621,000
Less group relief	(64,000)	(58,000)	(0)
Taxable total profits	556,000	212,000	621,000

In the year to 31 March 2010 group relief has been claimed for Bramley Ltd's loss. This saves Apple Ltd corporation tax of £17,920 (£64,000 × 28%). If the loss had been carried forward as shown above it would have saved Bramley Ltd tax of £13,440 (21% × £64,000). The overall tax saving to the group arising as a result of the group relief claim is £4,480.

Rollover relief has been claimed to defer £100,000 of the chargeable gain arising in the year to 31 March 2011. The £20,000 gain remaining chargeable is equal to the amount of proceeds not reinvested by Cox Ltd in the freehold factory. The lower limit for the year to 31 March 2011 is £75,000 so the rollover relief saves Apple Ltd corporation tax of £29,750 (£100,000 × 29.75%).

It is assumed that Delicious Ltd and Apple Ltd will make an election to transfer the loss on the leasehold factory to Apple Ltd. If this occurs, Apple Ltd will be able to relieve the £44,000 loss by setting it against its chargeable gain for the year, saving tax of £12,320 (£44,000 × 28%).

In the year to 31 March 2011 group relief has been claimed for Cox Ltd's loss. This saves corporation tax of £17,255 (£58,000 × 29.75%). If the loss had been carried back as shown above, it would have saved Cox Ltd corporation tax of £12,180 (£58,000 × 21%). The overall tax saving to the group of a group relief claim is therefore £5,075 (£17,255 − £12,180).

Delicious Ltd could surrender its loss of £15,000 in the year to 31 March 2012 to Cox Ltd. This would not be beneficial as the tax saving would be at 21% whereas the tax saving will be at 29.75% if the carry back relief claim shown in (a) above is made.

47 Tock-Tick Ltd

Text references. Calculation of taxable total profits and corporation tax in Chapters 19 and 20. Capital allowances covered in Chapter 8. Group relief is covered in Chapter 23. Rollover relief in Chapter 21.

Top tips. Make sure you know the tax consequences of a company being in different type of group and can apply the rules accordingly.

Easy marks. Part (a) was an adjustment of profits with many standard items to adjust for easy marks. Always show workings and state why you are/are not adjusting profits for items in the question to gain all possible marks (see examiner's comments below). Follow question requirements carefully, for example calculation of CT was **not** required. Don't waste your time and effort doing things the examiner doesn't ask for – no marks for doing this.

Examiner's comments. This question was generally very well answered, with many candidates achieving maximum marks. Parts (a) and (b) caused few problems. However, some candidates lost marks by not showing their workings for disallowed items when calculating the trading profit. Many candidates wasted time by calculating the corporation tax liability when this was not required. It was pleasing to see that part (c) was also generally well answered, given that the areas covered were not so straightforward as those in parts (a) and (b).

Marking scheme

			Marks
(a)	Depreciation	½	
	Impairment losses (½ each)	1½	
	Gifts (½ each)	1	
	Long service award	½	
	Donations (½ each)	1½	
	Professional fees (½ each)	3	
	Repairs and renewals (½ each)	1	
	Other expenses (½ each)	1½	
	Disposal of office building	½	
	Loan interest received	½	
	Interest payable	½	
	Capital allowances – Pool	1½	
	– AIA	½	
	– Expensive motor car	2	
	– Short-life asset sold	1½	
	– FYA @ 100%	1	
	– Deduct to compute trading income	½	
			19
(b)	Trading income	½	
	Interest income	1	
	Capital gain	2	
	Gift aid donation	1½	
			5
(c)	**Group relief**		
	Group relief claim	2	
	Taxable total profits effect	1	
	Rollover relief		
	Rollover relief claim	2	
	Taxable total profits effect	1	
			6
			30

(a)   **Tock-Tick Ltd – trading income**

		£	£
Profit before taxation			186,960
Add	depreciation	99,890	
	impairment loss – recovery from previous years	0	
	impairment loss – trade	0	
	impairment loss – non-trade	6,200	
	gifts to customers – pens (N1)	0	
	gifts to customers – hampers (N1)	720	
	long service award	0	
	gift aid donation (N2)	600	
	donation to national charity – not gift aid	250	
	donation to local charity	0	
	accountancy fees	0	
	legal fees – share capital issue	2,900	
	legal fees – registering trademark	0	
	legal fees – renewing short lease	0	
	legal fees – debt collection	0	
	legal fees – court action	900	
	repairs and renewals – roof (N3)	0	
	repairs and renewals – extension (N3)	53,300	
	other expenses – counselling on redundancy	0	
	other expenses – seconding employee to charity	0	
	other expenses – customer entertaining	2,160	
			166,920
			353,880
Less:	profit on disposal of office building	78,100	
	loan interest	12,330	
	CAs (W)	13,380	
			(103,810)
Trading income			250,070

Notes

(1)   The gifts of pens are allowable as they cost less than £50 per recipient in the tax year and carry a conspicuous advertisement for the company making the gift. The hampers are not allowed as they are food gifts.

(2)   If a donation has been made under the gift aid scheme this is deductible from total income.

(3)   The cost of the extension is capital expenditure and therefore is not allowable. The replacement of the roof should be fully allowable so long as it can be shown that the company could not carry on its business at the premises without the repair.

Working: Capital allowances

	FYA@ 100% £	AIA £	Main pool £	Exp car £	SLA £	Allowances £
TWDV b/f			12,200	20,800	3,100	
Additions qualifying for AIA						
15.8.10 Equipment		6,700				
AIA		(6,700)				6,700
Disposals						
28.5.10 Car (cost)				(33,600)		
BC				(12,800)		(12,800)
1.8.10 SLA					(460)	
BA					2,640	2,640
WDA @ 20%			(2,440)			2,440
Additions qualifying for FYA						
7.6.10 Car	14,400					
FYA @ 100%	(14,400)					14,400
TWDV c/f			9,760			
Allowances						13,380

(b) **Taxable total profits**

	£
Trading income	250,070 $\circlearrowleft$
Interest income (N)	12,330
Chargeable gain (W)	30,802
Total profits	293,202
Less gift aid donation	(600)
Taxable total profits	292,602

Note. Interest received is taxed as interest income on accruals basis.

Working

Chargeable gain	£
Proceeds	300,925
Less: cost	(197,900)
Unindexed gain	103,025
Less: IA	(72,223)
Indexed gain	30,802

(c) (i) **Group relief**

Only 9 months of the two companies' accounting periods overlap (1 April 2010 to 31 December 2010) and therefore the maximum group relief available would be the lower of:

(a)   9/12 × Tock-Tick's taxable total profits of £292,602 ie £219,452; and

(b)   9/12 × subsidiary's loss of £62,400 ie £46,800.

Therefore Tock-Tick Ltd's total profits before gift aid of £293,202 would be reduced by £46,800 to £246,402. Its taxable total profits would therefore be reduced to £245,802.

(ii) **Rollover relief**

The sale proceeds of the disposal of the freehold office building (£300,925) are partially reinvested in the new office building (£284,925).

To the extent that they are not reinvested, £(300,925 – 284,925) = £16,000, the gain remains in charge.

The balance of the gain (£30,802 – 16,000) = £14,802 can be rolled over and thus reduce the company's taxable total profits by that amount.

48 Sofa Ltd

> **Text references.** Chapter 19 deals with adjustment of profit for companies. Chapter 23 covers groups.
>
> **Top tips.** Make sure you read the information given in the question very carefully. You were told the figure to start your adjustment of profit.
>
> **Easy marks.** The capital allowances computation was straightforward if you used the standard format. The items to be disallowed should also have been well-known.
>
> **Examiner's comments.** Part (a) of this question was very well answered with only the calculation of the industrial buildings allowance consistently causing problems. A certain amount of bad examination technique was evident as regards the adjustments in computing the trading loss. Some candidates went into far too much detail explaining the adjustments made, thus wasting time, whilst others produced figures without any workings at all. Where no adjustment was necessary, such as for the interest payable, then this fact should have been clearly shown or stated. Most candidates did not answer part (b) very well. Many candidates wasted a lot time by performing detailed calculations showing the amount of group relief that should have been claimed rather than the amount that actually could be claimed.

		Marks
(a)	**Adjustment to profit**	
	Loss before taxation	½
	Depreciation	½
	Accountancy fees	½
	Legal fees – share capital	½
	Legal fees – renewal of short lease	½
	Legal fees – loan relationship	½
	New wall	½
	Repair to existing wall	½
	Business entertaining	½
	Staff entertaining	½
	Redundancy counselling	½
	Health and safety fine	½
	Profit on sale of shares	½
	Bank interest receivable	½
	Debenture interest payable	1
	Capital allowances on P&M	
	TWDVs b/f	½
	Additions qualifying for AIA: equipment	½
	fixtures	½
	AIA	1
	Special rate pool	1
	Disposals	1
	Balancing charge on car	1
	WDAs	1
	Additions qualifying for FYA: low emission car	½
	FYA @ 100%	½
	TWDVs c/f	½
	Allowances	1
	Industrial buildings allowance	
	Eligible expenditure	1
	Showroom	1
	WDA	1
		20

(b)   **Settee Ltd**

Availability of group relief	½
Corresponding period 1	1
Corresponding period 2	1
Couch Ltd	
No group relief – not in 75% group	1
Futon Ltd	
Availability of group relief	½
Corresponding period	<u>1</u>
	<u>5</u>
	<u>25</u>

(a)   **Sofa Ltd – tax adjusted trading loss**

	£	£
Loss before taxation		(217,800)
Add: depreciation	87,100	
professional fees: accountancy and audit	0	
professional fees (N1): share capital	7,800	
professional fees (N1): renewal of short lease	0	
professional fees (N1): issue of debentures	0	
repairs and renewals (N2): new wall	9,700	
repairs and renewals (N2): repair to existing wall	0	
other expenses (N3): entertaining suppliers	1,360	
other expenses (N3): entertaining employees	0	
other expenses (N3): counselling on redundancy	0	
other expenses (N3): fine	<u>420</u>	106,380
		(111,420)
Less: profit on sale of shares	3,300	
bank interest – taxed as interest income	8,400	
CAs on plant and machinery (W1)	65,280	
IBAs (W2)	<u>4,000</u>	<u>(80,980)</u>
Tax adjusted trading loss		(192,400)

Notes

1   The legal fees related to the renewal of a short lease (less than 50 years) are allowable. The cost of obtaining loan finance is allowable as a trading expense under the loan relationship rules as the loan was used for trading purposes. The cost of legal fees relating to the issue of share capital is not allowable as it is a capital expense.

2   The cost of the new wall is not allowable because it is a capital expense. The repair to the existing wall is allowable as a revenue expense.

3   Business entertaining is not allowable. Staff entertaining is allowable. Counselling on redundancy is specifically allowable. The health and safety fine is not allowable.

Workings

1 *Capital allowances on plant and machinery*

	FYA @ 100%	AIA	Main pool	Exp. car	Special rate pool	Allowances
	£	£	£	£	£	£
TWDV b/f			27,800	16,400		
Additions qualifying for AIA						
12.5.10 Equipment		1,400				
10.2.11 Fixtures (N)		44,800				
		46,200				
AIA		(46,200)				46,200
Additions not qualifying for AIA						
8.6.10 Car					22,200	
2.8.10			10,900			
Disposals						
8.6.10 Car				(17,800)		
BC				(1,400)		(1,400)
8.1.11 Lorry			(7,600)			
18.1.11 Car			(8,800)			
			22,300			
WDA @ 20%			(4,460)			4,460
WDA @ 10%					(2,220)	2,220
Additions qualifying for FYA @ 100%						
19.10.10 Car	13,800					
FYA @ 100%	(13,800)					13,800
TWDV c/f			17,840		19,980	
Allowances						65,280

Note

The sale price put on the fixtures can be an amount up to their original cost. Since it has been agreed that Sofa Ltd is to obtain maximum capital allowances on the fixtures, the election must have been the maximum amount possible.

2 *Industrial buildings allowance*

	£
Original cost	558,000
Less: cost of land	(158,000)
Eligible expenditure (note)	400,000

Note

The cost of the showroom is allowable because it is less than 25% of the eligible cost (£400,000 × 25% = £100,000).

WDA = £400,000 × 1% = £4,000

(b)   **Settee Ltd**

Group relief is available between Sofa Ltd and Settee Ltd because they are part of a 75% group.

Group relief applies to corresponding accounting periods.

Corresponding period 1 (1 April 2010 to 30 June 2010)
Loss of Sofa Ltd
3/12 × £192,400   £48,100

Profit of Settee Ltd
3/12 × £240,000   £60,000

Maximum group relief is lower of these two figures ie   £48,100

Corresponding period 2 (1 July 2010 to 31 March 2011)
Loss of Sofa Ltd
9/12 × £192,400   £144,300

Profit of Settee Ltd
9/12 × £90,000   £67,500

Maximum group relief is lower of these two figures ie   £67,500

Couch Ltd

There is no group relief available between Sofa Ltd and Couch Ltd because they are not members of a 75% group as Couch Ltd is only a 60% subsidiary.

Futon Ltd

Group relief is available between Sofa Ltd and Futon Ltd because they are part of a 75% group.

Corresponding period (1 January 2011 to 31 March 2011)
Loss of Sofa Ltd
3/12 × £192,400   £48,100

Profit of Futon Ltd   £60,000

Maximum group relief is lower of these two figures ie   £48,100

49 Gastron Ltd

Text references. Chapter 19 deals with adjustment of profit for companies. Chapter 23 covers groups.

Top tips. Make sure that you attempt all parts of a multi-part question such as this.

Easy marks. Once again, the administration aspects of this question should have yielded easy marks.

Examiner's comments. This question was very well answered, with only part (e) consistently causing problems. In part (a) candidates were instructed to list all of the items referred to in the notes, and to indicate by the use of zero any items that did not require adjustment. Candidates are advised that this will be a standard approach in future and they should ensure they follow this instruction to be able to score full marks. Despite the instruction some candidates did not list those items not requiring any adjustment. Parts (a) and (b) were kept separate for a very good reason – namely to help candidates. Therefore those candidates who attempted to combine both parts into one calculation not surprisingly often had problems. It was pleasing to see many candidates correctly calculate the correct figure for capital allowances. Although I can applaud candidate's attempts to save paper, it is not good examination technique to try and squeeze a capital allowances computation of this size into 5 or 6 lines at the end of a page. In part (c) a disappointing number of candidates gave 31 January as the payment date. Only a few candidates appreciated that interest would be due, and fewer still correctly calculated the actual amount payable. In part (d) most candidates appreciated that a 75% shareholding was necessary, but were then often unsure where the 50% limit fitted in. The holding company must have an effective interest of 50%. In part (e) many candidates simply stated that losses could be set against profits, without making any attempt to use the information given in the question.

Marks

(a)
Profit before taxation	½
Depreciation	½
Amortisation of leasehold property	½
Gifts of pens to customers	½
Gifts of hampers to customers	½
Donation	½
Legal fees re renewal of lease	½
Legal fees re issue of debentures	½
Entertaining suppliers	½
Entertaining employees	½
Lease premium – Assessable amount	1½
– Deduction	1
Income from investments	1
Disposal of shares	½
Interest payable	½
P & M – Pool with WDA	2
– AIA	1½
– Expensive motor car	1
– FYA @ 100%	1

15

(b)
Trading profit	½
Property business profit	2
Bank interest	½
Chargeable gain	½
Franked investment income	1
Group dividends	½
Corporation tax	2

7

(c)
Due date	1
Interest	2

3

(d)
75% shareholding	1
50% effective interest	1

2

(e)
Time limit	1
Set off of capital losses	1
Tax rate	1

3

30

(a)   **Gastron Ltd – Trading profit for the year ended 31 March 2011**

	£	£
Profit before taxation		640,000
Add		
Depreciation	85,660	
Amortisation of leasehold property	6,000	
Gifts of pens to customers (N1)	1,200	
Gifts of hampers to customers (N1)	1,100	
Donation to local charity	0	
Legal fees re renewal of lease (N2)	0	
Legal fees re issue of debentures	0	
Entertaining suppliers (N3)	1,300	
Entertaining employees (N3)	0	
		95,260
Deduct		
Lease premium (W1)	4,920	
Income from property	20,600	
Bank interest	12,400	
Dividends	54,000	
Profit on disposal of shares	80,700	
Interest payable (N4)	0	
Capital allowances (W2)	62,640	
		(235,260)
Trading profit		500,000

Notes

1   Gifts to customers are only an allowable deduction if they cost less than £50 per recipient per year, are not of food, drink, tobacco, or vouchers for exchangeable goods, and carry a conspicuous advertisement for the company making the gift.

2   The costs of renewing a short-lease (less than 50 years) and of obtaining loan finance are allowable.

3   The only exception to the non-deductibility of entertainment expenditure is when it is in respect of employees.

4   Interest on a loan used for trading purposes is deductible in calculating the trading loss on an accruals basis.

Workings

1   The office building has been used for business purposes, and so the proportion of the lease premium assessed on the landlord can be deducted, spread over the life of the lease.

The amount assessed on the landlord is £49,600 calculated as follows:

	£
Premium received	60,000
Less: £60,000 × 2% × (10 – 1)	(10,800)
	49,200

This is deductible over the life of the lease, so the deduction for the year ended 31 March 2010 is £(49,200/10) = £4,920.

2   *Plant and machinery*

	FYA @ 100% £	AIA £	Main pool £	Expensive motor car £	Allowances £
TWDV b/f			16,700	18,400	
Additions qualifying for AIA					
Equipment		21,600			
Lorry		17,200			
		38,800			
AIA		(38,800)			38,800
Addition not qualifying for AIA					
Motor car			9,800		
			26,500		
Disposal					
Equipment (N)			(3,300)		
			23,200		
WDA @ 20%			(4,640)		4,640
WDA – restricted				(3,000)	3,000
			18,560		
Addition qualifying for 100% FYA					
Motor car	16,200				
FYA @ 100%	(16,200)				16,200
TWDV c/f			18,560	15,400	
Total allowances					62,640

Note. The cost of the equipment sold will have originally been added to the pool, so the disposal proceeds of £3,300 are deducted from the pool.

(b)   **Gastron Ltd – Corporation tax computation for the year ended 31 March 2011**

	£
Trading profit	500,000
Property business profit (W1)	12,800
Bank interest	12,400
Chargeable gain	74,800
Taxable total profits	600,000
Franked investment income £36,000 × 100/90 (N)	40,000
Augmented profits	640,000
Corporation tax £600,000 @ 28%	168,000
Marginal relief 7/400 (750,000 – 640,000) × 600,000/640,000 (W2)	(1,805)
	166,195

Note
Group dividends are not included as franked investment income.

Workings

1   The property business profit is £12,800 calculated as follows:

	£	£
Rent receivable – First tenant £1,800 × 9		16,200
– Second tenant £1,950 × 2		3,900
		20,100
Impairment loss £1,800 × 2	3,600	
Decorating	3,700	
		(7,300)
		12,800

2   Gastron Ltd has one associated company, so the upper limit is reduced to £750,000 (£1,500,000/2).

(c) (1) Gastron Ltd's corporation tax liability for the year ended 31 March 2011 must be paid by 1 January 2012.

(2) If the company does not pay its corporation tax until 31 August 2012, then interest of £166,195 @ 3% × 8/12 = £3,324 will be charged by HM Revenue and Customs for the period between 1 January 2012 and 31 August 2012.

(d) (1) Companies form a capital gains group if at each level in the group structure there is a 75% shareholding.

(2) However, the parent company must also have an effective interest of over 50% in each group company.

(e) (1) Gastron Ltd and Culinary Ltd must make the election by 31 March 2013 (within two years of the end of the accounting period in the gain arose).

(2) The election will enable the capital gain of £74,800 to be set off against capital loss of £66,000.

(3) It is also beneficial for the balance of the chargeable gain of £(74,800 – 66,000) = £8,800 to arise in Culinary Ltd as it will only be taxed at the rate of 21%, instead of at the marginal rate (29.75%) in Gastron Ltd.

50 Lithograph Ltd

Text references. Chapters 26 and 27 deal with VAT.

Top tips. Read the question carefully to determine whether the figures you have been given include the VAT or not.

Marking scheme

			Marks
(a)	Monthly payments	½	
	Based on prior year	½	
	10%	½	
	Months 4 to 12	½	
	Calculation	1	
			3
(b)	(i)	Sales @ 17.5%	½
		Office equipment sale @ 17.5%	½
		Fuel scale charge @ 7/47	1
		Purchases	½
		Expenses	½
		Machinery	½
		Bad debt	1
		Output VAT less input VAT @ 17.5%	½
			5
	(ii)	Balancing payment	1
		Due date	1
			2
			10

(a) **Monthly payments on account**

As Lithograph Ltd uses the annual accounting scheme it will be paying monthly payments on account based on its previous year's liability.

It will make payments in months 4 to 12 of its VAT accounting period, each payment being 10% of the previous year's liability.

Lithograph Ltd will therefore have made payments of 10% x £10,200 = £1,020 from April 2010 to December 2010.

(b) (i) **VAT for y/e 31 December 2010**

	£		£
Output VAT			
Sales	160,000	@ 17.5%	28,000
Office equipment sale	8,000	@ 17.5%	1,400
Fuel scale charge (N1)	1,385	@ $^7/_{47}$	206
			29,606
Less: Input VAT			
Purchases	38,000		
Expenses			
28,000 – 3,600 (N2)	24,400		
Machinery purchase	24,000		
Bad debt (N3)	4,800		
	91,200	@ 17.5%	(15,960)
VAT due			13,646

Notes

1 Fuel scale charge

As the whole of the fuel VAT expense, including private fuel, has been deducted (included in the expenses) we need to restrict by using the fuel scale charge.

As this is a VAT inclusive figure we need to adjust by multiplying by $^7/_{47}$

2 Expenses

Customer entertaining is never allowable for VAT purposes.

3 Bad debt

As the debt is over 6 months old and has been written off in the company's books, it is possible to claim bad debt relief.

(ii) **Balancing payment and due date**

The balancing payment due would be:

	£
VAT due	13,646
Less: paid on account (9 payments)	(9,180)
Due by 28 February 2011	4,466

51 Tardy Ltd

> **Text references.** VAT is covered in Chapters 26 and 27.
>
> **Top tips.** Do not ignore the administrative side of VAT as most exam questions will test both numerical and written aspects of the tax.
>
> **Easy marks.** Bad debts are often examined and the conditions and how to deal with the debts should have been easy marks. The examiner frequently mentions that students are weak at applying their knowledge to the given facts in a question. Part (a) dealt with default surcharge. You need to outline which returns were in default but **also** discuss the impact of the default. There were 7 marks for doing this – easy marks for the knowledgeable student.
>
> **Examiner's comments.** Part (a) caused problems for a number of candidates. The main problem was that candidates explained the default surcharge rules, without applying them to the information given. Many candidates did not appreciate that the submission of four consecutive VAT returns on time resulted in a clean default surcharge record.

Marking scheme

			Marks
(a)	Quarter ended 30 September 2008	1	
	Quarter ended 31 December 2008	1	
	Quarter ended 30 June 2009	1½	
	Quarter ended 30 September 2009	1	
	Extension of surcharge period	½	
	Four consecutive VAT returns on time	1	
	Quarter ended 31 December 2010	1	
			7
(b)	Limits for errors that can be corrected on next VAT return	2	
	Notify in writing	1	
			3
			10

(a) Surcharge Liability Notices

Following the first default for the quarter ended 30 September 2008, a Surcharge Liability Notice (SLN) will have been issued for a period of 12 months ie to 30 September 2009. There is no penalty at this stage.

When Tardy Ltd defaulted for the quarter ended 31 December 2008, which fell within the SLN period, there will have been a surcharge of 2% of the outstanding tax, ie £644 (£32,200 × 2%). The SLN period would have been extended until 31 December 2009.

Tardy Ltd is late again for the quarter ended 30 June 2009. The SLN period will now extend until 30 June 2010. The surcharge would strictly be 5% of the unpaid VAT, £170 (as it is the second default within the period to 31 December 2009). However, as this is would be less than the de minimis limit of £400, no surcharge assessment would have been issued.

The next return for the quarter ended 30 September 2009 is also late, so the SLN period would be extended to 30 September 2010. However there would be no surcharge as there is a repayment due and only late payment incurs a surcharge.

The next four returns for the period to 30 September 2010 are submitted on time and therefore the SLN period expires on 30 September 2010.

The return for the quarter ended 31 December 2010 is late. The company has had a clean record for one whole 12 months period and therefore the SLN period starts again, running to 31 December 2011, and there will be no surcharge for this default.

(b)   **Disclosure of Errors**

Errors can be corrected on the next VAT return if they do not exceed the greater of

- £10,000 (net error)
- 1% of net VAT turnover for the return period (maximum £50,000).

Other errors should be notified to HMRC in writing eg by letter.

52 Ram-Rom Ltd

Text references. VAT is dealt with in Chapters 26 and 27.

Top tips. In part (a) you are given the input VAT recoverable so you must make sure that your answer reconciles with this figure. For part (b), make a rough list of the contents of the VAT invoice and then see which items are missing from the sample invoice given.

Easy marks. There were plenty of easy marks in this question. You should have been able to work out the items for part (a) since the examiner gave the amount of input tax recovered. Discounts are often examined, so you should ensure that you are very familiar with them.

Examiner's comments. Candidates often failed to show their workings of how they calculated pre-registration input VAT.

			Marks
(a)	Goods – explanation	1	
	– stock	½	
	– fixed assets	1½	
	Services – explanation	½	
	– calculation	1½	5
(b)	Registration number	½	
	Invoice number	½	
	Rate of VAT	½	
	VAT exclusive amount	½	
	Total VAT exclusive price	½	
	Total VAT	½	3
(c)	Charge to VAT	1	
	No change if not taken up	1	2
			10

(a)   Input VAT recovery – pre registration inputs

Input VAT is recoverable on goods if they are:

- Acquired within 4 years prior to registration
- For business purposes
- Not supplied onwards or consumed prior to registration

	£
Fixed assets – January 2010 acquisition £42,000 × 17.5%	7,350
– August 2010 acquisition £66,600 × 17.5%	11,655
Stock still held £92,000 × 17.5%	16,100
Input VAT on goods recoverable	35,105

Input VAT is recoverable on services if they are:

- Supplied within six months prior to registration
- For purposes of business

	£
March 2010	7,400
April 2010	6,300
May 2010	8,500
June 2010	9,000
July 2010	9,200
August 2010	8,200
	48,600

$\times$ 17.5% = £8,505

Total VAT recoverable £(35,105 + 8,505) = £43,610

(b) Alterations to invoice – must include

- Registration number
- Invoice number
- Rate of VAT for each supply of goods
- VAT exclusive amount for each supply of goods
- Total invoice price excluding VAT
- The total amount of VAT

(c) Where a discount is offered for prompt payment, VAT is chargeable on the net amount, regardless of whether the discount is taken up.

53 Sandy Brick

Text references. Chapters 26 and 27 for VAT.

Top tips. As with any question which requires a calculation, setting out the figures in a proforma will help both you and the examiner marking your paper.

Easy marks. The tax point and invoice issuing rules were easy marks.

Examiner's comments. Well answered but some candidates were penalised for not clearly showing which of their calculations were output VAT and which were input VAT.

	Marks
Sales – VAT registered customers	1½
– Non-VAT registered customers	1½
Advance payment	1
Materials	1
Office equipment	2
Telephone	1
Motor repairs	1
Equipment	1
	10

VAT return

	£	£
Output VAT		
Sales to VAT registered customers		
£(44,000 × 95%) = £41,800 × 20%		8,360
Sales to non-VAT registered customers		
£(16,920 − 5,170) = £11,750 × 1/6		1,958
Payment on account		
£5,000 × 1/6		833
Total output VAT		11,151
Less: Input VAT		
Materials £(11,200 − 800) = £10,400 × 20%	2,080	
Office equipment £(21 x 6) + £(24 x 3) (N1)	198	
Telephone £(400 × 70%) = 280 × 20%	56	
Motor repairs £920 × 20% (N2)	184	
Equipment £6,000 × 20%	1,200	(3,718)
Net VAT payable		7,433

Notes

(1) Pre-registration VAT can be recovered on services for six months before the registration date. Therefore nine months of input tax can be recovered.

(2) If a car is used for business purposes, then any VAT charged on repairs and maintenance costs can be treated as input tax. No apportionment has to be made for private use.

54 Anne Attire

Text references. Chapters 26 and 27 for VAT.

Top tips. Make sure that you read all the information given in the question – you are given this information by the examiner for a reason so you must make use of it when answering the question.

Easy marks. The due date for payment of VAT was an easy mark.

Examiner's comments. In part (a) candidates often did not appreciate that the calculation of output VAT on credit sales had to take account of the discount for prompt payment even if it was not taken by customers. In part (b) the answers of many candidates lacked sufficient depth to gain full marks. For example, the turnover limit of £1,350,000 was usually known, but only a minority of candidates correctly stated that it applied for the following 12-month period. The same comment applies to part (c). For example, candidates generally appreciated that the taxpayer's VAT registration would be cancelled, but few stated that the reason for the cancellation was the cessation of making taxable supplies. Many candidates stated that on a sale of the business as a going concern the VAT registration could be taken over by the purchaser despite the question clearly stating that the purchaser was already registered for VAT.

			Marks
(a)	Output VAT	– Cash sales	1
		– Credit sales	1½
	Input VAT	– Purchases and expenses	1
		– Impairment loss	1½
	Due date		1
			6
(b)	Limit		1
	VAT returns and VAT payments		1
	Output VAT		1
	Input VAT		1
	Bad debt relief		1
			5
(c)	(i)	*Sale of assets on a piecemeal basis*	
		Cancellation of VAT registration	1
		Output VAT	1
			2
	(ii)	*Sale of business as a going concern*	
		Cancellation of VAT registration	1
		Output VAT not due	1
			2
			15

(a) **VAT return – Quarter ended 30 November 2010**

	£	£
Output VAT		
Cash sales £28,000 × 17.5%		4,900
Credit sales £12,000 × 95% × 17.5% (N1)		1,995
Input VAT		
Purchases and expenses £11,200 × 17.5%	1,960	
Impairment loss £800 × 95% × 17.5% (N2)	133	
		(2,093)
VAT payable		4,802

The VAT return for the quarter ended 30 November 2010 should have been submitted by 31 December 2010 (one month after the end of the VAT period) or 7 January 2011 if filed online.

Notes

(1) The calculation of output VAT on the credit sales takes into account the discount for prompt payment, even for those 10% of customers that did not take it.

(2) Relief for an impairment loss is not given until six months from the time that payment is due. Therefore relief can only be claimed in respect of the invoice due for payment on 10 April 2010. Relief is based on the amount of output VAT that would originally have been paid, taking into account the discount for prompt payment.

(b) Anne can use the cash accounting scheme if her expected taxable turnover for the next 12 months does not exceed £1,350,000. Anne must also be up-to-date with her VAT returns and VAT payments.

Output VAT on most credit sales will be accounted for up to one month later than at present since the scheme will result in the tax point becoming the date that payment is received from customers. However, the recovery of input VAT will be delayed by two months.

The scheme will provide automatic bad debt relief should a credit sale customer default on the payment of a debt.

(c) (i) **Sale of assets on a piecemeal basis**

On the cessation of trading Anne will cease to make taxable supplies, so her VAT registration will be cancelled on the date of cessation or an agreed later date.

Output VAT will be due in respect of the value of the fixed assets at the date of deregistration on which VAT has been claimed (although output VAT is not due if it is less than £1,000).

(ii) **Sale of business as a going concern**

Since the purchaser is already registered for VAT, Anne's VAT registration will be cancelled as above.

A sale of a business as a going concern (TOGC) is outside the scope of VAT and therefore output VAT will not be due.

Mock exams

ACCA

Paper F6

Taxation (United Kingdom)

Mock Examination 1

Question Paper	
Time allowed	
Reading and Planning	*15 minutes*
Writing	*3 hours*
ALL FIVE questions are compulsory and MUST be attempted.	

During reading and planning time only the question paper may be annotated.

**DO NOT OPEN THIS PAPER UNTIL YOU ARE READY TO START UNDER
EXAMINATION CONDITIONS**

ALL FIVE questions are compulsory and MUST be attempted

1 Mark Kett (Pilot paper)

On 31 December 2010 Mark Kett ceased trading as a marketing consultant. He had been self-employed since 6 April 2004, and had always made his accounts up to 5 April. On 1 January 2011 Mark commenced employment as the marketing manager of Sleep-Easy plc. The company runs a hotel. The following information is available for the tax year 2010/11:

Self-employment

(1) Mark's tax adjusted trading profit for the nine-month period ended 31 December 2010 is £20,700. This figure is before taking account of capital allowances.

(2) The tax written down values for capital allowances purposes at 6 April 2010 were as follows:

	£
Main pool	13,800
Expensive motor car (acquired June 2008)	14,600

The expensive motor car was used by Mark, and 40% of the mileage was for private purposes.

(3) On 15 June 2010 Mark had purchased office furniture for £1,900. All of the items included in the general pool were sold for £18,800 on 31 December 2010. On the cessation of trading Mark personally retained the expensive motor car. Its value on 31 December 2010 was £11,800.

Employment

(1) Mark is paid a salary of £3,250 (gross) per month by Sleep-Easy plc, from which income tax of £620 per month has been deducted under PAYE.

(2) During the period from 1 January 2011 to 5 April 2011 Mark used his private motor car for business purposes. He drove 2,500 miles in the performance of his duties for Sleep-Easy plc, for which the company paid an allowance of 16 pence per mile. The relevant HM Revenue & Customs authorised mileage rate to be used as the basis of an expense claim is 40 pence per mile.

(3) On 1 January 2011 Sleep-Easy plc provided Mark with an interest free loan of £76,000 so that he could purchase a new main residence.

(4) During the period from 1 January 2011 to 5 April 2011 Mark was provided with free meals in Sleep-Easy plc's staff canteen. The total cost of these meals to the company was £400.

Property income

(1) Mark let out a furnished property throughout the tax year 2010/11. He received gross rents of £8,600, 5% of which was paid to a letting agency. During December 2010 Mark spent £540 on replacing dilapidated furniture and furnishings.

(2) From 6 April 2010 to 31 December 2010 Mark let out a spare room in his main residence, receiving rent of £350 per month.

Investment income

(1) During the tax year 2010/11 Mark received dividends of £2,880, interest from government stocks (gilts) of £4,900, and interest of £430 from an individual savings account (ISA). These were the actual cash amounts received.

(2) On 3 May 2010 Mark received a premium bond prize of £100.

Other information

(1) On 15 December 2010 Mark made a gift aid donation of £800 (net) to a national charity.
(2) Mark's payments on account of income tax in respect of the tax year 2010/11 totalled £11,381.

Required

(a) Compute the income tax payable by Mark for the tax year 2010/11 and the balancing payment or repayment that will be due for the year. **(22 marks)**

(b) Advise Mark as to how long he must retain the records used in preparing his tax return for the tax year 2010/11, and the potential consequences of not retaining the records for the required period. **(3 marks)**

(Total = 25 marks)

2 Scuba Ltd (Pilot paper)

(a) Scuba Ltd is a manufacturer of diving equipment. The following information is relevant for the year ended 31 March 2011:

Operating profit

The operating profit is £168,680. The expenses that have been deducted in calculating this figure include the following:

	£
Depreciation	45,200
Entertaining customers	7,050
Entertaining employees	2,470
Gifts to customers (diaries costing £25 each displaying Scuba Ltd's name)	1,350
Gifts to customers (food hampers costing £80 each)	1,600

Leasehold property

On 1 July 2010 Scuba Ltd acquired a leasehold office building that is used for business purposes. The company paid a premium of £80,000 for the grant of a twenty-year lease.

Purchase of industrial building

Scuba Ltd purchased a new factory from a builder on 1 July 2010 for £240,000, and this was immediately brought into use. The cost was made up as follows:

	£
Drawing office serving the factory	34,000
General offices	40,000
Factory	98,000
Land	68,000
	240,000

Plant and machinery

On 1 April 2010 the tax written down values of plant and machinery were as follows:

	£
Main pool	47,200
Expensive motor car (acquired July 2008)	22,400

The following transactions took place during the year ended 31 March 2011:

		Cost (Proceeds) £
3 April 2010	Purchased machinery	18,020
29 May 2010	Purchased a computer	1,100
4 July 2010	Purchased a motor car CO_2 emissions 135g/km	10,400
18 August 2010	Purchased machinery	7,300
15 November 2010	Sold a lorry	(12,400)

The motor car purchased on 4 July 2010 for £10,400 is used by the factory manager, and 40% of the mileage is for private journeys. The lorry sold on 15 November 2010 for £12,400 originally cost £19,800.

Property income

Scuba Ltd lets a retail shop that is surplus to requirements. The shop was let until 31 March 2010 but was then empty from 1 April 2010 to 31 July 2010. During this period Scuba Ltd spent £6,200 on decorating the shop, and £1,430 on advertising for new tenants. The shop was let from 1 August 2010 to 31 March 2011 at a quarterly rent of £7,200, payable in advance.

Interest received

Interest of £430 was received from HM Revenue & Customs on 31 January 2011 in respect of the overpayment of corporation tax for the year ended 31 March 2010.

Other information

Scuba Ltd has no associated companies, and the company has always had an accounting date of 31 March.

Required

(i)   Compute Scuba Ltd's tax adjusted trading profit for the year ended 31 March 2011. You should ignore value added tax (VAT).

     Note: Your computation should start with operating profit for the period of £168,680 and should list all of the items in the income statement indicating by the use of a zero (0) any items that do not require adjustment;   **(15 marks)**

(ii)   Compute Scuba Ltd's corporation tax liability for the year ended 31 March 2011.   **(4 marks)**

(b)   Scuba Ltd registered for value added tax (VAT) on 1 July 2008. The company's VAT returns have been submitted as follows:

Quarter ended	VAT paid (refunded) £	Submitted
30 September 2008	18,600	One month late
31 December 2008	32,200	One month late
31 March 2009	8,800	On time
30 June 2009	3,400	Two months late
30 September 2009	(6,500)	One month late
31 December 2009	42,100	On time
31 March 2010	(2,900)	On time
30 June 2010	3,900	On time
30 September 2010	18,800	On time
31 December 2010	57,300	Two months late
31 March 2011	9,600	On time

Scuba Ltd always pays any VAT that is due at the same time that the related return is submitted.

During May 2011 Scuba Ltd discovered that a number of errors had been made when completing its VAT return for the quarter ended 31 March 2011. As a result of these errors the company will have to make an additional payment of VAT to HM Revenue & Customs.

Required

(i)   State, giving appropriate reasons, the default surcharge consequences arising from Scuba Ltd's submission of its VAT returns for the quarter ended 30 September 2008 to the quarter ended 31 December 2010 inclusive.   **(8 marks)**

(ii)   Explain how Scuba Ltd can voluntarily disclose the errors relating to the VAT return for the quarter ended 31 March 2011. You are not required to discuss penalties for errors.   **(3 marks)**

(Total = 30 marks)

3 Sophia Tang (BTX)

Sophia Tang, a widow aged 78, has been in business as a sole trader since 1 April 1988. On 31 March 2011 she transferred the business to her daughter Wong, at which time the following assets were sold to Wong:

(1)   A freehold shop with a market value of £260,000. The shop had been purchased on 1 July 2004 for £113,000, and has always been used by Sophia for business purposes. Wong paid Sophia £160,000 for the shop.

(2)   A freehold warehouse with a market value of £225,000. The warehouse had been purchased on 1 April 1988 for £70,000, and has never been used by Sophia for business purposes. Wong paid Sophia £100,000 for the warehouse.

Where possible, Sophia and Wong have elected to hold over any gains arising. Sophia does not wish to claim entrepreneurs' relief on the disposal of the business.

Sophia also made the following unconnected disposal during the year.

In July 2010 she sold a house for £350,000. The house had been acquired in July 1989 for £35,000. Sophia used the house as her main residence until July 1993 when she went to work overseas. She returned to the house in July 1995 and lived there until July 1997. Sophia went travelling for a year, returning in July 1998 when she moved into the house owned by her fiancé. The property was let from July 1998 up to the date of sale. The remainder of the time it was empty.

She made no other capital disposals in the 2010/11 tax year and has losses brought forward of £12,350. She had taxable income of £40,000 in 2010/11.

Required

Calculate Sophia's capital gains tax liability for the tax year 2010/11 and state when it is due.   **(15 marks)**

4 Li Fung (Pilot paper)

Li Fung commenced in self-employment on 1 October 2006. She initially prepared accounts to 30 June, but changed her accounting date to 31 March by preparing accounts for the nine-month period to 31 March 2010. Li's trading profits since she commenced self-employment have been as follows:

	£
Nine-month period ended 30 June 2007	18,600
Year ended 30 June 2008	24,900
Year ended 30 June 2009	22,200
Nine-month period ended 31 March 2010	16,800
Year ended 31 March 2011	26,400

Required

(a)   State the qualifying conditions that must be met for a change of accounting date to be valid.   **(3 marks)**

(b)   Compute Li's trading income assessments for each of the five tax years, 2006/07, 2007/08, 2008/09, 2009/10 and 2010/11.   **(9 marks)**

(c)   Advise Li of the advantages and disadvantages for tax purposes of changing her accounting date from 30 June to 31 March.   **(3 marks)**

(Total = 15 marks)

5 Andrew Zoom (TX 06/09)

Andrew Zoom is a cameraman who started working for Slick-Productions Ltd on 6 April 2010. The following information is available in respect of the year ended 5 April 2011:

(1)   Andrew received gross income of £50,000 from Slick-Productions Ltd. He works a set number of hours each week and is paid an hourly rate for the work that he does. When Andrew works more than the set number of hours he is paid overtime.

(2)   Andrew is under an obligation to accept the work offered to him by Slick-Productions Ltd, and the work is carried out under the control of the company's production manager. He is obliged to do the work personally, and this is all performed at Slick-Productions Ltd's premises.

(3)   All of the equipment that Andrew uses is provided by Slick-Productions Ltd.

Andrew has several friends who are cameramen, and they are all treated as self-employed. He therefore considers that he should be treated as self-employed as well in relation to his work for Slick-Productions Ltd.

Required

(a)   List those factors that indicate that Andrew Zoom should be treated as an employee in relation to his work for Slick-Productions Ltd rather than as self-employed.

   Note: you should confine your answer to the information given in the question.   **(4 marks)**

(b)   Calculate Andrew Zoom's income tax liability and national insurance contributions for the tax year 2010/11 if he is treated:

   (i)   As an employee in respect of his work for Slick-Productions Ltd;

   Note: You are not required to calculate employers' national insurance contributions.   **(3 marks)**

   (ii)   As self-employed in respect of his work for Slick-Productions Ltd.   **(3 marks)**

(c)   Assuming that Andrew Zoom is treated as being self-employed in respect of his work for Slick-Productions Ltd, state the date by which Andrew must notify Her Majesty's Revenue and Customs of his liability to pay income tax and outline the penalties that would be payable if Andrew's delay is deemed to be careless.

(5 marks)

(Total = 15 marks)

Answers

DO NOT TURN THIS PAGE UNTIL YOU HAVE
COMPLETED THE MOCK EXAM

A plan of attack

What's the worst thing you could be doing right now if this was the actual exam paper? Sharpening your pencil? Wondering how to celebrate the end of the exam in about three hours' time? Panicking, flapping and generally getting in a right old state?

Well, they're all pretty bad, so turn back to the paper and let's sort out a **plan of attack**!

First things first

You have fifteen minutes of reading time. Spend this looking carefully through the questions and deciding the order in which you will attempt them. As a general rule you should attempt the questions that you find easiest first and leave the hardest until last. Depending on how confident you are we recommend that you follow one of the following two options:

Option 1 (if you're thinking 'Help!')

If you're a bit worried about the paper, do the questions in the order of how well you think you can answer them. You may find the shorter questions less daunting than the longer questions. Alternatively, you may feel better prepared for questions 1 and 2 and wish to start there.

- The requirements for question 1 are broken down into parts which should help you to allocate your time. You could start with part (b) if you knew the answer to this part. Ensure you use the correct pro-forma in part (a) even of you cannot fill every number in.
- Question 2 is also broken down into parts. Make sure you make a good attempt at the corporation tax AND the VAT aspects.
- Approach question 3 by breaking it down into parts. Calculate each gain, deal with losses and then work out the tax due.
- Question 4 is change of accounting date question. If you find this topic hard, it might be worth leaving this question until last.
- Question 5 is a question comparing employment and self-employment with some tax administration. Even if you couldn't remember all of the distinctions between them for part (a), you should have been able to do the simple computations in part (b).

Lastly, what you mustn't forget is that you have to **answer all of the questions in the paper. They are all compulsory**. Do not miss out any questions or you will seriously affect your chance of passing the exam.

Option 2 (if you're thinking 'It's a doddle')

It never pays to be over confident but if you're reasonably confident about the exam then it is best to work through the questions sequentially starting with question 1.

No matter how many times we remind you....

Always, always **allocate your time** according to the marks for the question in total and then according to the parts of the question. And **always, always follow the requirements** exactly. Did you calculate the payment or repayment in Question 1, not just the income tax liability: these was an easy mark and you should make sure you get it.

You've got spare time at the end of the exam.....?

If you have allocated your time properly then you **shouldn't have time on your hands** at the end of the exam. But if you find yourself with five or ten minutes to spare, check over your work to make sure that there are no silly arithmetical errors.

Forget about it!

And don't worry if you found the paper difficult. More than likely other candidates did too. If this were the real thing you would need to **forget** the exam the minute you leave the exam hall and **think about the next one**. Or, if it's the last one, **celebrate**!

1 Mark Kett

Marking scheme

			Marks
(a)	Trading profit		½
	Capital allowances – Pool		2
	– Motor car		2
	Salary		1
	Beneficial loan		1
	Staff canteen		½
	Expense claim		1½
	Property business profit		2
	Furniture and furnishings		½
	Rent-a-room scheme		1
	Interest from government stocks		1
	Dividends		1
	Individual savings account		½
	Premium bond prize		½
	Personal allowance		½
	Extension of basic rate band		1
	Income tax		2½
	Tax suffered at source – PAYE		1
	– Dividends		1
	Balancing repayment		1
			22
(b)	Business records		1
	Other records		1
	Penalty		1
			3
			25

(a) Mark Kett income tax computation 2010/11

	Non-savings income £	Savings income £	Dividend income £	Total £
Trading income (W1)	22,120			
Employment income (W3)	9,910			
Property income (W6)	7,310			
Gilt interest (received gross)		4,900		
Dividends × 100/90			3,200	
Net income	39,340	4,900	3,200	47,440
Less PA	(6,475)			(6,475)
Taxable income	32,865	4,900	3,200	40,965

Tax

	£
Tax on non-savings income	
£32,865 @ 20%	6,573
Tax on saving income	
£4,535 @ 20%	907
£365 @ 20% (W8)	73
Tax on dividend income	
£635 @ 10% (W8)	64
£2,565 @ 32.5%	834
Tax liability	8,451
Less tax credits	
PAYE (3 × £620)	(1,860)
Dividends	(320)
Tax payable	6,271
Less POAs	(11,381)
Repayment due from HMRC	(5,110)

Note. Both the ISA interest and premium bond winnings are exempt from tax.

Workings

1 *Trading income*

	£
Trading profit	20,700
Balancing charge (W2)	1,420
	22,120

2 *Capital allowances*

	Main pool £	Exp car (60%) £	CAs £
TWDV b/f	13,800	14,600	
Additions	1,900		
	15,700	14,600	
Disposal	(18,800)	(11,800)	
Balancing charge	(3,100)		(3,100)
Balancing allowance		2,800 @ 60%	1,680
No WDA in year of cessation			
Balancing charge			(1,420)

3 *Employment income*

	£
Salary (1.1.11 – 5.4.11)	9,750
Loan (W5)	760
Canteen meals – not taxable	nil
Less mileage deduction (W4)	(600)
Employment income	9,910

4 *Mileage allowance*

	£
Company pays: 2,500 @ 16p	400
Less: mileage allowance	
2,500 @ 40p	(1,000)
Deduction (expense claim)	600

5 *Loan*

£76,000 × 4% × 3/12 = £760

6   *Property income*

	£
Income	
Rent	8,600
Less expenses	
letting agent fees	(430)
wear & tear (£8,600 @ 10%)	(860)
	7,310

Note. There is no relief for expenditure on furniture as wear and tear allowance is given.

7   *Rent-a-room relief*

Received: £350 × 9 = £3,150

This is below the limit of £4,250 and therefore this income will be exempt.

8   *Basic rate band*

Extended by gift aid: £800 × 100/80 = £1,000

(b)   **Retaining records**

(i)   As Mark has self employment and property income he must retain his records for five years and ten months from the end of the tax year ie until 31 January 2017.

(ii)   He must also retain the records for his other income until this date (even though the usual period would be one year ten months).

(iii)   If he does not retain his records for this period of time HMRC can fine him up to £3,000 (although this is usually only collected in serious cases).

2 Scuba Ltd

Text references. Calculation of taxable profits, taxable total profits and corporation tax in Chapters 19 and 20. Chapter 8 for IBAs and capital allowances. Administration in Chapter 25. VAT in Chapters 26 and 27.

Top tips. When dealing with an adjustment to profits, make a brief note to the examiner about why you have treated an item in a particular way. Ensure that you comment on every item in the question to obtain maximum marks.

Most of the calculations are fairly straightforward with perhaps the lease premium being the most challenging and only possible if you have studied this topic.

The most likely trap is not reading the question carefully and missing some information. It is good to mark the question in some way when you have dealt with each item (eg tick off or highlight each item dealt with).

With plant and machinery be careful with dates of purchase.

Easy marks. The adjustment to profit was straightforward, as was the calculation of corporation tax.

Once again using a proforma for

- adjustments of profit
- capital allowances
- calculation of taxable total profits

would have helped gain marks. You can slot the appropriate item into the proformas as you read through the question in many cases.

			Marks
(a)	(i)	**Trading profit**	
		Operating profit	½
		Depreciation	½
		Entertaining (½ each)	1
		Gifts to customers (½ each)	1
		Lease premium – Assessable amount	1½
		– Deduction	1½
		IBA – land	½
		– general offices	1
		– eligible expenditure	1½
		– allowance	1
		P&M – pool	2½
		– motor car	1½
		– AIA	1
			15
	(ii)	**Corporation tax computation**	
		Trading profit	½
		Property business profit – rent receivable	1
		– expenses	1
		Interest	½
		Corporation tax	1
			4
(b)	(i)	**Default surcharge**	
		Quarter ended 30 September 2008	1
		Quarter ended 31 December 2008	1
		Quarter ended 30 June 2009	2
		Quarter ended 30 September 2009	1
		Extension of surcharge period	1
		Four consecutive VAT returns on time	1
		Quarter ended 31 December 2010	1
			8
	(ii)	**Errors on VAT return**	
		Limits	2
		Notify in writing	1
			3
			30

(a) (i) **Scuba Ltd – tax adjusted trading profit year ended 31 March 2011**

	£	£
Profit before tax		168,680
Add depreciation	45,200	
customer entertaining (N1)	7,050	
employee entertaining (N1)	0	
gifts to customers: diaries (N2)	0	
gifts to customers: food hampers (N2)	1,600	
		53,850
Less lease premium (W1)		(1,860)
Adjusted profits		220,670
Less IBAs (W2)		(1,720)
Capital allowances (W3)		(38,460)
Taxable trading profit		180,490

Notes

(1) Customer entertaining is never an allowable expense. Staff entertaining is allowable.

(2) Expenditure on gifts to customers is only allowable if the gift (i) costs less than £50 per item, (ii) is not food, tobacco, alcohol or vouchers, and (iii) clearly advertises the business's name.

(ii) **CT liability year ended 31 March 2011**

	£
Taxable trading profit (above)	180,490
Property income (W4)	11,570
Interest (W5)	430
Taxable total profits/augmented profits	192,490

Small profits rate applies (augmented profits < £300,000)

		£
CT liability		
FY 2010	£192,490 × 21%	40,423

Workings

1 *Lease premium*

	£
Premium (P)	80,000
Less 2% × (n – 1) × P	
2% × (20 – 1) × 80,000	(30,400)
Taxable as Landlord's income	49,600

This amount is deductible for the company over the life of the lease:

$$\frac{£49,600}{20} = £2,480$$

Allowable on an accruals basis ie 1 July 2010 to 31 March 2011 = 9/12 × £2,480 = £1,860

2 *IBAs*

	£
Allowable cost	
Expenditure	240,000
Less land	(68,000)
Total cost	172,000

Expenditure on offices only allowable if represents < 25% × total cost:

$$\frac{40,000}{172,000} = 23\% \text{ therefore allowable}$$

IBA: 1% × £172,000 = £1,720

3   Capital allowances

	AIA £	Main pool £	Exp. car £	Allowances £
TWDV b/f		47,200	22,400	
Additions qualifying for AIA				
3.4.10 Machinery	18,020			
29.5.10 Computer	1,100			
18.8.10 Machinery	7,300			
	26,420			
AIA	(26,420)			26,420
Additions not qualifying for AIA				
4.7.10 Car		10,400		
Disposals				
15.11.10 Lorry		(12,400)		
		45,200		
WDA @ 20%		(9,040)		9,040
WDA £3,000 max			(3,000)	3,000
TWDV c/f		36,160	19,400	
Allowances				38,460

4   Property income

1 August 2010 to 31 March 2011 = 8m

	£
£7,200 × 4 = £28,800 × 8/12 =	19,200
Less expenses:	
decorating	(6,200)
advertising	(1,430)
Property income	11,570

5   Interest

Non-trading loan relationship therefore £430 is taxable as non-trading interest receivable.

(b)   (i)   **Default surcharge**

	Quarter ended	Circumstance	Default surcharge consequence
1	30 September 2008	Late return and payment	Surcharge liability notice (SLN) issued, ending 30 September 2009. As this is the first default there is no surcharge
2	31 December 2008	Late return and payment	SLN extended to 31 December 2009 Surcharge @ 2% = £644
3	31 March 2009	On time	SLN remains in place until 31 December 2009
4	30 June 2009	Late return and payment	SLN extended to 30 June 2010 Surcharge @ 5% = £170 Not collected as < £400
5	30 September 2009	Late return but no VAT due	SLN extended to 30 September 2010 No surcharge as no VAT due
6	31 December 2009 to 30 September 2010	On time	As returns and payments have been on time until the end of the SLN period, the SLN record is wiped clean
7	31 December 2010	Late return and payment	New SLN issued to 31 December 2011 As this is the first default there is no surcharge
8	31 March 2011	On time	SLN remains in place until 31 December 2011

(ii) Errors can be connected on the next VAT return if they do not exceed the greater of:

- £10,000 (under-declaration minus over-declaration)
- 1% of VAT turnover for the return period (maximum £50,000)

Other errors must be notified to HMRC in writing (eg by letter).

3 Sophia Tang

Text references. Chapters 13 to 16 on CGT.

Top tips. You can answer the final part of the requirement (about the due date for CGT) first. This will ensure that you do not forget to answer this part and lose an easy mark.

Easy marks. The gains on disposals were not difficult to calculate.

Examiner's comments. Confusion over basics. Gift relief given incorrectly.

Marking scheme

	Marks
Shop – MV/cost	1
– gift relief	2
Warehouse – MV/cost	1
House – gain	1
– actual occupation	2
– deemed occupation	2
– PPR relief	1
– lettings relief	1
Brought forward loss	1
AE	1
CGT	1
Due date	1
	15

Sophia Tang

	£
Shop (W1)	47,000
Warehouse (W2)	155,000
House	110,000
Less loss b/f	(12,350)
	299,650
Less annual exempt amount	(10,100)
Taxable gains	289,550
CGT £289,550 @ 28%	81,074

CGT due 31 January 2012

Workings

1   *Shop*

		£
Market value		260,000
Less: cost		(113,000)
Gain		147,000
Excess sale proceeds over cost £(160,000 – 113,000) chargeable		(47,000)
Gain held over under gift relief		100,000

Gain chargeable = £47,000

2   *Warehouse*

	£
Market value	225,000
Less cost	(70,000)
Gain	155,000

No gift relief is available as the asset is not used in the business.

3   *House*

	£
Disposal proceeds	350,000
Less cost	(35,000)
Gain	315,000
Less: PPR relief (note 1) £315,000 × 11/21	(165,000)
	150,000
Less: lettings relief (note 2)	(40,000)
Gain	110,000

Notes

1   *PPR periods*

	Occupation (years)	Non-Occupation (years)
July 1989 – July 1993 – actual occupation	4	
July 1993 – July 1995 working overseas (deemed occupation)	2	
July 1995 – July 1997 – actual occupation	2	
July 1997 – July 1998*		1
July 1998 – July 2007 (let)		9
July 2007 – July 2010 – last 36 months	3	
	11	10

The last 36 months of ownership is always treated as a period of deemed occupation.

*Travelling overseas would be deemed occupation under the 4 years absence for any reason rule, but Sophia did not live in the house on her return.

2   *Lettings relief*

Relief available is the lowest of:

		£
(i)	PPR relief	165,000
(ii)	Gain in the let period: £315,000 × 9/21	135,000
(iii)	Maximum	40,000

ie £40,000

4 Li Fung

> **Text references.** Self-employment is covered in Chapters 7 to 9.
>
> **Top tips.** There are 3 marks for part (a); you should aim to state 3 conditions.

				Marks
(a)	Notification date		1	
	18 month limit		1	
	Change within five years		1	
				3
(b)	Assessments	– 2006/07	1	
		– 2007/08	1½	
		– 2008/09	1	
		– 2009/10	1½	
		– 2010/11	1	
	Overlap profits	– 1.10.06-5.4.07	1	
		– 1.7.07-30.9.07	1	
		– Relieved in 2009/10	1	
				9
(c)	Basis periods correspond		1	
	Overlap profits		1	
	Disadvantages		1	
				3
				15

(a) Change of accounting date conditions

(i) Must notify HMRC by 31 January following the tax year of the change of accounting date.

(ii) The new accounts must not exceed 18 months in length.

(iii) There must not have been a change of accounting date in the previous 5 years unless there is a commercial reason for this later change.

(b) Trading income assessments

	£	£
2006/07		
Actual basis: 1.10.06 – 5.4.07		
6/9 × £18,600		12,400
2007/08		
<12 months therefore tax first 12 months		
9m to 30.6.07	18,600	
1.7.07 – 30.9.07: 3/12 × £24,900	6,225	
		24,825
2008/09		
CYB: y/e 30.6.08		24,900

	£	£

2009/10
Year of change (two periods ending in same tax year)
Tax both periods and relieve overlap profits

	£	£
Y/e 30.6.09	22,200	
9m to 31.3.10	16,800	
21 months worth of profit	39,000	
Less overlap relief (W1) (9 months worth)	(18,625)	
12 months worth of profit		20,375
2010/11		
CYB: y/e 31.3.11		26,400

Working

Overlap profits are any profits that are taxed twice when a business starts (or on a change of accounting date):

		£
1.10.06 – 5.4.07	= 6m	12,400
1.7.07 – 30.9.07	= 3m	6,225
Total	= 9m	18,625

(c) **Advantages and disadvantages of changing accounting date**

Advantages	Disadvantages
All of the overlap profits will be relieved	Tax on the profits of a tax year will be due sooner
The year end will now correspond with the tax year so will make basis periods easier	The profits taxable for a tax year will not be known until after the end of the tax year.
On cessation, only the profits earned in the tax year of cessation will be taxed.	

5 Andrew Zoom

Text references. Employment is covered in Chapters 3 and 4. National insurance contributions are covered in Chapter 12. Tax administration for individuals is dealt with in Chapter 17.

Top tips. Don't forget about Class 2 NICs for self-employed individuals.

Easy marks. The calculation of income tax should have been easy marks.

Examiner's comments. This question was very well answered by the majority of candidates. However, in part (a) only a few candidates pointed out that the taxpayer did not take any financial risk or profit from sound management. The only common mistake in part (b) was that candidates often based their NIC calculations on the taxable income figure rather than on employment income or trading profit.

Marks

(a)	Control		½
	Financial risk		½
	Basis of remuneration		1
	Sound management		½
	Required to do the work personally		½
	Obligation to accept work offered		½
	Equipment		½
			4
(b)	(i)	*Treated as an employee*	
		Employment income	½
		Personal allowance	½
		Income tax liability	½
		Class 1 NIC	1½
			3
	(ii)	*Treated as self-employed*	
		Income tax liability	½
		Class 2 NIC	1
		Class 4 NIC	1½
			3
(c)	Notification date		1
	Penalties – maximum		2
	Penalties – minimum		2
			5
			10

(a) **Factors for employment rather than self-employment**

- Andrew is under the control of Slick-Productions Ltd.
- Andrew is not taking any financial risk.
- Andrew works a set number of hours, is paid by the hour and is paid for overtime.
- Andrew cannot profit from sound management.
- Andrew is required to do the work personally.
- There is an obligation to accept work that is offered.
- Andrew does not provide his own equipment.

(b) (i) **Treated as an employee**

Andrew's income tax liability 2010/11

	£
Employment income/net income	50,000
Less: personal allowance	(6,475)
Taxable income	43,525

Income tax

£	
37,400 @ 20%	7,480
6,125 @ 40%	2,450
43,525	

Income tax liability	9,930

Andrew's national insurance contributions 2010/11

Class 1 NIC
£(43,875 − 5,715) = 38,160 @ 11% + £(50,000 − 43,875) = 6,125 @ 1% = <u>£4,259</u>.

(ii) **Treated as self-employed**

Andrew's income tax liability 2010/11
Andrew's trading profit for 2010/11 will be £50,000, so his income tax liability will be unchanged at <u>£9,930</u>.

Andrew's National insurance contributions 2010/11

Class 2 NIC
52 × £2.40 = <u>£125</u>

Class 4 NIC
£(43,875 − 5,715) = 38,160 @ 8% + £(50,000 − 43,875) = 6,125 @ 1% = <u>£3,114</u>.

(c) Andrew starts being self-employed in 2010/11. He must notify HMRC that he has a new source of income by 5 October 2011.

If Andrew notifies HMRC after these dates and his delay is careless, he will be liable to pay a penalty based on the potential lost revenue (PLR) as the result of his delay. This is usually the tax liability. The maximum penalty is 30% of PLR.

If Andrew notifies HMRC without prompting, the minimum penalty is 10% if the delay is more than 12 months or 0% within 12 months.

If the notification is with prompting by HMRC, the minimum penalties are 20% and 10% respectively.

ACCA

Paper F6

Taxation (United Kingdom)

Mock Examination 2

Question Paper	
Time allowed	
Reading and Planning	**15 minutes**
Writing	**3 hours**
ALL FIVE questions are compulsory and MUST be attempted.	

During the reading and planning time only the question paper may be annotated.

DO NOT OPEN THIS PAPER UNTIL YOU ARE READY TO START UNDER EXAMINATION CONDITIONS

ALL FIVE questions are compulsory and MUST be attempted

1 Noel and Liam Wall (BTX)

(a) Noel and Liam Wall are brothers, aged 38 and 40 respectively. Noel has more income than Liam, so he is surprised that for the tax year 2010/11 his total income tax liability and national insurance contributions were much lower than Liam's. The following information is available for the tax year 2010/11:

Noel Wall

(1) Noel is a self-employed musician. His income statement for the year ended 5 April 2011 was as follows:

	£	£
Fee income		84,245
Depreciation	1,980	
Motor expenses (note 2)	5,600	
Professional fees (note 3)	2,110	
Repairs and renewals (note 4)	2,360	
Travelling and entertaining (note 5)	960	
		(13,010)
Net profit		71,235

(2) During the year ended 5 April 2011 Noel drove a total of 8,400 miles, of which 7,560 were for business journeys.

Noel's motor car (acquired in August 2008) had a tax written down value of £32,800 at 6 April 2010.

(3) The figure for professional fees includes £510 for personal tax advice in respect of the tax year 2009/10.

(4) The figure for repairs and renewals consists of £1,900 for a new guitar, and £460 for repairing this guitar when it was damaged.

(5) The figure for travelling and entertaining includes £370 for entertaining clients, and £120 for parking fines.

(6) In addition to his self-employed income, Noel received dividends of £7,560 during the tax year 2010/11. This was the actual cash amount received.

Liam Wall

(1) Liam is employed as a music producer by Forever Ltd. The company runs a recording studio. During the tax year 2010/11 he was paid a gross annual salary of £65,270.

(2) Throughout the tax year 2010/11 Forever Ltd provided Liam with a diesel powered motor car which has a list price of £32,400. The official CO_2 emission rate for the motor car is 211 grams per kilometre. The company also provided Liam with fuel for private journeys.

(3) On 1 December 2010 Forever Ltd paid a golf club membership fee of £580 for the benefit of Liam.

(4) On 1 January 2011 Liam paid a professional subscription of £220 to the Guild of Producers, a HM Revenue & Customs' approved professional body.

(5) In addition to his employment income, Liam received building society interest of £6,640 during the tax year 2010/11. This was the actual cash amount received.

Required

(i) Calculate Noel's income tax liability and national insurance contributions for the tax year 2010/11.

Note: your computation of Noel's trading income should start with net profit for the period of £71,235 and should list all of the items in the income statement indicating by the use of a zero (0) any items that do not require adjustment. **(12 marks)**

(ii) Calculate Liam's income tax liability and national insurance contributions for the tax year 2010/11.

(8 marks)

(b) Denzil Dyer has been a self-employed printer since 2007. He has recently registered for value added tax (VAT).

Denzil's sales consist of printed leaflets, which are standard rated. He sells to both VAT registered customers and to non-VAT registered customers.

For a typical printing contract, Denzil receives a 10% deposit at the time that the customer makes the order. The order normally takes fourteen days to complete, and Denzil issues the sales invoice three to five days after completion. Some customers pay immediately upon receiving the sales invoice, but many do not pay for up to two months.

Customers making an order of more than £500 are given a discount of 5% from the normal selling price. Denzil also offers a discount of 2.5% of the amount payable to those customers that pay within one month of the date of the sales invoice.

All of Denzil's printing supplies are purchased from a VAT registered supplier. He pays by credit card and receives a VAT invoice. However, Denzil also purchases various office supplies by cash without receiving any invoices.

Denzil does not use the annual accounting scheme, the cash accounting scheme or the flat rate scheme.

Required

(i) Advise Denzil as to when he should account for the output VAT relating to a typical standard rated printing supply. **(4 marks)**

(ii) Explain the VAT implications of the two types of discount that Denzil gives or offers to his customers.

(3 marks)

(iii) Advise Denzil of the conditions that will have to be met in order for him to recover input VAT. You are not expected to list those goods and services for which input VAT is non-recoverable. **(3 marks)**

(Total = 30 marks)

2 Helium Ltd (BTX)

Helium Ltd is a UK resident company. Helium operates in the UK, and via two overseas branches in the countries Argon and Boron. Helium Ltd has no associated companies. The following information is available for Helium Ltd for the year ended 31 March 2011:

UK Trading income

The UK trading profit is £150,000. This figure is before taking account of capital allowances.

Industrial building   *IBA CA*

Helium Ltd had a new factory constructed on 1 July 2010 at a cost of £330,000. The factory was immediately brought into industrial use.

Plant and machinery   *CA -*

Helium Ltd purchased the following assets in respect of the year ended 31 March 2011:

		£
15 April 2010	Machinery	88,750
13 September 2010	Van	23,840
10 October 2010	Motor car	14,500

The motor car was purchased for one of the company's directors who will use the car 45% for business purposes. It has 150g/km CO_2 emissions.

On 7 August 2010, Helium Ltd sold machinery which had originally cost £12,000. The proceeds of sale were £14,000.   *Bal clA -*

The tax written down value of the main pool at 1 April 2010 was £137,365.

Property income   *Property income.*

Helium Ltd let out an office building from 1 June 2010 on a 7 year lease. It received a premium of £10,000 on the grant of the lease. The rental payable under the lease was £600 per month.

Helium Ltd paid an insurance premium of £2,040 on 1 June 2010 for the period between 1 June 2010 and 31 May 2011.

Loan interest received   *investment inccne.*

Loan interest of £7,500 was received on 30 September 2010, and £7,500 on 31 March 2011. There were no accruals at the year end. The loan was made for non-trading purposes.

Overseas trading income   *DTR.   DTR. oversea sep con.*

Helium's overseas branches generated after tax profits of £90,000 in Argon and £10,000 in Boron. Withholding taxes are 10% in Argon and 25% in Boron.   *income oversea*

Dividends received   *FLL*

The company also received dividends of £13,500 from Carbon plc, an unconnected UK company. This figure was the actual cash amount received.

Charitable donations   *Loss GA*

Helium Ltd made donations to charity of £30,000 under the Gift Aid scheme during the period.

Future expansion

Helium Ltd is considering expanding overseas operations. This would be achieved by buying shares in a company in the country of Xenon. Helium Ltd would expect to receive dividends from the company, which is expected to make profits.

Required

(a) Calculate Helium Ltd's corporation tax liability for the year ended 31 March 2011. **(22 marks)**

(b) Explain briefly, without calculations, possible effects of the Xenon company on Helium Ltd's future corporation tax calculations. **(3 marks)**

(Total = 25 marks)

3 Rotate, Spin and Turn (BTX)

You are a trainee accountant and your manager has asked for your help in advising three unconnected corporate clients that have each sold freehold factories.

Rotate Ltd

On 2 September 2010 Rotate Ltd sold a freehold factory for £470,000. The indexed cost of the factory on that date was £240,100. On 8 August 2010 Rotate Ltd had purchased a replacement freehold factory for £415,000.

Spin Ltd

On 14 November 2010 Spin Ltd sold a freehold factory for £360,000. The indexed cost of the factory on that date was £333,200. On 5 January 2011 Spin Ltd purchased a replacement leasehold factory, with a lease period of 15 years, for £394,000.

Turn Ltd

On 22 December 2010 Turn Ltd sold a freehold factory for £290,000. The indexed cost of the factory on that date was £230,000. 80% of this factory had been used in a manufacturing business run by Turn Ltd. However, the remaining 20% of this factory has never been used for business purposes. On 18 January 2011 Turn Ltd purchased a replacement freehold factory for £340,000.

Other information

Unless otherwise stated, each of the factories has always been used for business purposes. Where possible, Rotate Ltd, Spin Ltd and Turn Ltd have all elected to hold over the gain arising on the disposal of their respective freehold factories under the rollover relief (replacement of business assets) rules.

Required

(a) State the conditions that must be complied with in order that rollover relief can be claimed. You are not expected to list the categories of asset that qualify for rollover relief. **(3 marks)**

(b) Advise Rotate Ltd, Spin Ltd and Turn Ltd of the rollover relief available on the disposal of their respective freehold factories. Your answer should include:

(1) Calculations of the capital gains immediately chargeable, and

(2) An explanation of the future tax implications arising from the gains that have been deferred.

(12 marks)

(Total = 15 marks)

4 Duke and Earl (BTX)

Duke and Earl Upper-Crust, aged 44, are twin brothers.

Duke is employed by the High-Brow Bank plc as a financial adviser. During the tax year 2010/11 Duke was paid a gross salary of £120,000. He also received a bonus of £40,000 on 15 March 2011. On 31 March 2011 Duke made a contribution of £85,000 (gross) into a personal pension scheme. He is not a member of High-Brow Bank plc's occupational pension scheme.

Earl is self-employed as a financial consultant. His trading profit for the year ended 5 April 2011 was £34,000. On 31 March 2011 Earl made a contribution of £40,000 (gross) into a personal pension scheme.

Neither Duke nor Earl has any other income. In previous years, both Duke and Earl have made pension contributions equal to the maximum amounts qualifying for tax relief.

Required

(a) Calculate Duke and Earl's income tax liabilities for the tax year 2010/11, together with the actual net of tax amounts that Duke and Earl will have paid to their personal pension companies. **(8 marks)**

(b) Advise Duke and Earl of the maximum additional amounts that they could have contributed into personal pension schemes for the tax year 2010/11, whether or not such additional contributions would have qualified for tax relief, and the date by which any qualifying contributions would have had to have been paid.

(4 marks)

(c) Explain the effect of the pension scheme annual allowance, and the tax implications if contributions are made in excess of this amount. **(3 marks)**

(Total = 15 marks)

5 Rahul

Rahul died on 22 December 2010. During his lifetime he made the following gifts:

Date	Gift	Recipient
15 August 2001	Quoted shares worth £280,000	Daughter
10 March 2005	House worth £290,000	Son
7 July 2007	Cash of £315,000	Trust
		(Rahul agreed to pay
		the IHT due)

The nil rate bands in previous years were as follows:

2001/02	£242,000
2004/05	£263,000
2007/08	£300,000

Rahul left the following assets in his death estate:

	£
Quoted shares	180,000
House	400,000
Life assurance policy	see below

The life assurance policy was worth £30,000 immediately before Rahul's death. The sum assured by the policy was £110,000 and this was paid to his executors on 10 March 2011.

Rahul also had the following debts at his death:

	£
Repayment mortgage secured on house	125,000
Income tax	2,400

Rahul's executors paid his funeral expenses of £5,600 on 31 January 2011.

In his Will, Rahul left the quoted shares to his wife and the remainder of his estate to his son. The executors filed an account for inheritance tax on 10 April 2011.

Required

(a) Calculate the inheritance tax payable on the lifetime gifts made by Rahul:

   (i) during his lifetime; and

   (ii) on his death,

   Where relevant, state the due date of payment and who is liable to pay the inheritance tax. **(10 marks)**

(b) Calculate the inheritance tax payable on Rahul's death estate. State the due date of payment and who is liable to pay the inheritance tax. **(5 marks)**

(Total = 15 marks)

Answers

DO NOT TURN THIS PAGE UNTIL YOU HAVE
COMPLETED THE MOCK EXAM

A plan of attack

What's the worst thing you could be doing right now if this was the actual exam paper? Sharpening your pencil? Wondering how to celebrate the end of the exam in about 3 hours time? Panicking, flapping and generally getting in a right old state?

Well, they're all pretty bad, so turn back to the paper and let's sort out a **plan of attack**!

First things first

You have fifteen minutes of reading time. Spend this looking carefully through the questions and deciding the order in which you will attempt them. As a general rule you should attempt the questions that you find easiest first and leave the hardest until last. Depending on how confident you are we recommend that you follow one of the following two options:

Option 1 (if you're thinking 'Help!')

If you're a bit worried about the paper, do the questions in the order of how well you think you can answer them. You may find the shorter questions less daunting than the longer questions. Alternatively, you may feel better prepared for questions 1 and 2 and wish to start there.

- Question 1 is on standard income tax topics. Part (b) is about VAT and you must make sure you make a good attempt at this part of the question as well.
- Question 2 is a corporation tax computation. Use the standard pro-forma in your answer and ensure that you deal with all the information given in the question.
- Question 3 dealt with capital gains for a number of companies. Work through the gains or losses systematically and don't forget to apply relevant reliefs.
- Question 4 dealt with pensions. There were easy marks on the basic income tax computations even if you were unsure about the details of the pension rules.
- Question 5 is an inheritance tax question. This is a new topic in the 2011 F6 syllabus so you really need to understand it well.

Lastly, what you mustn't forget is that you have to **answer all of the questions in the paper. They are all compulsory**. Do not miss out any questions or you will seriously affect your chance of passing the exam.

Option 2 (if you're thinking 'It's a doddle')

It never pays to be over confident but if you're reasonably confident about the exam then it is best to work through the questions sequentially starting with question 1.

No matter how many times we remind you....

Always, always **allocate your time** according to the marks for the question in total and then according to the parts of the question. And **always, always follow the requirements** exactly.

You've got spare time at the end of the exam.....?

If you have allocated your time properly then you **shouldn't have time on your hands** at the end of the exam. But if you find yourself with five or ten minutes to spare, check over your work to make sure that there are no silly arithmetical errors.

Forget about it!

And don't worry if you found the paper difficult. More than likely other candidates did too. If this were the real thing you would need to **forget** the exam the minute you leave the exam hall and **think about the next one**. Or, if it's the last one, **celebrate**!

1 Noel and Liam Wall

Text references. Chapters 2 to 4, 7 to 9 and 12. VAT in Chapters 26 and 27.

Top tips. Using familiar proformas for the adjustment to profits and computation of employment income should ensure that you present your workings in a clear and logical way.

To make sure that you don't miss anything it is a good idea to mark the question in some way, eg tick off items as you deal with them.

Easy marks. The adjustment to profits was fairly straightforward, as was the computation of the income tax liability in both cases. Make sure you allocate your time correctly to enable you to have time to calculate both liabilities.

Marking scheme

				Marks
(a)	(i)	Net profit	½	
		Depreciation	½	
		Motor expenses	1	
		Professional fees	½	
		Repairs and renewals (½ each)	1	
		Travelling and entertaining (½ each)	1	
		Capital allowances – Motor car	1	
		– Guitar	1	
		Dividends	1	
		Personal allowance	½	
		Income tax	1½	
		Class 2 NIC	1	
		Class 4 NIC	1½	
				12
	(ii)	Salary	½	
		Car benefit – relevant percentage	1	
		– calculation	½	
		Fuel benefit	1	
		Golf club membership	½	
		Professional subscription	½	
		Building society interest	1	
		Personal allowance	½	
		Income tax	1	
		Class 1 NIC	1½	
				8

(b) (i) VAT period   1
          Basic tax point   1
          Payment received   1
          Issue of invoice within 14 days   1
                                                                    4

     (ii) Large order discount   1
          Prompt payment discount   2
                                                                    3

     (iii) Made to taxable person   1
          Supported by evidence   1
          Supplied for business purposes   1
                                                                    3
                                                                   30

(a) (i) **Noel Wall – income tax computation 2010/11**

	Non-savings income £	Dividend income £	Total £
Trading profits (W1)	72,075		
Dividends (£7,560 × 100/90)		8,400	
Net income	72,075	8,400	80,475
Less: PA	(6,475)		(6,475)
Taxable income	65,600	8,400	74,000

Tax	£
£37,400 @ 20%	7,480
£28,200 @ 40%	11,280
£8,400 @ 32.5 %	2,730
Tax liability	21,490

Class 2 NIC: 52 × £2.40	125
Class 4 NIC: £(43,875 – 5,715) × 8% + (72,075 – 43,875) × 1%	3,335

Workings

1   *Trading profit*

	£
Net profit	71,235
Add: depreciation	1,980
Motor expenses (5,600 × $\frac{8,400 - 7,560}{8,400}$)	560
Professional fees: personal tax advice fees	510
Repairs and renewals: new guitar (capital)	1,900
Repairs and renewals: repairs to guitar	0
Travelling and entertaining: entertaining clients	370
Travelling and entertaining: parking fines	120
	5,440
	76,675
Less: capital allowances (W2)	(4,600)
Taxable trading profit	72,075

2   Capital allowances

	AIA	Trader's car (90%)	Allowances
	£	£	£
TWDV b/f		32,800	
Addition – guitar	1,900		
AIA	(1,900)		1,900
WDA – restricted (note 1)		(3,000) × 90%	2,700
TWDV c/f		29,800	
Total allowances			4,600

Note: 90% (7,560/8,400) of the use of the car is for business purposes.

(ii)   **Liam Wall – income tax computation 2010/11**

	Non-savings Income	Savings income	Total
	£	£	£
Employment income (W1)	82,766		
BSI (£6,640 × 100/80)		8,300	
Net income	82,766	8,300	91,066
Less: PA	(6,475)		(6,475)
Taxable income	76,291	8,300	84,591

Tax

	£
£37,400 @ 20%	7,480
£38,891 @ 40%	15,556
£8,300 @ 40%	3,320
Tax liability	26,356

Class 1 NIC: £(43,875 – 5,715) × 11% + £(65,270 – 43,875) × 1%	4,412

Note. Taxable employment benefits are not subject to Class 1 NIC.

Workings

1   *Employment income*

	£
Salary	65,270
Car benefit (W2)	11,016
Fuel benefit (W3)	6,120
Golf club membership	580
	82,986
Less: professional subscription	(220)
Employment income	82,766

2   *Car benefit*

Round CO_2 emissions down to nearest 5, ie 210

210 – 130 = 80 gkm

Divided by 5 = 16

Taxable % = 15 + 16 + 3 (diesel powered) – 34%

List price = £32,400

Value of benefit   £32,400 × 34% = £11,016

3   *Fuel benefit*

£18,000 × 34% = £6,120

(b) (i) **Accounting for output VAT**

Output VAT must be accounted for according to the VAT period in which the supply is treated as being made. This is determined by the tax point.

The printing contracts are supplies of services, so the basic tax point for each contract will be the date that it is completed.

Where payment is received before the basic tax point, then this date becomes the actual tax point. The tax point for each 10% deposit is therefore the date that it is received.

If an invoice is issued within 14 days of the basic tax point, the invoice date will usually replace the basic tax point outlined above. This will apply to the balance of the contract price since Denzil issues invoices within three to five days of completion.

(ii) **Discounts**

Where a discount of 5% is given for an order of more than £500 then output VAT is simply calculated on the revised, discounted, selling price.

As regards the 2.5% discount offered for prompt payment, output VAT is calculated on the selling price less the amount of discount offered.

There is no amendment to the amount of output VAT charged if the customer does not take the discount but instead pays the full selling price.

(iii) **Input VAT**

The supply must be made to Denzil since he is the taxable person making the claim.

The supply must be supported by evidence, and this will normally take the form of a VAT invoice. Denzil will therefore not be able to recover any input VAT in respect of the purchases of office supplies for cash where there is no invoice.

Denzil must use the goods or services supplied for business purposes, although an apportionment can be made where supplies are acquired partly for business purposes and partly for private purposes.

2 Helium Ltd

Text references. Chapters 19 and 20 for taxable total profits and CT calculation. Chapter 24 deals with the overseas aspects.

Top tips. Use a columnar approach when working out the double taxation relief for the UK holding company.

Easy marks. The residence of companies should be well known and the examiner has already given a clue about the significance of board meetings. Use of proformas to calculate the UK and overseas taxable profits as well as DTR ensures you do not make mistakes and lose marks.

Examiner's comments. Only a minority of candidates correctly calculated the overseas income and very few appreciated that the Gift Aid payment should be set against UK income.

Marks

(a) Trading income ½
    IBA 1
    PM – additions 1½
    – AIA 1
    – disposal 1
    – WDA 1
    Property income – premium taxed as property income 2
    – rents received 1
    – insurance premium 1
    Interest income 1
    Overseas income: Argon 1
    Overseas income: Boron 1
    Gift Aid 2
    FII 1
    Small profits rate 1½
    CT 2
    DTR 3
    22

(b) Associated company 1
    Dividends exempt 1
    FII 1
    3
    25

(a) **Helium Ltd – CT liability year ended 31 March 2011**

	Total £	UK £	Overseas £
Trading income	150,000	150,000	
Less IBAs (W1)	(3,300)	(3,300)	
CAs (W2)	(130,491)	(130,491)	
Taxable trading income	16,209	`16,209	
Property income (W3)	13,100	13,100	
Interest income (accruals basis)	15,000	15,000	
Overseas income			
– Argon (W4)	100,000		100,000
– Boron (W5)	13,333		13,333
Total profits	157,642	44,309	113,333
Less Gift Aid donation	(30,000)	(30,000)	–
Taxable total profits	127,642	14,309	113,333
FII £13,500 × 100/90	15,000		
Augmented profits	142,642		
CT @ 21% (N)	26,805	3,005	23,800
Less DTR			
Argon (W4)	(10,000)		(10,000)
Boron (W5)	(2,800)		(2,800)
CT liability	14,005	3,005	11,000

Note. Helium Ltd has no associated companies and so the small profits rate applies.

Workings

1   *Industrial buildings allowance*

     WDA @ 1% × £330,000 = £3,300

2   *Capital allowances on plant and machinery*

	AIA £	Main pool £	Allowances £
TWDVs c/f		137,365	
Additions qualifying for AIA			
15.4.10 Machinery	88,750		
13.9.10 Van	23,840		
	112,590		
AIA	(100,000)		100,000
	12,590		
Transfer balance to pool	(12,590)	12,590	
Additions not qualifying for AIA			
10.10.10 Car		14,500	
		164,455	
Disposal			
7.8.10 Machinery (restricted to cost)		(12,000)	
		152,455	
WDA @ 20%		(30,491)	30,491
TWDV c/f		121,964	
Allowances			130,491

3   *Property income*

	£	£
Premium received	10,000	
Less: (7-1) x 2% x £10,000	(1,200)	
Taxable as property income		8,800
Rent received 10 x £600	6,000	
Less: insurance premium 10/12 x £2,040	(1,700)	
Net rental income		4,300
Total property income		13,100

4   *DTR Argon branch profits*

     Gross overseas income: £90,000 × 100 / (100 – 10) = £100,000

     Overseas tax: £100,000 - £90,000 = £10,000

     UK tax: £100,000 × 21% = £21,000

     DTR: lower ie £10,000

5   *DTR Boron branch profits*

     Gross overseas income: £10,000 x 100 / (100 – 25) = £13,333

     Overseas tax: £13,333 – £10, 000 = £3,333

     UK tax: £13,333 × 21% = £2,800

     DTR: lower ie £2,800

(b)   If the overseas company is a subsidiary, it would be an associated company, so the small profits lower and upper limits would be reduced to £150,000 and £750,000 respectively. This may increase the rate of UK corporation tax.

       The dividends received from the Xenon company are exempt from UK corporation tax.

However franked investment income includes all dividends received by UK and foreign companies (other than group income). Therefore, if the holding is less than 51%, the dividends could affect the calculation of corporation tax.

Note: the question was deliberately vague about Helium Ltd's percentage holding so that you could make all the above points without contradiction.

3 Rotate, Spin and Turn

Text references. Chapter 21 covers the rules for chargeable gains companies.

Top tips. This question tests thoroughly the rollover relief rules. Remember that you always need to calculate the indexed gain first, before you can think about taking advantage of any reliefs.

Easy marks. The calculation of the three indexed gains were easy marks.

(a)   **Conditions for rollover relief**

(i)   The reinvestment must take place between one year before and three years after the date of disposal of the original asset.

(ii) The old and new assets must both be qualifying assets and be used for business purposes.

(iii) The new asset must be brought into business use at the time that it is acquired.

(b)   **Rotate Ltd**

	£
Proceeds	470,000
Less: Indexed cost	(240,100)
	229,900
Less: Rollover relief (balancing figure)	(174,900)
Chargeable gain	55,000

The gain that remains chargeable is the amount of proceeds received that have not been reinvested in the purchase of the replacement asset, ie £(470,000 – 415,000) = £55,000.

When the replacement factory is ultimately disposed of the base cost will be £240,100 (415,000 – 174,900).

Spin Ltd

	£
Proceeds	360,000
Less: indexed cost	(333,200)
	26,800
Less: rollover relief	(26,800)
Chargeable gain	–

The sale proceeds are fully reinvested, and so the whole of the gain can be rolled over.

The leasehold factory is a depreciating asset, and so the base cost of this factory is not adjusted.

The gain of £26,800 will be held over until the earlier of 5 January 2021 (ten years from the date of acquisition), the date that the factory is disposed of, or the date that the factory ceases to be used for business purposes, at which point it will be chargeable.

Turn Ltd

	£
Proceeds	290,000
Less: indexed cost	(230,000)
	60,000
Less: rollover relief (balancing figure)	(48,000)
Chargeable gain	12,000

The proportion of the gain relating to non-business use is £12,000 (60,000 x 20%), and this amount does not qualify for rollover relief.

The business proportion of the sale proceeds (290,000 x 80% = 232,000) is fully reinvested, and so the balance of the gain can be rolled over.

When the replacement factory is ultimately disposed of the base cost will be £292,000 (340,000 – 48,000).

4 Duke and Earl

Text references. Chapter 2 covers the income tax computation. Pension contributions are covered in Chapter 5.

Top tips. Tax relief is available on pension contributions up to an amount of 100% of relevant earnings. Personal pension contributions are always paid net of basic rate tax; higher rate relief is given, where appropriate, by extending the basic rate band.

Easy marks. Part (a) required two straightforward income tax computations.

			Marks
(a)	**Duke Upper-Crust**		
	Employment income	1	
	Personal allowance	1	
	Income tax	1½	
	Net contribution	1	
	Earl Upper-Crust		
	Trading profit	½	
	Personal allowance	½	
	Income tax	1	
	Net contribution	1½	
			8
(b)	No restriction regarding contributions	1	
	Tax relief – Duke	1	
	– Earl	1	
	Period of payment	1	
			4
(c)	Effective limit	1	
	Tax charge on excess contribution	1	
	Cancellation of relief given	1	
			3
			15

(a) **Duke Upper-Crust – Income tax computation 2010/11**

	£
Employment income (120,000 + 40,000)	160,000
Less personal allowance (W)	(6,475)
Taxable income	153,525
Income tax	
£37,400 @ 20%	7,480
£85,000 @ 20%	17,000
£31,125 @ 40%	12,450
Income tax liability	36,930

All of Duke's pension contribution of £85,000 qualifies for tax relief, so he will have paid £68,000 (80% × £85,000) to his personal pension company.

The basic rate limit will be extended to £(37,400 + 85,000) = £122,400 and the higher rate limit will be extended to £(150,000 + 85,000) = £235,000.

Working

Calculation of adjusted net income for restriction of personal allowance

	£
Net income	160,000
Less personal pension contribution	(85,000)
Adjusted net income	75,000

Since the adjusted nil income is less than the limit of £100,000, the personal allowance is given in full.

Earl Upper-Crust – Income tax computation 2010/11

	£
Trading profit	34,000
Less personal allowance	(6,475)
Taxable income	27,525

	£
Income tax	
£27,525 @ 20%	5,505
Income tax liability	5,505

Only £34,000 of Earl's pension contribution of £40,000 qualifies for tax relief, since relief is only available up to the amount of earnings.

The amount of tax relief is £6,800 (£34,000 at 20%), so Earl will have paid £33,200 £(40,000 – 6,800) to his personal pension company.

(b)   There is no restriction regarding the amounts that Duke and Earl could have contributed into a personal pension scheme for 2010/11.

However, tax relief is only available on an amount up to earnings. Therefore, Duke would only receive tax relief on additional pension contributions of up to £75,000 £(160,000 – 85,000).

Earl has already made a pension contribution in excess of his earnings for 2010/11, and so any additional pension contribution would not have qualified for any tax relief.

Pension contributions for 2010/11 would have had to have been paid between 6 April 2010 and 5 April 2011, since it is not possible to carry back contributions.

(c)   Although there is tax relief on pension contributions up to relevant earnings, the annual allowance acts as an effective limit.

Any tax relieved contributions in excess of the annual allowance are taxed at a rate dependent on other income on the individual, with the tax being paid under the self assessment system.

The annual allowance charge therefore cancels out the tax relief that would have been given. There is no charge where contributions have not qualified for tax relief.

5 Rahul

Marking scheme

				Marks
(a)	(i)	***Lifetime IHT on lifetime gifts***		
		15 August 2001	PET	1
		10 March 2005	PET	1
		7 July 2007	CLT	
			AE 2007/08	½
			AE 2006/07 b/f	½
			nil rate band	½
			tax using 20/80 to gross up	½
			gross transfer	½
			due date	½
			liability	½
	(ii)	*Death IHT on lifetime gifts*		
		15 August 2001	PET exempt	½
		10 March 2005	PET chargeable	½
			within nil band so no IHT due	½
		7 July 2007	CLT	
			nil rate band available	½
			tax at 40% on balance	½
			taper relief	½
			deduct lifetime tax	½
			due date	½
			liability	½
					10
(b)		*Death estate*		
		Shares		½
		House less mortgage		1
		Life policy		½
		Income tax		½
		Funeral expenses		½
		Spouse exemption		½
		Tax at 40%		½
		Due date		½
		Liability		½
					5
					15

(a)   (i)   **Lifetime IHT on lifetime gifts**

15 August 2001

Potentially exempt transfer after annual exemptions 2001/02, 2000/01

10 March 2005

Potentially exempt transfer after annual exemptions 2004/05, 2003/04

7 July 2007

Chargeable lifetime transfer

No chargeable transfers in 7 years before this transfer, so full nil rate band of £300,000 available.

				£
Gift				315,000
Less:	AE 2007/08			(3,000)
	AE 2006/07 b/f			(3,000)
Net transfer of value				309,000
				£
IHT	£300,000	× 0% =		Nil
	£ 9,000	× 20/80 =		2,250
	£309,000			2,250

The gross transfer is £(309,000 + 2,250) = £311,250.

Check

IHT	£300,000	× 0% =		Nil
	£ 11,250	× 20% =		2,250
	£311,250			2,250

The tax is due on 30 April 2008 and is payable by Rahul.

(ii)   **Death IHT on lifetime gifts**

15 August 2001

Potentially exempt transfer – exempt because donor survived 7 years

10 March 2005

Potentially exempt transfer - chargeable because donor did not survive 7 years

		£
Gift		290,000
Less:	AE 2004/05	(3,000)
	AE 2003/04 b/f	(3,000)
Gross transfer of value		284,000

No chargeable transfers in 7 years before this transfer, so full nil rate band of £325,000 available.

Transfer within nil band so no IHT payable on this transfer.

7 July 2007

Chargeable lifetime transfer

Additional tax due because donor did not survive 7 years.

There was a lifetime transfer of value of £284,000 in seven years before 7 July 2007 (transfers after 7 July 2000) so the nil rate band available is £(325,000 – 284,000) = £41,000.

		£
Gross transfer of value		<u>311,250</u>
		£
IHT £41,000 × 0% =		Nil
<u>£270,250</u> × 40% =		108,100
£311,250		108,100
Less taper relief @ 20% (death between 3 and 4 years after transfer)		(21,260)
Death IHT		86,480
Less lifetime IHT paid		(2,250)
IHT payable		<u>84,230</u>

The tax is due on 30 June 2011 and is payable by the trustees.

(b) **Death estate**

	£	£
Quoted shares		180,000
House (N1)	400,000	
Less: mortgage	(125,000)	
		275,000
Life policy (proceeds payable as a result of death)		110,000
		565,000
Less: income tax	2,400	
funeral expenses	5,600	
		(8,000)
		557,000
Less: spouse exemption (legacy of quoted shares)		(180,000)
Chargeable death estate		377,000

Transfers in the 7 years before death were £(284,000 + 311,250) = £595,250 so the nil rate band of £325,000 at death is used up by these lifetime transfers.

Death tax @ 40% on £377,000 is <u>£150,800.</u>

Due date 10 April 2011, payable by executors.

ACCA

Paper F6

Taxation (United Kingdom)

Mock Examination 3
(December 2010 paper)

Question Paper	
Time allowed	
Reading and Planning	*15 minutes*
Writing	*3 hours*
ALL FIVE questions are compulsory and MUST be attempted.	

During reading and planning time only the question paper may be annotated.

BPP note: This examination has been adapted from the actual December 2010 paper examination to reflect the F6 syllabus, and the format of the examinations, in 2011. Question 3 has been reduced from 20 marks to 15 marks. Question 5 has been replaced by a new question written by BPP Learning Media and reviewed by the examiner.

DO NOT OPEN THIS PAPER UNTIL YOU ARE READY TO START UNDER EXAMINATION CONDITIONS

ALL FIVE questions are compulsory and MUST be attempted

Question 1

On 31 December 2010 Joe Jones resigned as an employee of Firstly plc, and on 1 January 2011 commenced employment with Secondly plc. Joe was employed by both companies as a financial analyst. The following information is available for the tax year 2010/11:

Employment with Firstly plc

(1)   From 6 April 2010 to 31 December 2010 Joe was paid a salary of £6,360 per month. In addition to his salary, Joe was paid a bonus of £12,000 on 12 May 2010. He had become entitled to this bonus on 22 March 2010.

(2)   Joe contributed 6% of his monthly gross salary of £6,360 into Firstly plc's HM Revenue and Customs' registered occupational pension scheme.

(3)   On 1 May 2010 Firstly plc provided Joe with an interest free loan of £120,000 so that he could purchase a holiday cottage. Joe repaid £50,000 of the loan on 31 July 2010, and repaid the balance of the loan of £70,000 when he ceased employment with Firstly plc on 31 December 2010.

(4)   During the period from 6 April 2010 to 31 December 2010 Joe's three-year-old daughter was provided with a place at Firstly plc's workplace nursery. The total cost to the company of providing this nursery place was £11,400 (190 days at £60 per day).

(5)   During the period 6 April 2010 to 31 December 2010 Firstly plc paid gym membership fees of £1,371 for Joe.

(6)   Firstly plc provided Joe with a home entertainment system for his personal use costing £4,400 on 6 April 2010. The company gave the home entertainment system to Joe for free, when he left the company on 31 December 2010, although its market value at that time was £3,860.

Employment with Secondly plc

(1)   From 1 January 2011 to 5 April 2011 Joe was paid a salary of £6,120 per month.

(2)   During the period 1 January 2011 to 5 April 2011 Joe contributed a total of £3,000 (gross) into a personal pension scheme.

(3)   From 1 January 2011 to 5 April 2011 Secondly plc provided Joe with living accommodation. The property has an annual value of £10,400 and is rented by Secondly plc at a cost of £2,250 per month. On 1 January 2011 Secondly plc purchased furniture for the property at a cost of £16,320. The company pays for all of the running costs relating to the property, and for the period 1 January 2011 to 5 April 2011 these amounted to £1,900.

(4)   During the period 1 January 2011 to 5 April 2011 Secondly plc provided Joe with 13 weeks of childcare vouchers costing £100 per week. Joe used the vouchers to provide childcare for his three-year-old daughter at a registered nursery near to his workplace.

(5)   During the period 1 January 2011 to 5 April 2011 Joe used Secondly plc's company gym which is only open to employees of the company. The cost to Secondly plc of providing this benefit to Joe was £340.

(6)   During the period 1 January 2011 to 5 April 2011 Secondly plc provided Joe with a mobile telephone costing £560. The company paid for all of Joe's business and private telephone calls.

Required

(a)   Calculate Joe Jones' taxable income for the tax year 2010/11.   **(17 marks)**

(b)   (i)   Briefly explain the basis of calculating Joe Jones' PAYE tax code for the tax year 2010/11, and the purpose of this code;   **(2 marks)**

       (ii)   For each of the PAYE forms P45, P60 and P11D, briefly describe the circumstances in which the form will be completed, state who will provide it, the information to be included, and the dates by which they should have been provided to Joe Jones for the tax year 2010/11.   **(6 marks)**

Note: your answer to both sub-parts (i) and (ii) should be confined to the details that are relevant to Joe Jones.   **(Total = 25 marks)**

Question 2

(a)   Neung Ltd is a UK resident company that runs a business providing financial services. The company's business is mainly based in the UK, but Neung Ltd also has two overseas branches. The company's summarised income statement for the year ended 31 March 2011 is as follows:

	Note	£
Operating profit	1 & 2	307,900
Income from investments		
Loan interest	3	37,800
Dividends	4	54,000
Profit before taxation		399,700

Note 1 – Operating profit

The operating profit does not include the results from either of Neung Ltd's two overseas branches (see note 2 below).

Depreciation of £11,830 and amortisation of leasehold property of £7,000 have been deducted in arriving at the operating profit of £307,900.

Note 2 – Overseas branches

Neung Ltd's first overseas branch made a trading profit of £41,000 for the year ended 31 March 2011. No overseas corporation tax was paid on this profit.

The second overseas branch made a trading loss of £15,700 for the year ended 31 March 2011.

Note 3 – Loan interest receivable

The loan was made for non-trading purposes on 1 July 2010. Loan interest of £25,200 was received on 31 December 2010, and interest of £12,600 was accrued at 31 March 2011.

Note 4 – Dividends received

Neung Ltd holds shares in four UK resident companies as follows:

	Percentage shareholding	Status
Second Ltd	25%	Trading
Third Ltd	60%	Trading
Fourth Ltd	100%	Dormant
Fifth Ltd	100%	Trading

During the year ended 31 March 2011 Neung Ltd received a dividend of £37,800 from Second Ltd, and a dividend of £16,200 from Third Ltd. These figures were the actual cash amounts received.

Additional information

Leasehold property

On 1 April 2010 Neung Ltd acquired a leasehold office building, paying a premium of £140,000 for the grant of a 20-year lease. The office building was used for business purposes by Neung Ltd throughout the year ended 31 March 2011.

Plant and machinery

On 1 April 2010 the tax written down values of Neung Ltd's plant and machinery were as follows:

	£
Main pool	4,800
Motor car [1] (acquired June 2008)	22,800
Special rate pool	12,700

The company purchased the following assets during the year ended 31 March 2011:

		£
19 July 2010	Motor car [2]	15,400
12 December 2010	Motor car [3]	28,600
20 December 2010	Ventilation system	35,000

Motor car [1] has a CO_2 emission rate of 220 grams per kilometre. Motor car [2] purchased on 19 July 2010 has a CO_2 emission rate of 242 grams per kilometre. Motor car [3] purchased on 12 December 2010 has a CO_2 emission rate of 148 grams per kilometre.

The ventilation system purchased on 20 December 2010 for £35,000 is integral to the freehold office building in which it was installed.

Required

(i)   State, giving reasons, which companies will be treated as being associated with Neung Ltd for corporation tax purposes;   **(2 marks)**

(ii) Calculate Neung Ltd's corporation tax liability for the year ended 31 March 2011;

Note: you should assume that the whole of the annual investment allowance is available to Neung Ltd, and that the company wishes to maximise its capital allowances claim.   **(15 marks)**

(iii) Advise Neung Ltd of the taxation disadvantages of converting its two overseas branches (see note 2) into 100% overseas subsidiary companies.   **(3 marks)**

(b)   Note that in answering this part of the question you are not expected to take account of any of the information provided in part (a) above.

The following information is available in respect of Neung Ltd's value added tax (VAT) for the quarter ended 31 March 2011:

(1)   Invoices were issued for sales of £44,600 to VAT registered customers. Of this figure, £35,200 was in respect of exempt sales and the balance in respect of standard rated sales. The standard rated sales figure is exclusive of VAT.

(2)   In addition to the above, on 1 March 2011 Neung Ltd issued a VAT invoice for £8,000 plus VAT of £1,600 to a VAT registered customer. This was in respect of a contract for standard rated financial services that will be completed on 15 April 2011. The customer paid for the contracted services in two instalments of £4,800 on 31 March 2011 and 30 April 2011 respectively.

(3)   Invoices were issued for sales of £289,300 to non-VAT registered customers. Of this figure, £242,300 was in respect of exempt sales and the balance in respect of standard rated sales. The standard rated sales figure is inclusive of VAT.

(4)   The managing director of Neung Ltd is provided with free fuel for private mileage driven in her company motor car. During the quarter ended 31 March 2011 this fuel cost Neung Ltd £260. The relevant quarterly scale charge is £463. Both these figures are inclusive of VAT.

(5)   There were no transactions during the period 1 to 3 January 2011.

For the quarters ended 30 September 2009 and 30 June 2010 Neung Ltd was one month late in submitting its VAT returns and in paying the related VAT liabilities. All of the company's other VAT returns have been submitted on time.

Required

(i)   Calculate the amount of output VAT payable by Neung Ltd for the quarter ended 31 March 2011;

(4 marks)

(ii)   Advise Neung Ltd of the default surcharge implications if it is one month late in submitting its VAT return for the quarter ended 31 March 2011 and in paying the related VAT liability;   **(3 marks)**

(iii)   State the circumstances in which Neung Ltd is and is not required to issue a VAT invoice, and the period during which such an invoice should be issued.   **(3 marks)**

(Total = 30 marks)

Question 3

Lim Lam is the controlling shareholder and managing director of Mal-Mil Ltd, an unquoted trading company that provides support services to the oil industry.

Lim Lam

Lim disposed of the following assets during the tax year 2010/11:

(1)   On 8 July 2010 Lim sold five acres of land to Mal-Mil Ltd for £260,000, which was the market value of the land on that date. The land had been inherited by Lim upon the death of her mother on 17 January 2004, when the land was valued at £182,000. Lim's mother had originally purchased the land for £137,000.

(2)   On 13 August 2010 Lim made a gift of 5,000 £1 ordinary shares in Oily plc, a quoted trading company, to her sister. On that date the shares were quoted on the Stock Exchange at £7.40–£7.56, with recorded bargains of £7.36, £7.38 and £7.60. Lim had originally purchased her 5,000 shares in the company on 23 November 2004 for £15,925.

Entrepreneurs' relief and holdover relief are not available in respect of this disposal.

(3)   On 22 March 2011 Lim sold 40,000 £1 ordinary shares in Mal-Mil Ltd for £280,000. She had originally purchased 125,000 shares in the company on 8 June 2003 for £142,000, and had purchased a further 60,000 shares on 23 May 2005 for £117,000. Mal-Mil Ltd has a total share capital of 250,000 £1 ordinary shares.

Entrepreneurs' relief is available in respect of this disposal. Lim has made no previous disposals eligible for entrepreneurs' relief.

Lim had taxable income of £28,000 in 2010/11.

Mal-Mil Ltd

On 20 December 2010 Mal-Mil Ltd sold two of the five acres of land that had been purchased from Lim on 8 July 2010. The sale proceeds were £162,000 and legal fees of £3,800 were incurred in connection with the disposal. The market value of the unsold three acres of land as at 20 December 2010 was £254,000. During July 2010 Mal-Mil Ltd had spent £31,200 levelling the five acres of land. The relevant retail price indexes (RPIs) are as follows:

July 2010   226.4
December 2010   232.1

Mal-Mil Ltd's only other income for the year ended 31 December 2010 was a trading profit of £163,000.

Required

(a) Calculate Lim Lam's capital gains tax liability for the tax year 2010/11, and state by when this should be paid. **(8 marks)**

(b) Calculate Mal-Mil Ltd's corporation tax liability for the year ended 31 December 2010, and state by when this should be paid. **(7 marks)**

(Total = 15 marks)

Question 4

You should assume that today's date is 20 March 2010.

Sammi Smith is a director of Smark Ltd. The company has given her the choice of being provided with a leased company motor car or alternatively being paid additional director's remuneration and then privately leasing the same motor car herself.

Company motor car

The motor car will be provided throughout the tax year 2010/11, and will be leased by Smark Ltd at an annual cost of £26,740. The motor car will be petrol powered, will have a list price of £92,000, and will have an official CO_2 emission rate of 315 grams per kilometre.

The lease payments will cover all the costs of running the motor car except for fuel. Smark Ltd will not provide Sammi with any fuel for private journeys.

Additional director's remuneration

As an alternative to having a company motor car, Sammi will be paid additional gross director's remuneration of £26,000 during the tax year 2010/11. She will then privately lease the motor car at an annual cost of £26,740.

Other information

The amount of business journeys that will be driven by Sammi will be immaterial and can therefore be ignored.

Sammi's current level of director's remuneration is over £150,000 which means that she will pay income tax at the additional rate of 50% in 2010/11. Smark Ltd prepares its accounts to 5 April, and pays corporation tax at the main rate of 28%. The lease of the motor car will commence on 6 April 2010.

Required

(a) Advise Sammi Smith of the income tax and national insurance contribution implications for the tax year 2010/11 if she (1) is provided with the company motor car, and (2) receives additional director's remuneration of £26,000. **(5 marks)**

(b) Advise Smark Ltd of the corporation tax and national insurance contribution implications for the year ended 5 April 2011 if the company (1) provides Sammi Smith with the company motor car, and (2) pays Sammi Smith additional director's remuneration of £26,000.

Note: you should ignore value added tax (VAT). **(5 marks)**

(c) Determine which of the two alternatives is the most beneficial from each of the respective points of view of Sammi Smith and Smark Ltd. **(5 marks)**

(Total = 15 marks)

Question 5

(a)   State FOUR advantages of making lifetime transfers for inheritance tax.   **(4 marks)**

(b)   Evelyn died on 1 February 2011. During her lifetime the following events occurred:

10 June 2006	Gave £100,000 to her sister
19 April 2007	Sold a painting to an art dealer for £10,000. Following revaluation by an expert, the painting was found to be worth £150,000
10 March 2008	Gave shares worth £320,000 to a trust. The trustees agreed to pay the lifetime inheritance tax. The nil rate band in 2007/08 was £300,000.

Evelyn left a net estate of £750,000 at her death including a house worth £150,000 and personal effects worth £25,000. In her Will, she left her house and personal effects to her husband Lewis, and the residue of her estate to a trust for her nephews and nieces. The executors submitted their inheritance tax account to HM Revenue and Customs on 16 June 2011.

Required

(i)   Explain the inheritance tax implications of the events during Evelyn's lifetime, and state the due date(s) for any tax that is payable.

Note: Your answer should be supported by appropriate calculations.   **(6 marks)**

(ii)   Explain the inheritance tax implications arising from Evelyn's death, and state the due date(s) for any tax that is payable.

Note: Your answer should be supported by appropriate calculations.   **(5 marks)**

(Total = 15 marks)

Answers

DO NOT TURN THIS PAGE UNTIL YOU HAVE
COMPLETED THE MOCK EXAM

A plan of attack

What's the worst thing you could be doing right now if this was the actual exam paper? Sharpening your pencil? Wondering how to celebrate the end of the exam in about 3 hours time? Panicking, flapping and generally getting in a right old state?

Well, they're all pretty bad, so turn back to the paper and let's sort out a **plan of attack**!

First things first

You have fifteen minutes of reading time. Spend this looking carefully through the questions and deciding the order in which you will attempt them. As a general rule you should attempt the questions that you find easiest first and leave the hardest until last. Depending on how confident you are we recommend that you follow one of the following two options:

Option 1 (if you're thinking 'Help!')

If you're a bit worried about the paper, do the questions in the order of how well you think you can answer them. You may find the shorter questions less daunting than the longer questions. Alternatively, you may feel better prepared for questions 1 and 2 and wish to start there.

- Question 1 is on employment benefits and PAYE. Make sure that you deal with all the benefits – perhaps tick each one off as you deal with it in your answer. Remember to state why any benefit is exempt.

- Question 2 is a corporation tax computation. Use the standard pro-forma in your answer and ensure that you deal with all the information given in the question.

- Question 3 dealt with capital gains of an individual and a company. Work through the gains in order and don't forget to deal with reliefs.

- Question 4 is about getting the best tax effect either by an employer providing a car or giving extra salary to the employee to lease a car. There were lots of figures in this question and you need to keep a cool head so that you don't mix them up.

- Question 5 is an inheritance tax question. This is a new topic in the 2011 F6 syllabus so you really need to understand it well.

Lastly, what you mustn't forget is that you have to **answer all of the questions in the paper. They are all compulsory**. Do not miss out any questions or you will seriously affect your chance of passing the exam.

Option 2 (if you're thinking 'It's a doddle')

It never pays to be over confident but if you're reasonably confident about the exam then it is best to work through the questions sequentially starting with question 1.

No matter how many times we remind you....

Always, always **allocate your time** according to the marks for the question in total and then according to the parts of the question. And **always, always follow the requirements** exactly.

You've got spare time at the end of the exam.....?

If you have allocated your time properly then you **shouldn't have time on your hands** at the end of the exam. But if you find yourself with five or ten minutes to spare, check over your work to make sure that there are no silly arithmetical errors.

Forget about it!

And don't worry if you found the paper difficult. More than likely other candidates did too. If this were the real thing you would need to **forget** the exam the minute you leave the exam hall and **think about the next one**. Or, if it's the last one, **celebrate**!

Question 1

Marking scheme

			Marks
(a)	Salary – Firstly plc	½	
	Occupational pension scheme contributions	1	
	Bonus	½	
	Salary – Secondly plc	½	
	Personal pension contributions	½	
	Beneficial loan — Average method	1½	
	— Strict method	1½	
	Workplace nursery	1	
	Gym membership	½	
	Home entertainment system — Use	1½	
	— Acquisition	1½	
	Living accommodation	2	
	Furniture	1½	
	Running costs	½	
	Childcare vouchers	1	
	Company gym	½	
	Mobile telephone	½	
	Personal allowance	½	
			17
(b)	(i) Basic of calculation	1	
	Deduction from salary	1	
			2
	(ii) **Form P45**		
	By Firstly plc when employment ceases	½	
	Details	1	
	Date provided	½	
	Form P60		
	By Secondly plc at end of tax year	½	
	Details	1½	
	Date provided	½	
	Form P11D		
	Both employers	½	
	Details	½	
	Date provided	½	
			6
			25

(a)   **Joe Jones – Taxable income 2010/11**

	£
Employment income	
Salary – Firstly plc (6,360 x 9)	57,240
Pension contributions (57,240 x 6%) (N2)	(3,434)
	53,806
Bonus (N1)	nil
Salary – Secondly plc (6,120 x 3)	18,360
Beneficial loan (W1)	2,367
Workplace nursery (N3)	nil
Gym membership (N3)	1,371
Home entertainment system – Use (W2)	660
– Acquisition (W2)	3,860
Living accommodation (W3)	6,750
Furniture (W3)	816
Running costs	1,900
Childcare vouchers (W4)	585
Company gym (N3)	nil
Mobile telephone	nil
Net income	90,475
Less: personal allowance	(6,475)
Taxable income	84,000

Workings

1   *Loan benefit*

The benefit of the beneficial loan using the average method is £2,533 ((120,000 + 70,000)/2 = 95,000 at 4% x 8/12).

Using the strict method the benefit is £2,367 ((120,000 at 4% x 3/12) + (70,000 at 4% x 5/12)).

Joe will therefore elect to have the taxable benefit calculated according to the strict method.

2   *Home entertainment system*

The benefit for the use of the home entertainment system is £660 (4,400 x 20% x 9/12).

The benefit for the acquisition of the home entertainment system is the market value of £3,860, as this is greater than £3,740 (4,400 – 660).

3   *Living accommodation and furniture*

The benefit for the living accommodation is the higher of the annual value of £2,600 (10,400 x 3/12) and the rent paid of £6,750 (2,250 x 3).

The benefit for the use of the furniture is £816 (16,320 x 20% x 3/12).

4   *Childcare vouchers*

The exemption for childcare vouchers is £55 per week. The benefit for the provision of the vouchers is therefore £585 (100 – 55 = 45 x 13).

Notes

1   The bonus of £12,000 will have been treated as being received during 2009/10 as Joe became entitled to it during that tax year.

2   The personal pension contributions will extend Joe's basic rate tax band, and are therefore irrelevant as regards the calculation of taxable income.

3   The provision of a place in a workplace nursery, the use of a company gym (sporting facility), and the provision of one mobile telephone do not give rise to a taxable benefit.

(b) (i) **Joe's tax code**

Joe's tax code will have been calculated by starting with his personal allowance of £6,475, and then reducing it by the value of the taxable benefits.

An employee's tax code is used to adjust their salary when calculating the amount of income tax that has to be paid each week or month under the PAYE system.

(ii) **Form P45**

Form P45 will be prepared by Firstly plc when Joe's employment ceases. It will show his taxable earnings and income tax deducted up to the date of leaving, together with his tax code at the date of leaving.

Firstly plc should have provided this form to Joe immediately following his cessation of employment with the company.

Form P60

Form P60 will be prepared by Secondly plc at the end of the tax year. It will show Joe's taxable earnings, income tax deducted, final tax code, national insurance contributions, and Secondly plc's name and address.

Secondly plc should have provided this form to Joe by 31 May 2011.

Form P11D

A separate form P11D will be prepared by both Firstly plc and Secondly plc, detailing the cash equivalents of the benefits provided to Joe.

Both companies should have provided a form to Joe by 6 July 2011.

Question 2

Text references. Taxable total profits are covered in Chapter 19 and the computation of corporation tax in Chapter 20. VAT is dealt with in Chapters 26 and 27.

Top tips. Set out your capital allowance computation in the standard columnar format – you might want to do this computation at the start of the question and then slot the total into the calculation of taxable total profits.

Easy marks. The rules on associated companies should be well known and so part (a)(i) should have given easy marks. Keep your points short and relevant to the question asked. For example, you did not need to deal with the position of non-UK companies in this part, although this was relevant in part (a)(iii).

					Marks
(a)	(i)	Second Ltd and Fourth Ltd		1	
		Third Ltd and Fifth Ltd		1	
					2
	(ii)	Operating profit		½	
		Depreciation		½	
		Amortisation		½	
		Lease premium	– Assessable amount	1½	
			– Deduction	1	
		Capital allowances	– AIA	1	
			– Main pool	1½	
			– Motor car [1]	1½	
			– Special rate pool	1½	
		Overseas branches		1	
		Loan interest		1	
		Franked investment income		1	
		Group dividend		½	
		Corporation tax		2	
					15
	(iii)	Relief for trading losses		1	
		Availability of capital allowances		1	
		Associated company		1	
					3
(b)	(i)	Sales – VAT registered customers		1	
		– Additional contract		1	
		– Non-VAT registered customers		1	
		Fuel scale charge		1	
					4
	(ii)	Previous late submissions		1	
		Surcharge		1	
		Extension of surcharge period		1	
					3
	(iii)	Circumstances		2	
		Period		1	
					3
					30

(a)   (i)   **Associated companies**

Second Ltd and Fourth Ltd are not associated companies as Neung Ltd has a shareholding of less than 50% in Second Ltd, and Fourth Ltd is dormant.

Third Ltd and Fifth Ltd are associated companies as Neung Ltd has a shareholding of over 50% in each case, and both are trading companies.

(ii)   **Neung Ltd – Corporation tax computation for the year ended 31 March 2011**

	£
Operating profit	307,900
Depreciation	11,830
Amortisation	7,000
Deduction for lease premium (W1)	(4,340)
Capital allowances (W2)	(47,490)
UK trading profit	274,900
First overseas branch trading profit	41,000
Second overseas branch trading loss	(15,700)
Net trading profit	300,200
Loan interest (25,200 + 12,600)	37,800
Taxable total profits	338,000
Franked investment income (37,800 x 100/90)	42,000
Augmented profits	380,000
Corporation tax (338,000 at 28%)	94,640
Marginal relief	
7/400 (500,000 – 380,000) x 338,000/380,000	(1,868)
	92,772

Neung Ltd has two associated companies, so the upper limit is reduced to £500,000 (1,500,000/3).

Tutorial note

The dividend of £16,200 from Third Ltd is not included as franked investment income as it is a group dividend.

Workings

1   *Deduction for lease premium*

The amount assessed on the landlord is £86,800 calculated as follows:

	£
Premium received	140,000
Less: 140,000 x 2% x (20 – 1)	(53,200)
	86,800

This is deductible over the life of the lease, so the deduction for the year ended 31 March 2011 is £4,340 (86,800/20).

Tutorial note

The office building has been used for business purposes, and so the proportion of the lease premium assessed on the landlord can be deducted, spread over the life of the lease.

2 Capital allowances

	AIA £	Main pool £	Motor car [1] £	Special rate pool £	Allowances £
WDV brought forward		4,800	22,800	12,700	
Additions qualifying for AIA					
Ventilation system	35,000				
AIA	(35,000)				35,000
Other additions					
Motor car [2]				15,400	
Motor car [3]		28,600			
		33,400		28,100	
WDA – 20%		(6,680)			6,680
WDA – Restricted			(3,000)		3,000
WDA – 10%				(2,810)	2,810
WDV carried forward		26,720	19,800	25,290	
Total allowances					47,490

Tutorial notes:

1   Motor car [1] was owned at 1 April 2009 and therefore continues to qualify for writing down allowance at the rate of 20% subject to a maximum of £3,000.

2   Motor car [2] has CO_2 emissions over 160 grams per kilometre and therefore only qualifies for writing down allowances at the rate of 10% as part of the special rate pool.

3   Motor car [3] has CO_2 emissions between 111 and 160 grams per kilometre and therefore qualifies for writing down allowances at the rate of 20% as part of the main pool.

(iii) **Branch or subsidiary**

UK relief is not usually available for trading losses incurred by an overseas subsidiary company, whereas relief is usually available for trading losses incurred by an overseas branch.

UK capital allowances will be available for capital expenditure incurred by an overseas branch. For expenditure incurred by an overseas subsidiary company, relief is not available in the UK, and may not be available overseas.

An overseas subsidiary company will be an associated company, and so the UK corporation tax limits will be reduced accordingly. An overseas branch cannot be an associated company.

(b) (i) **Neung Ltd – Output VAT for the quarter ended 31 March 2011**

Sales	£
VAT registered customers (44,600 – 35,200 = 9,400 x 20%)	1,880
Additional contract	1,600
Non-VAT registered customers (289,300 – 242,300 = 47,000 x 20/120)	7,833
Fuel scale charge (463 x 20/120)	77
	11,390

Tutorial note

The basic tax point for a supply of services is the date that they are completed, but if a VAT invoice is issued or payment received before the basic tax point, then this becomes the actual tax point. Therefore the tax point for the contract is when the VAT invoice was issued on 1 March 2011.

Default surcharge

Neung Ltd was late in submitting VAT returns and paying the related VAT liability for two previous quarters. The company has not managed to revert to a clean default surcharge record by submitting four consecutive VAT returns on time.

The late payment of VAT for the quarter ended 31 March 2011 will therefore result in a surcharge of 5% of the VAT liability for that period, although this will not be collected if it is less than £400.

In addition, the surcharge period will be extended to 31 March 2012.

(iii) **VAT invoices**

Neung Ltd must issue a VAT invoice when it makes a standard rated supply to a VAT registered customer, but there is no requirement to do so if the supply is exempt or if the supply is to a non-VAT registered customer.

A VAT invoice should be issued within 30 days of the date that the supply is treated as being made.

Question 3

> **Text references.** Computing chargeable gains for individuals is covered in Chapter 13 and business reliefs in Chapter 15. Shares are dealt with in Chapter 16. Chargeable gains for companies are dealt with in Chapter 21.
>
> **Top tips.** Remember to set the annual exempt amount against gains not qualifying for entrepreneurs' relief first. This gives the lowest overall capital gains tax. However, you must treat the gains qualifying for entrepreneurs' relief as the lowest part of the gains thus using up the available basic rate band.
>
> **Easy marks.** Don't forget the easy marks for stating the due dates for payment of the tax liabilities.

Marking scheme

				Marks
(a)	Land	– Proceeds	½	
		– Cost	½	
	Oily plc	– Deemed proceeds	2	
		– Cost	1	
	Mal-Mil Ltd	– Proceeds	½	
		– Cost	1	
	Annual exempt amount	– Use first against gains not qualifying for ER	1	
	Capital gains tax @ 28%		½	
	Capital gains tax @ 10%		½	
	Due date		½	
				8
(b)	**Chargeable gain**			
	Proceeds		½	
	Incidental costs of disposal		½	
	Cost		1½	
	Enhancement expenditure		1	
	Indexation		1½	
	Corporation tax liability			
	Calculation		1½	
	Due date		½	
				7
				15

(a) **Lim Lam – Capital gains tax liability 2010/11**

Summary

	£	Gains not qualifying for entrepreneurs' relief £	Gains qualifying for entrepreneurs' relief £
Land			
Disposal proceeds	260,000		
Less: cost	(182,000)		
		78,000	
Ordinary shares in Oily plc			
Deemed proceeds	37,200		
(5,000 x £7.44) (W1)			
Less: cost	(15,925)		
		21,275	
Ordinary shares in Mal-Mil Ltd			
Disposal proceeds	280,000		
Less: cost (W2)	(56,000)		
			224,000
Chargeable gains		99,275	224,000
Less: annual exempt amount (N1)		(10,100)	
Taxable gains		89,175	224,000
Capital gains tax on 89,175 @ 28% (N2)		24,969	
Capital gains tax on 224,000 @ 10%			22,400
Capital gains tax liability 2010/11			£47,369

Lim's capital gains tax liability should be paid by 31 January 2012.

Workings

1   The shares in Oily plc are valued at £7.44 (£7.40 + ¼(£7.56 – £7.40)) as this is lower than £7.48 ((£7.36 + £7.60)/2).

2   Share pool

	Number	Cost £
Purchase 8 June 2003	125,000	142,000
Purchase 23 May 2005	60,000	117,000
	185,000	259,000
Disposal 22 March 2011 (259,000 x 40,000/185,000)	(40,000)	(56,000)
Balance carried forward	145,000	203,000

Tutorial notes

1   The annual exempt amount is set against the gains not qualifying for entrepreneurs' relief as this gives the best use of the annual exempt amount as it reduces tax at 28%.

2   The gains qualifying for entrepreneurs' relief are the lowest part of the gains and therefore use up the remaining basic rate band of £9,400 (37,400 – 28,000). This means that the gains not qualifying for entrepreneurs' relief are all taxed at 28%.

(b)   **Mal-Mil Ltd – Chargeable gain on the disposal of the land**

	£	£
Disposal proceeds		162,000
Incidental costs of disposal		(3,800)
		158,200
Cost (W1)	101,250	
Enhancement expenditure (W2)	12,150	
		(113,400)
Less: indexation allowance (113,400 x 0.025 (W3))		(2,835)
Chargeable gain		41,965

Workings

1   *Cost of land*

The cost relating to the two acres of land sold is £101,250 (260,000 x 162,000/416,000 (162,000 + 254,000)).

2   *Enhancement expenditure*

The levelling of the land is enhancement expenditure. The cost relating to the two acres of land sold is £12,150 (31,200 x 162,000/416,000).

3   *Indexation factor*

Both the cost and the enhancement expenditure were incurred during July 2010. The relevant indexation factor is therefore 0.025 ((232.1 – 226.4)/226.4).

Corporation tax liability

Mal-Mil Ltd's corporation tax liability for the year ended 31 December 2010 is £43,043 (163,000 + 41,965 = 204,965 at 21%). This is due on 1 October 2011.

Question 4

Text references. Chapter 4 deals with employment benefits. National insurance contributions are covered in Chapter 12. Computing taxable total profits is in Chapter 19 and computing corporation tax in Chapter 20.

Top tips. Use headings to show the examiner which of two options you are dealing with.

Easy marks. There were easy marks for computing the car benefit and computing the national insurance contributions.

Marks

(a)	**Company motor car**		
	Car benefit		2
	Income tax		1
	NIC implications		½
	Additional director's remuneration		
	Income tax		½
	Class 1 NIC		1
			5
(b)	**Company motor car**		
	Class 1A NIC		1
	Allowable leasing costs		1
	Corporation tax saving		1
	Additional director's remuneration		
	Class 1 NIC		1
	Corporation tax saving		1
			5
(c)	**Sammi**		
	Director's remuneration	- Net of tax income	1
		- Overall result	1
	Conclusion		1
	Smark Ltd		
	Director's remuneration		1
	Conclusion		1
			5
			15

(a) **Sammi Smith – Company motor car**

The list price used in the car benefit calculation is restricted to a maximum of £80,000. The relevant percentage is restricted to a maximum of 35% (15% + 37% (315 – 130 = 185/5) = 52%).

Sammi will therefore be taxed on a car benefit of £28,000 (80,000 x 35%).

Sammi's marginal rate of income tax is 50%, so her additional income tax liability for 2010/11 will be £14,000 (28,000 at 50%).

There are no national insurance contribution implications for Sammi.

Tutorial note

There is no fuel benefit as fuel is not provided for private journeys.

Sammi Smith – Additional director's remuneration

Sammi's additional income tax liability for 2010/11 will be £13,000 (26,000 at 50%).

The additional employee's Class 1 NIC liability will be £260 (26,000 at 1%).

Tutorial note

Sammi's director's remuneration exceeds the upper earnings limit of £43,875, so her additional class 1 NIC liability is at the rate of 1%.

(b) **Smark Ltd – Company motor car**

The employer's class 1A NIC liability in respect of the car benefit will be £3,584 (28,000 at 12.8%).

The motor car has a CO_2 emission rate in excess of 160 grams per kilometre, so only £22,729 (26,740 less 15%) of the leasing costs are allowed for corporation tax purposes.

Smark Ltd's corporation tax liability will be reduced by £7,368 (22,729 + 3,584 = 26,313 at 28%).

Smark Ltd – Additional director's remuneration

The employer's class 1 NIC liability in respect of the additional director's remuneration will be £3,328 (26,000 at 12.8%).

Smark Ltd's corporation tax liability will be reduced by £8,212 (26,000 + 3,328 = 29,328 at 28%).

(c) **Most beneficial alternative for Sammi Smith**

Under the director's remuneration alternative, Sammi will receive additional net of tax income of £12,740 (26,000 – 13,000 – 260).

However, she will have to lease the motor car at a cost of £26,740, so the overall result is additional expenditure of £14,000 (26,740 – 12,740).

If Sammi is provided with a company motor car then she will have an additional tax liability of £14,000, so she is in exactly the same financial position.

Most beneficial alternative for Smark Ltd

The net of tax cost of paying additional director's remuneration is £21,116 (26,000 + 3,328 – 8,212).

This is more beneficial than the alternative of providing a company motor car since this has a net of tax cost of £22,956 (26,740 + 3,584 – 7,368).

Question 5

Text references. Chapter 18 covers inheritance tax.

Top tips. Watch out for exemptions – remember that the only exemption in the F6 syllabus which applies to both lifetime and death transfers is the spouse/civil partner exemption.

Easy marks. There were easy marks for allocating the annual exemptions correctly and spotting that the sale at an undervalue was not a transfer of value.

				Marks
(a)	One mark for each advantage			4
(b)	(i)	*10 June 2006*		
		Annual exemptions	1	
		PET - exempt	½	
		19 April 2007		
		Diminution in value of estate	½	
		No gratuitous intent	1	
		10 March 2008		
		Annual exemption	½	
		CLT – calculation of tax	2	
		Due date for tax	½	
				6

<table>
<tr><td>(b)</td><td>(ii)</td><td>*10 June 2006*</td><td></td><td>**Marks**</td></tr>
<tr><td></td><td></td><td>PET now chargeable but within nil band</td><td>½</td><td></td></tr>
<tr><td></td><td></td><td>*10 March 2008*</td><td></td><td></td></tr>
<tr><td></td><td></td><td>CLT – calculation of additional tax</td><td>1</td><td></td></tr>
<tr><td></td><td></td><td>Due date for tax</td><td>½</td><td></td></tr>
<tr><td></td><td></td><td>*1 February 2011*</td><td></td><td></td></tr>
<tr><td></td><td></td><td>Spouse exemption</td><td>1</td><td></td></tr>
<tr><td></td><td></td><td>Chargeable death estate</td><td>½</td><td></td></tr>
<tr><td></td><td></td><td>Calculation of tax</td><td>1</td><td></td></tr>
<tr><td></td><td></td><td>Due date for tax</td><td>½</td><td></td></tr>
</table>

5

15

(a) **Advantages of making lifetime transfers**

A potentially exempt transfer is completely exempt after seven years.

A chargeable lifetime transfer will not incur any additional IHT liability on death after seven years.

Taper relief will reduce the amount of IHT payable after three years if the donor dies between three to seven years.

Lifetime transfers are valued at the time they are made, so it is beneficial to make gifts of assets which may increase in value such as land and shares.

(b) (i) **Lifetime implications of event during Evelyn's lifetime**

10 June 2006

The gift of £100,000 to her sister is an exempt transfer of £6,000 (annual exemptions 2006/07 and 2005/06 b/f) and a potentially exempt transfer of £(100,000 – 6,000) = £94,000. There is no lifetime tax as the PET is treated as exempt during Evelyn's lifetime.

19 April 2007

This is a sale at an undervalue resulting in a diminution of Evelyn's estate by £(150,000 – 10,000) = £140,000. However, this is not a transfer of value for inheritance tax as there was no gratuitous intent.

10 March 2008

The gift of £320,000 is an exempt transfer of £3,000 (annual exemption 2007/08) and a chargeable lifetime transfer of £(320,000 – 3,000) = £317,000. The full nil band at the date of the transfer is available as this is the first chargeable lifetime transfer.

The lifetime tax is calculated as follows:

<table>
<tr><td></td><td></td><td></td><td></td><td>£</td></tr>
<tr><td colspan="4">Chargeable lifetime transfer</td><td>317,000</td></tr>
<tr><td></td><td></td><td></td><td></td><td>£</td></tr>
<tr><td>IHT</td><td>£300,000</td><td>× 0% =</td><td></td><td>Nil</td></tr>
<tr><td></td><td>£ 17,000</td><td>× 20% =</td><td></td><td>3,400</td></tr>
<tr><td></td><td>£ 317,000</td><td></td><td></td><td>3,400</td></tr>
</table>

Due date 30 September 2008

(ii) **Inheritance tax implications of Evelyn's death**

10 June 2006

The PET of £94,000 becomes chargeable because Evelyn dies within seven years of making it.

There is no tax on the PET itself as it is within the nil band at death of £325,000.

10 March 2008

Additional death tax is due on this chargeable lifetime transfer because Evelyn dies within seven years of making it. There is now a chargeable transfer of value of £94,000 in seven years before 10 March 2008 (transfers after 10 March 2001) so the nil rate band available is £(325,000 – 94,000) = £231,000.

The additional death tax is therefore:

				£
Chargeable lifetime transfer				317,000
				£
IHT	£231,000	× 0% =		Nil
	£ 86,000	× 40% =		34,400
	£ 317,000			34,400
Less: lifetime tax paid				(3,400)
				31,000

Due date 31 August 2011

Tutorial note

There is no taper relief as death was within three years of the gift.

1 February 2011

Death estate of £750,000. The gift of the house and personal effects totalling £175,000 are exempt because of the spouse exemption.

The remainder of the estate of £(750,000 – 175,000) = £575,000 is chargeable at 40% because the nil band has been used in full by the lifetime transfers.

£575,000 @ 40%	£230,000

Due date 16 June 2011

Tax tables

SUPPLEMENTARY INFORMATION

1. Calculations and workings need only be made to the nearest £.
2. All apportionments may be made to the nearest month.
3. All workings should be shown.

TAX RATES AND ALLOWANCES

The following tax rates and allowances are to be used in answering the questions

Income tax

		Normal rates %	Dividend rates %
Basic rate	£1 – £37,400	20	10
Higher rate	£37,401 – £150,000	40	32.5
Additional rate	£150,001 and over	50	42.5

A starting rate of 10% applies to savings income where it falls within the first £2,440 of taxable income.

Personal allowances

	£
Personal allowance	6,475
Personal allowance aged 65 to 74	9,490
Personal allowance aged 75 and over	9,640
Income limit for age-related allowances	22,900
Income limit for standard personal allowance	100,000

Car benefit percentage

The base level of CO_2 emissions is 130 grams per kilometre.

A rate of 5% applies to petrol cars with CO_2 emissions of 75 grams per kilometre or less and a rate of 10% applies where CO_2 emissions are between 76 and 120 grams per kilometre.

Car fuel benefit

The base figure for calculating the car fuel benefit is £18,000.

Pension scheme limits

The maximum contribution that can qualify for tax relief without any earnings is £3,600.

Authorised mileage allowances: cars

Up to 10,000 miles	40p
Over 10,000 miles	25p

Capital allowances

Plant and machinery	%
Main pool	20
Special rate pool	10

Motor cars (purchases since 6 April 2009 (1 April 2009 for companies))

CO_2 emissions up to 110 grams per kilometre	100
CO_2 emissions between 111 and 160 grams per kilometre	20
CO_2 emissions over 160 grams per kilometre	10

Annual investment allowance

First £100,000 of expenditure	100

Industrial buildings

Writing-down allowance	1%

Corporation tax

Financial year	2008	2009	2010
Small profits rate	21%	21%	21%
Main rate	28%	28%	28%
Lower limit	£300,000	£300,000	£300,000
Upper limit	£1,500,000	£1,500,000	£1,500,000
Standard fraction	7/400	7/400	7/400

Marginal relief

Standard fraction × (U – A) × N/A

Value Added Tax

Standard rate	Up to 3 January 2011	17.5%
	From 4 January 2011 onwards	20%
Registration limit		£70,000
Deregistration limit		£68,000

Inheritance tax: tax rates

		%
£1 – £325,000		Nil
Excess	Death rate	20
	Lifetime rate	40

Inheritance tax: taper relief

Years before death	% reduction
Over 3 but less than 4 years	20
Over 4 but less than 5 years	40
Over 5 but less than 6 years	60
Over 6 but less than 7 years	80

Capital gains tax

		%
Rates of tax	Lower rate	18
	Higher rate	28
Annual exemption		£10,100
Entrepreneurs' relief		
	Lifetime limit	£5,000,000
	Rate of tax	10%

National insurance (not contracted-out rates)

		%
Class 1 employee	£1 – £5,715 per year	Nil
	£5,716 – £43,875 per year	11.0
	£43,876 and above per year	1.0
Class 1 employer	£1 – £5,715 per year	Nil
	£5,716 and above per year	12.8
Class 1A		12.8
Class 2	Small earnings exception limit - £5,075	
	£2.40 per week	
Class 4	£1 – £5,715 per year	Nil
	£5,716 – £43,875 per year	8.0
	£43,876 and above per year	1.0

Rates of Interest

Official rate of interest	4.0%
Rate of interest on underpaid tax	3.0% (assumed)
Rate of interest on overpaid tax	0.5% (assumed)

Review Form– Paper F6 Taxation (1/11)

Name: _____   Address: _____

_____

_____

How have you used this Kit?
(Tick one box only)

☐ Home study (book only)

☐ On a course: college _____

☐ With 'correspondence' package

☐ Other _____

Why did you decide to purchase this Kit?
(Tick one box only)

☐ Have used the complementary Study Text

☐ Have used other BPP products in the past

☐ Recommendation by friend/colleague

☐ Recommendation by a lecturer at college

☐ Saw advertising

☐ Other _____

During the past six months do you recall seeing/receiving any of the following?
(Tick as many boxes as are relevant)

☐ Our advertisement in *Student Accountant*

☐ Our advertisement in *Pass*

☐ Our advertisement in *PQ*

☐ Our brochure with a letter through the post

☐ Our website www.bpp.com

Which (if any) aspects of our advertising do you find useful?
(Tick as many boxes as are relevant)

☐ Prices and publication dates of new editions

☐ Information on product content

☐ Facility to order books off-the-page

☐ None of the above

Which BPP products have you used?

Text	☐	Success CD	☐	Learn Online	☐
Kit	☑	i-Learn	☐	Home Study Package	☐
Passcard	☐	i-Pass	☐	Home Study PLUS	☐

Your ratings, comments and suggestions would be appreciated on the following areas.

	Very useful	Useful	Not useful
Passing ACCA exams	☐	☐	☐
Passing F6	☐	☐	☐
Planning your question practice	☐	☐	☐
Questions	☐	☐	☐
Top Tips etc in answers	☐	☐	☐
Content and structure of answers	☐	☐	☐
'Plan of attack' in mock exams	☐	☐	☐
Mock exam answers	☐	☐	☐

Overall opinion of this Kit	Excellent ☐	Good ☐	Adequate ☐	Poor ☐

Do you intend to continue using BPP products?   Yes ☐   No ☐

The BPP author of this edition can be e-mailed at: suedexter@bpp.com

Please return this form to: Lesley Buick, ACCA Publishing Manager, BPP Learning Media Ltd, FREEPOST, London, W12 8BR

Review Form (continued)

TELL US WHAT YOU THINK

Please note any further comments and suggestions/errors below.